Charles '**Charlie**' Robert **Watts**, born in University College June 1941 became famous worldwide as the drummer of their record sleeves and tour stages. He was one of the gr from January 1963 until his death on 24th August 2021. C his drumming style.

He worked as a graphic designer for advertising compan developed an interest in jazz as a youth, joining Alexis Kc playing drums in London's Rhythm 'n' Blues clubs, where Richards. Charlie left Blues Incorporated in January 1963 to join the Rolling Stones as their drummer, making his 1st public appearance as a permanent member at the Ealing Jazz Club on 2nd February 1963. Watts, Jagger and Richards are the only members to have featured on all of the group's studio albums.

Apart from his career with the Rolling Stones, Charlie toured with his own band, the Charlie Watts Quintet, having also appeared in London at Ronnie Scott's Jazz Club with the Charlie Watts Tentet. Watts was inducted into the Modern Drummer Hall of Fame during 2006, the same year that Vanity Fair elected him into the International Best Dressed List Hall of Fame. Music critic Robert Christgau rated Charlie as 'rock's greatest drummer'. He was ranked 12th on Rolling Stone's '100 Greatest Drummers of All Time' list in 2016.

Charles Robert Watts was the son of Charles Richard Watts, a lorry driver, delivering parcels for the London, Midland and Scottish Railway & his wife Lillian Charlotte (née Eaves), a former factory worker. He had a sister, Linda, the family living in a prefab in Wembley, at 23 Pilgrims Way, where many of the houses had been destroyed by Luftwaffe bombs during World War II. Charlie's neighbour Dave Green, who lived opposite at 22 Pilgrims Way, was a childhood friend, the pair remaining friends until Watts' death.

Dave, who became a jazz bass player, recalled that as boys, "We discovered 78 rpm records. Charlie had more records than I did ... We used to go to Charlie's bedroom then just get these records out". Watts's earliest records were jazz recordings; he remembered owning 78 rpm records of early jazz pianist Jelly Roll Morton and bop saxophonist Charlie Parker. Green recalled that Charlie also "had the one with Monk and the Johnny Dodge Trio. Charlie was ahead of me in listening and acquisitions".

The Watts family moved to Kingsbury, north-west London, where he attended Tylers Croft Secondary Modern School from 1952 to 1956, showing a talent for art, music, cricket & football. When he and Dave were both c. 13, Charlie became interested in drumming: "I bought a banjo but I didn't like the dots on the neck, so I took the neck off & at the same time I heard a drummer called Chico Hamilton, who played with Gerry Mulligan and I wanted to play like that, with brushes. I didn't have a snare drum, so I put the banjo head on a stand".

Watts' parents gave him his first drum kit during 1955 then he practised drumming along to jazz records that he collected. After finishing secondary school, Charlie attended Harrow Art School until 1960, which later became the Harrow campus of the University of Westminster. After leaving art school, he played drums occasionally with local groups in coffee shops & clubs, while working as a graphic designer for an advertising company called Charlie Daniels Studios.

Watts and Green began their musical careers together from 1958 to 1959, playing in a jazz band in Middlesex named the 'Jo Jones All Stars'. Charlie initially found his transition to R 'n' B puzzling: "I went into rhythm & blues. When they asked me to play, I didn't know what it was. I thought it meant Charlie Parker, played slow". Watts met Alexis Korner in 1961, who invited him to join his group, Blues Incorporated, when Charlie was on his way to work as a graphic designer in Denmark, but he accepted Korner's offer when he returned to London during February 1962. Watts played regularly with Blues Incorporated while employed by advertising firm Charles, Hobson and Grey.

Charlie first met Brian Jones, Ian 'Stu' Stewart, Mick Jagger & Keith Richards in mid-1962, who also frequented the London rhythm 'n' blues clubs, but it wasn't until January 1963 that he agreed to join the Rolling Stones. Initially, the band couldn't afford to pay Watts, who'd been earning a regular salary from his gigs. His 1st public appearance as a permanent member was at the Ealing Jazz Club on 2nd February 1963.

As well as his work as a musician, Charlie contributed graphic art and comic strips to early Rolling Stones records including the Between the Buttons record sleeve & was responsible for the tour announcement press conference in New York City of 1975. The group surprised the throng of waiting reporters by playing Brown Sugar on the back of a flat-bed truck in the middle of Manhattan traffic, Watts having known that it was a common way for New Orleans jazz bands to promote upcoming dates. He also designed the elaborate stages for tours with Mick, 1st contributing to the lotus-shaped design of that Tour of the Americas [1975], as well as the Steel Wheels/Urban Jungle Tour of 1989–1990, the Bridges to Babylon Tour [1997–1998], the Licks Tour [2002–2003] then A Bigger Bang Tour of 2005–2007.

Charlie had many other interests outside his life as a member of the Rolling Stones, having published a cartoon tribute to Charlie Parker during December 1964, titled Ode to a High Flying Bird. Although he made his name in rock, his personal tastes were mainly in jazz. Watts joined Ian Stewart in the back-to-the-roots boogie-woogie group Rocket 88 in the late '70s, which featured many of Britain's top jazz, rock and R 'n'B musicians. He toured worldwide with a big band during the '80s that included Evan Parker, Courtney Pine & Jack Bruce, who was also a member of Rocket 88.

Charlie formed a jazz quintet in 1991, as another tribute to Charlie Parker, Warm and Tender [1993], being issued by the Charlie Watts Quintet, which included vocalist Bernard Fowler. The group then released Long Ago & Far Away [1996], both records including a collection of Great American Songbook standards. After a successful collaboration with Jim Keltner on the Rolling Stones L.P. Bridges to Babylon, they put out a techno/instrumental album titled Charlie Watts/Jim Keltner Project.

Watts stated that even though the tracks were given names like the 'Elvin Suite', in honour of the late Elvin Jones, Max Roach and Roy Haynes, rather than copying their style of drumming, they were capturing a feeling by those artists. Watts at Scott's was recorded with his band, 'the Charlie Watts Tentet', at Ronnie Scott's Jazz Club in London. He started to perform concerts with the ABC&D of Boogie Woogie during April 2009, including pianists Axel Zwingenberger and Ben Waters, with his lifelong friend Dave Green on bass.

The Rolling Stones were inducted into the Rock and Roll Hall of Fame in 1989, although Charlie didn't attend the ceremony. He was voted into the Modern Drummer Hall of Fame in the July 2006 issue of Modern Drummer magazine, joining Ringo Starr, Keith Moon, Steve Gadd, Buddy Rich & other highly rated, influential drummers from the history of rock and jazz.

Watts wed the sculptor Shirley Ann Shepherd (born 11th September 1938) on 14th October 1964, whom he met before the Rolling Stones became successful. The couple had a daughter, Seraphina, born during March 1968, who gave birth to their only grandchild, a girl named Charlotte. Charlie lived near Dolton, a rural village in west Devon, where he owned an Arabian horse stud farm. He also owned a percentage of The Rolling Stones' corporate entities.

Watts was known for his sartorial elegance, The Daily Telegraph naming him one of the World's Best Dressed Men. Vanity Fair named him on their International Best Dressed Hall of Fame List in 2006. Charlie collected cars, as did all the other Rolling Stones members, despite never having had a driving licence, viewing his motors as beautiful objects.

He had a love–hate attitude towards touring, stating during 2003 that he "loved playing with Keith and the band" but "wasn't interested in being a pop idol, sitting there with girls screaming". Watts said in 1996 that he'd sketched every bed that he'd slept on while on tour since 1967. His personal life was much more stable than those of his band-mates & many of his rock-'n'-roll contemporaries. Charlie projected a calm, amused counterpoint to his flamboyant band-mates on-stage.

Ever faithful to his wife Shirley, Watts consistently refused sexual offers from groupies on the road; in Robert Greenfield's STP: A Journey Through America with The Rolling Stones, a documentary of their American Tour of 1972, it was observed that when the band was invited to the Playboy Mansion, Watts went to Hugh Hefner's game room to play pool instead of taking advantage of the girls. He stated "I've never filled the stereotype of the rock star. Back in the '70s, Bill Wyman and I decided to grow beards, but the effort left us exhausted".

During the mid-'80s, a drunken Jagger phoned Charlie's hotel room in the middle of the night to ask, "Where's my drummer?" Watts got up, shaved, dressed in a suit, put on a tie & newly shined shoes, went down the stairs then punched Mick in the face, telling him: "Never call me your drummer again". He said he was sorry about it in 2003, putting it down to drink. Charlie's previously moderate use of alcohol and drugs became problematic during the mid-'80s: "They were my way of dealing with family problems ... I think it was a mid-life crisis. All I know is that I became totally another person around 1983 then came out of it c. 1986. I nearly lost my wife & everything over my behaviour".

Watts was diagnosed with throat cancer in June 2004, despite having given up smoking during the late '80s, undergoing a course of radiotherapy which sent the cancer into remission: "I went into hospital then 8 months later Mick said, 'We're going to make a record, but we'll only do it when you're ready'. They were buggering about, writing songs then when I was ready I went down and that was it, A Bigger Bang. I completed a 2-year tour. It seems that whenever we stop, I get ill, so maybe I should carry on".

It was reported on 5th August 2021 that Charlie had decided to sit out the resumption of the US 'No Filter Tour' due to an unspecified medical procedure, with Steve Jordan temporarily replacing him on drums.

Watts died in a London hospital on 24th August 2021 at the age of 80, surrounded by his family. Variety stated on the day of his death that he was "universally recognized as one of the greatest rock drummers of all time". Jagger & Richards paid tribute to him, as did Paul McCartney, Ringo Starr and Elton John, calling Charlie "One of the greatest", "a fantastic drummer" and "the most stylish of men".

Discography

As well as his work with the Rolling Stones, Watts released the following L.Ps:

The Charlie Watts Orchestra – Live at Fulham Town Hall (1986, Columbia Records)

The Charlie Watts Quintet – From One Charlie (1991, Continuum Records)

The Charlie Watts Quintet – A Tribute to Charlie Parker with Strings (1992, Continuum Records)

The Charlie Watts Quintet – Warm and Tender (1993, Continuum Records)

The Charlie Watts Quintet – Long Ago and Far Away (1996, Virgin Records)

The Charlie Watts-Jim Keltner Project (2000, Cyber Octave Records)

The Charlie Watts Tentet – Watts at Scott's (2004, Sanctuary Records)

The ABC&D of Boogie Woogie – The Magic of Boogie Woogie (2010, Vagabond Records)

The ABC&D of Boogie Woogie – Live in Paris (2012, Eagle Records)

Charlie Watts meets the Danish Radio Big Band (Live at the Danish Radio Concert Hall, Copenhagen 2010) (2017, Impulse! Records)

One of the most startling revelations ever concerning the effortlessly dapper Charlie Watts, which emerged in the late '80s, was that the Rolling Stones' most avuncular and apparently solid group member, had for years dabbled with heroin, having also regarded himself an alcoholic. Almost as surprising was the disclosure that in the middle of the night at an Amsterdam hotel, a drunken Mick phoned Watts' room:

"Is that my drummer boy? Why don't you get your arse down here?" "Charlie shaved, put on a suit & tie, came down, grabbed him then went boom! Charlie dished him a walloping right hook. He landed in a plateful of smoked salmon and slid along the table towards the window. I pulled his leg & saved him from going out into the canal below", related Keith Richards. It became part of rock 'n' roll folklore that Jagger was issued the warning: "Don't ever call me your drummer again. You're my f*ckin' singer!"

Faithful to his wife Shirley, in a band of compulsive philanderers, the man whose main on-the-road recreational activity seemed to be the sketches that he drew of every hotel room in which he stayed, apparently had another side to him. Wilfully eccentric, not really wanting to be in or enjoying the Rolling Stones, to whose music he didn't listen, on tour wanting to catch the next plane home, the drummer's countenance was one of gentle glumness and ironic resignation.

However, there was a suggestion that all along such an existentialist pose carried an element of studied affectation: Watts, who regarded himself as a jazz rather than R'n'B drummer, had been the first Rolling Stone to regularly smoke marijuana, at first hiding it from the other group members, believing that such youngsters would be shocked. With Jagger & Richards, he'd been tough enough to last the course in a group with its share of casualties.

A couple of years older than those other 2 survivors, Charlie was working as a graphic designer in prestigious advertising agency Charlie Daniels Studios when they first met him. He was a modernist. "We all thought Charlie was very kind of hip, because of his jackets and shirts. Because he was working in an advertising agency, he was very different. It was good for the band to have someone who was sort of sharp … We had the advantage that Keith & I both get along very well with Charlie. The fact that there's 3 of us who get along so well is very important", said Mick.

Watts's dad worked for British Railways as a parcel deliveryman, his mother having been a factory worker. He had a sister, Linda. The family lived in Kingsbury, north-west London, in a modest but fastidiously tidy house: his father would make him cover all his books in brown paper – "even my Buffalo Bill album".

Charlie remembered being brought up, running to the air-raid shelter. From an early age his talent at art was clear and his mother would recall him rapping out tunes on the kitchen table with his knife & fork. Watts bought a banjo when he was 14 but couldn't work out how to play it. Then he made a stand for the instrument "and hit the round skin part with brushes; it was a like a drum anyway". That Christmas his parents bought him his 1st drum kit for £12, on which Charlie practised intensively at home, playing along to jazz records, which were his great love. "Gradually, I built up my confidence".

Watts's drumming influences included Britain's Phil Seamen, but he thought that bebop icon Kenny Clarke was the world's best sticks-man. "To me, how an American plays the drums is how you should play the drums. That's how I play. I mean, I play regular snare drum, I don't play tympani style, although I know guys who play fantastically like that. I play march-drum style. Most rock drummers play like Ringo; a bastard version of tympani style. In reality that's what it is, because tympani style is fingers & most rock drummers play like that because it's heavy offbeat", he said many years later.

A couple of months after leaving school aged 16, during July 1957, Charlie began studying at Harrow School of Art. In the summer of 1960 he began work at Charles Hobson and Gray on Regent Street, a prestigious agency, starting off as a £2 / week tea-boy but soon progressing to be a graphic designer. Jazz remained his main interest. Watts was so awed by the work of the great saxophonist Charlie 'Bird' Parker, legendary for his use of heroin, that during this period he wrote a book about him, Ode to a Highflying Bird, published during 1965 : "It was a kid's book, with a bird character instead of Charlie Parker". The Rolling Stones' album Between the Buttons [1967] featured 6 cartoon drawings by Watts on the back cover.

At a show that he played at the Troubador in Earls Court, Charlie met Alexis Korner, doyen of British blues. Korner asked the drummer to join his group Blues Incorporated in the late summer of 1961, but he declined, the offer being repeated the following January, when he accepted. Joint leader of the band with Alexis was Cyril Davies, with Jack Bruce on bass. "On a good night it was amazing, a cross between R'n'B & Charlie Mingus, which was what Alexis wanted", Watts recalled. In the audience at a Blues Incorporated gig Charlie noticed Shirley Ann Shepherd, who was studying sculpture at the Royal College of Art: the pair wed in 1964.

Watts had stopped playing with Blues Incorporated, concerned that too many late nights were affecting his day job, being replaced by Ginger Baker, when the recently formed Rolling Stones, named after the Muddy Waters song 'Rollin' Stone' approached him. He wasn't convinced, but Korner persuaded him that they'd last and they all seemed to get on with each other, especially Charlie with Mick & Keith.

The group's founder Brian Jones warmed to Watts' commitment and idealism. "With Charlie we were thinking about the atmosphere in the band. In the early days I thought Keith might be an awkward person to get to know. I'd watch Keith with other people, and he always seemed to back away a bit, but he & Charlie were a f*ckin' comedy team. They had a dual sense of humour", said Ian Stewart, the group's keyboard player, during 1979.

"Charlie is incredibly honest, brutally honest. Lying bores him. He just sees right through you to start with, and he's not even that interested in knowing, he just does. That's Charlie Watts. He just knows you immediately. If he likes you, he'll tell you things, give you things & you'll leave feeling like you've been talking to Jesus Christ…The only word I can use for Charlie is deep", said Richards. Watts's biography in the first official Rolling Stones fan club letter, included the statement that his ambition was "to own a pink Cadillac". He never learned to drive, but purchased a Lagonda of 1930s vintage in 1983, which he'd sit in and look at.

By then his mum Lillian was washing the 14 shirts that Charlie had bought, his 1st symbols of success: "He's always been a good boy. Never had any police knocking on the door or anything like that and he's always been terribly kind to old folk. He was always a neat dresser. That's why I get perturbed when they call them ugly & dirty. When he's home you can't get him out of the bathroom. People think he's moody but he's not really. He's just quiet. He hates fuss and gossip", she said.

Charlie and Shirley moved to a substantial property in Lewes in East Sussex during 1967. By the early '70s they'd moved again, to north Devon, to an even more impressive abode, a 600-acre stud farm where they bred Arabian horses. Specialising in horses of Polish origin, eventually the business was worth over £10m, although the farm manager was imprisoned for false accounting in the year 2000.

The frequent squabbling between the band's 2 central protagonists during the '70s & '80s made Watts consider leaving the Rolling Stones, but instead he relieved his frustrations through a series of side projects. Charlie started playing drums in Rocket 88 in the late '70s, Ian Stewart's boogie-woogie group; during the '80s he toured across the globe with a line-up including Jack Bruce, Courtney Pine, and Evan Parker; Warm & Tender, by the Charlie Watts Quintet, was issued in 1993, followed by Long Ago and Far Away 3 years later. He also released a L.P. with Jim Keltner & with The Charlie Watts

Tentet put out as 'Watts at Scotts' then from 2009 he played concerts with another band that he put together; the ABC&D of Boogie Woogie.

Diagnosed with throat cancer during 2004, he underwent a course of radiotherapy then recovered, returning to his day job with the Stones, his time with the group netting Watts an estimated £70m. He spent some of his time and money seeking out rare artefacts, including one of Kenny Clarke's drum kits, as well as one once played by Big Sid Catlett – "one of the great '30s swing drummers". He also collected signed first editions of 20th-century writers: "Agatha Christie: I've got every book she wrote in paperback. Graham Greene, I have all of them. Evelyn Waugh, he's another one. Wodehouse: everything he wrote".

Looking back on over 50 years with the Rolling Stones, Charlie reflected: "You have to be a good drummer to play with the Stones & I try to be as good as I can. It's terribly simple what I do, actually. It's what I like, the way I like it. I'm not a para-diddle man. I play songs. It's not technical, it's emotional. One of the hardest things of all is to get that feeling across".

Watts wrote and drew a children's book, 'Ode to a Highflying Bird', during his Art School days, originally intended for a class project, which was a biography about one of his musical heroes, Charlie 'Bird' Parker, who was depicted as an anthropomorphic bird. The story was drawn in a simple graphic style, with narration handwritten above the images. The book came to the attention of the publisher of the fanzine Rolling Stones Monthly in 1965, who encouraged Watts to publish it, although it had nothing to do with the band.

Around the same time John Lennon also published a book with illustrated poems & stories, 'In His Own Write' (1964), later followed by 'A Spaniard in the Works' (1965). On 17th January 1965, 'Ode to A Highflying Bird' was published as a 5 by 7 inch, 36-page book, which soon sold out. It was reprinted as part of the Charlie Watts Quintet album 'From One Charlie...' (1991).

Watts created a comic strip for the Stones' U.S. tour during 1966, printed inside the concert program. Titled 'It's The Same Old Story (If Not The Song)', it depicted Mick Jagger singing on an ever growing platform. While adoring fans kept increasing, the platform rose into the sky. One man kept criticizing the group, no matter how popular they got. Charlie intended it as a commentary on the relativity of show business. The drawing became part of the collection of the Rock and Roll Hall of Fame Museum.

The band released their L.P. 'Between the Buttons' in 1967, on the back cover of which Watts drew another comic strip in the same vein as the one from the year before. The panels showed fans cheering for the group, while others kept changing their opinion about how good or bad they were. The speech balloons contained condescending commentary including: 'All head & no bread!' and 'Is that a boy or a girl?'. Once the band became famous, the former critics started to like them: 'You know, they ain't so bad after all'. Lyrics from the title song appeared as captions underneath each panel. Wyman addressed the readers with the message: 'Between the Buttons! To understand this little rhyme, you must tap your foot in time. Then the buttons come much nearer and the Stones you see much clearer'.

Most of Charlie's published comics were made available to the public from 1965 - 1967. While they are definitely amateurish, they remain charming curiosities created by a world famous rock artist. Among other musicians who've illustrated their own album covers are Serge Buyse, Kurt Cobain, Def P, Daniel Johnston, Lucia Pamela, Schoolly D, Urbanus, Dallas Tamaira & Adam Wallenta.

Charlie Watts, whose adept, powerful skin work propelled the Rolling Stones for 58 years, died in London on the morning of Tuesday 24th August '21, at the age of 80. A statement from the group and

Watts' spokesperson read: "It is with immense sadness that we announce the death of our beloved Charlie Watts. He passed away peacefully in a London hospital earlier today surrounded by his family. Charlie was a cherished husband, father & grandfather and also a member of the Rolling Stones, one of the greatest drummers of his generation. We kindly request that the privacy of his family, band members and close friends is respected at this difficult time".

Watts had abruptly withdrawn from the Stones' upcoming U.S. tour on August 4th, which had been postponed due to the pandemic, citing the need to recover from an unspecified but 'successful' recent medical procedure. A spokesperson stated, 'Charlie has had a procedure which was completely successful, but I gather that his doctors this week concluded that he now needs proper rest & recuperation. With rehearsals starting in a fortnight it's very disappointing to say the least, but it's also fair to say that no one saw this coming'.

Unconfirmed reports said that Watts had undergone heart surgery; drummer Steve Jordan, a long-time associate of Stones guitarist Keith Richards, was filling in for the tour, which was due to begin in St. Louis on Sept. 26th. Charlie had generally been healthy throughout his career with the Rolling Stones, having recovered from throat cancer during 2004, following problems with substance abuse in the '70s -'80s, which he also beat.

Widely recognized as one of the greatest rock drummers of all time, Watts and Richards had always been the core of the Rolling Stones' instrumental sound: Keith spent over half his time at the band's concerts turned around, facing Charlie, bobbing his head to the drummer's rhythm. A review of a Rolling Stones concert during 2012 read : 'For all of Mick & Keith's supremacy, there's no question that the heart of this group is and will always be Watts: At 71, his whip-crack snare and preternatural sense of swing drive the songs with peerless authority & define the contradictory uptight-laid-back-ness that's at the heart of the Stones' rhythm'.

Charlie was never a flashy drummer, but driving the beat for 'The World's Greatest Rock 'n' Roll Band' for a 2-hr set in a stadium was an act of great physical endurance that Watts performed until he was 78. His last concert with the group was in Miami on August 30th, 2019, although he had appeared with them during the 'One World Together' all-star live stream in April 2020, early in the pandemic. Reviewing a show earlier during the 2019 tour, Variety wrote, 'Sitting at a minimalist kit and moving even more minimally with his casual jazz grip, Charlie looks like the mild-mannered banker who no one in the heist movie realizes is the guy actually blowing up the vault".

The wiry, basset-faced musician was a jazz-schooled player who came to the Stones through London's 'trad' scene of the early '60s, being the missing piece in the band's early line-up, joining in January 1963; with Jagger & Richards, he remained a constant on record and on stage for over 58 years. Watts nimbly, energetically supported the group's long run of dirty, blues- and R&B-based hits of the early to mid-'60s. He reached the apex of his prowess on a series of mature recordings, made with producer Jimmy Miller during the late '60s - early '70s, on which his sharp playing caromed off Keith's serrated guitar riffs.

In the oral history 'According to the Rolling Stones'[2003], Richards said, "To have a drummer from the beginning who could play with the sensibility of Charlie Watts is one of the best hidden assets I've had, because I never had to think about the drummer and what he's going to do. I just say, 'Charlie, it goes like this' then we'll kick it around a bit & it's done. I can throw him ideas and I never have to worry about the beat...It's a blessing".

A flexible player, Watts displayed his malleable chops on the band's forays into off-brand styles – psychedelia, reggae & on the hit single 'Miss You' (1978), disco. Although he'd grown tired of the Stone's touring pace by the '80s, he soldiered on with the group for 3 more decades, on what was probably the most comfortable and lucrative drumming gig in music. He survived bouts of heroin addiction then a battle with throat cancer, facing these challenges as the spotlight shined brighter on his more flamboyant band mates.

Charlie remained a picture of domestic bliss & tranquillity amid the soap-operatic lives of his fellow Stones, staying together with his wife Shirley amid rough patches, from 1964 to the end. He had a life-long passion for jazz, and from the '80s recorded with ad hoc line-ups of his Charlie Watts Quintet, essaying the hard-swinging instrumental music that fired his early interest in music.

In 'The True Adventures of the Rolling Stones', Watts told Stanley Booth, 'Fortunately my parents were perceptive enough to buy me a drum kit. I'd bought a banjo myself, taken the neck off & started playing it as a drum... I played newspaper with wire brushes. My parents bought me one of those first drum kits every drummer knows all too well". Charlie emblazoned the bass drum head of his early kit with the name 'Chico', after saxophonist Gerry Mulligan's drummer Chico Hamilton. In his teens he played in some regional jazz groups.

Watts first encountered some of his future band mates in 1962, at London's Ealing Club, a subterranean venue where 1st-generation trad-to-blues players including Alexis Korner and Cyril Davies made their early attempts at replicating US R&B and blues. Following a stint doing design work in Copenhagen, Charlie returned to London where he accepted an offer from Alexis to drum in his group Blues Incorporated, which for a time had featured Mick as its singer.

Jagger was establishing his own blues-based band, originally named the Rollin' Stones, with Keith Richards, guitarist Brian Jones, bassist Bill Wyman and pianist Ian Stewart. The weak link was drummer Tony Chapman, so after pleas from Keith & Brian, Watts replaced Chapman in the nascent group, being replaced in Korner's band by Ginger Baker, later of Cream.

Charlie later stated, "It was from Brian, Mick and Keith that I first seriously learned about R&B. I knew nothing about it. The blues to me was Charlie Parker or New Orleans jazz clarinetist Johnny Dodds playing slow". He taught himself by listening to recorded performances of drummers including Earl Phillips, Jimmy Reed's accompanist, and Fred Below, who powered many of Chess Records' big blues hits of the '50s.

Watts was a good pupil, forcefully completing the sound of the Rolling Stones, who soon removed Stewart from their permanent line-up, employing him as a side-man & road manager. From the band's 1st single, a cranked-up cover of Chuck Berry's 'Come On' [1963], he pushed the unit with seemingly effortless power and swing. Charlie gave potent support to the R&B- and blues-derived material recorded in the era when purist Jones was an equal in the Stones with Richards & Jagger. However, he was much more than a 4-on-the-floor timekeeper, flourishing as Jagger-Richards originals took the Stones to the top of the U.S. and U.K. charts.

Watts stood out on the group's first U.S. chart-topper, (I Can't Get No) Satisfaction (1965) then on later exotica including Paint It Black (1966), Ruby Tuesday, Dandelion, We Love You & She's a Rainbow (1967). He came into his own with Jumpin' Jack Flash, Street Fighting Man (1968) and Honky Tonk Women (1969), convulsive singles produced by Jimmy Miller that marked the end of Brian's time with the group, as he drowned during 1969 & the arrival of guitarist Mick Taylor.

Those tracks, along with Brown Sugar (No. 1, 1969) then Tumbling Dice (1972), drawn from the Stones' landmark albums Sticky Fingers and Exile on Main St., all had the trademark sound of the Stones at their peak, with Charlie bouncing hard off Keith's lacerating guitar intro. Watts featured on 8 successive chart-topping studio L.Ps by the Stones from 1971-81 & played on 3 of the biggest-grossing tours of the era. He brought his design skills to bear from 1975 onwards, working with Jagger on configuring the elaborate stage sets that became a hallmark of their later tours.

Watts began using heroin in the late '70s, his addiction becoming so severe that he nodded out in the studio during the recording of Some Girls Charlie. He later said that Richards – a big user of the drug – shook him awake at the session telling him, "You should do this when you're older". Charlie said that he took Keith's advice, stopping taking the drug. Despite his problems during the era, Watts smoothly navigated the dance-floor back-beat that propelled 'Miss You' [1978] the Stones' final # 1 single. He brought his whip-cracking skills to the band's top-10 hits of the early '80s, the perennial show-opener Start Me Up (1981) then the dark fusillade Undercover of the Night (1983).

Charlie again struggled with alcohol and drug issues during the mid-'80s, but once again shook off his addictions, cleaning up for good in 1986.

In his book 'Rolling With the Stones' [2002], bassist Bill Wyman, who left the Stones during 1993, stated that Watts' enthusiasm for working with the group waned during the late '80s, when conflict between Jagger & Richards over the direction of the group threatened to permanently run it aground. Charlie increasingly recorded and toured on his own as a jazz band leader, cutting a big band album for Columbia in 1986; four sets with his own quintet from 1991-96 then worked on a collaborative project with fellow drummer Jim Keltner during 2000, before a L.P. featuring his tentet was recorded at Ronnie Scott's famous jazz venue in London in 2004.

Watts clocked back in with the Stones after Mick & Keith reconciled: Their 4 studio albums from 1989-2005 being succeeded by massive tours that broke global records. His tour duty wasn't broken by throat cancer, diagnosed during 2004 then treated successfully. Around their golden anniversary year the group made successful arena tours without any new product in stores, hitting the road in 2012-16. They filled the Empire Polo Field in Indio, California during October 2016, site of the annual Coachella music festival on a double bill with Bob Dylan, as part of the 3-day Desert Trip festival, featuring '60s classic rock acts.

The Rolling Stones last toured with Charlie in 2019, including an August 22nd show at the Pasadena Rose Bowl, of which Variety observed in a review, 'The faces have changed, while the bodies, cocky postures and enviable stamina levels haven't, in some kind of laughably wonderful cosmic disconnect. ... Charlie Watts is still our darling, sitting at a minimalist kit & moving even more minimally with his casual jazz grip, looking like the mild-mannered banker who no one in the heist movie realizes is the guy actually blowing up the vault'.

The band played what turned out to be its final show with Watts just a few nights later, at Florida's Hard Rock Stadium on August 30th, 2019. The Stone's final public appearance with Charlie on drums was a filmed appearance for the 'One World: Together at Home' broadcast during April 2020, for which a contented-looking Watts played 'air drums' to a pre-recorded track on a fresh version of 'You Can't Always Get What You Want'.

Rumours were starting to spread in early 1975 that the Rolling Stones were about to announce a mammoth North and South American tour running through that summer & autumn. A news conference had been scheduled for May 1st at an hotel on 5th Avenue, right next to Washington Square Park, but it didn't happen that day. While journalists huddled inside the hotel, waiting for the Stones & getting out of the rain on a sweltering, muggy spring day in New York, a rumbling was heard outside, followed by screams. The writers and photographers rushed out to see what was happening before they realized what was causing what by then had become near-chaos in the streets.

There the Rolling Stones were, accompanied by keyboardist Billy Preston, on the back of a flat-bed truck performing a raucous, wonderfully sloppy version of Brown Sugar. At the end of the 8-min. performance, Mick Jagger, wearing blue jeans, white T-shirt & black leather jacket, reached into a plastic rubbish bin then began tossing out flyers that listed all the tour dates, folk clamouring for them as they floated to the pavement.

That's how the world found out where and when the Rolling Stones would be playing, leading to much discussion about whether it'd be their final tour given the age of their members, with Jagger turning 32 during July of that year. The media had been had but in tricking them, the Stones had pulled off one of the greatest promotional tour announcements in history. Apparently, the idea came from Charlie Watts, who'd recalled that jazz bands up in Harlem used to ride around during the day performing on the backs of trucks to promote their evening concerts. Little did Charlie know that he'd created a new tour announcement standard for the group that they'd try to top over the years.

Since then the Rolling Stones had been inventive and ingenious when it came to letting the world know that they were about to tour again, but it was doubtful whether or not anything would ever come close to what they achieved on that dank, drizzly but ultimately dazzling May Day of 1975. To announce their comeback tour during August 1989, the Stones took to the rails. Steel Wheels would be the first Rolling Stones L.P. since 1986 & to help promote the supporting tour, the group appeared by antique caboose, pulling up at New York City's Grand Central Station to field questions from over 300 members of the media. As Mick said that day: "I don't see it as a retrospective or a farewell or any thing like that. It's the Rolling Stones in 1989". The band provided a short sample of their upcoming single, Mixed Emotions, with Jagger holding his microphone up to a boom-box.

The group chose water as their mode of tour announcement during May 1994, cruising by boat from the Manhattan docks at West 79th Street to Pier 60 at West 19th Street to announce their Voodoo Lounge tour. It was the 1st time that Bill Wyman wasn't along for the ride, being replaced on bass by Darryl Jones. In rather tamer fashion, in August 1997 the Stones arrived by red Cadillac convertible under the Brooklyn Bridge for the announcement of their Bridges to Babylon tour, in support of their album of the same name.

Sensing that maybe their last couple of tour announcements had been too lame, the band got back in stride with a spectacular entrance into New York City's Van Cortland Park during 2002, arriving in a dazzling blimp emblazoned with their famous tongue logo. The group has always made their tour announcements in New York City, 2005 being no different. Perhaps because it had been 8 years since their last new album, the Rolling Stones didn't just give a news conference at the Julliard School in New York to announce the Bigger Bang tour on May 10th, they also played a mini concert. Like back in 1975, New Yorkers were treated to a free, if slightly less spontaneous performance by the 'greatest rock 'n' roll band in the world'.

That would be that for big, splashy tour announcements, at least as far as in-person events and spontaneous performances. As they prepared to hit the road for more recent tours like '50 & Counting', the Rolling Stones relied almost exclusively on social media to tease, hype and spread the word, times having changed regarding how a tour was promoted, leaving behind fond memories of how they often went the extra mile to give us satisfaction.

Despite becoming one of the greats of rock 'n' roll, the dapper, deadpan Charlie Watts spent over 60 years doing his 2nd-favourite job. Watts applied himself diligently to being the rock-steady heartbeat of the Rolling Stones, but what he always really wanted to do was play jazz. Charlie Parker, Duke Ellington & Miles Davis were his musical idols, while his playing was inspired by jazz drummers including Elvin Jones, Roy Haynes and Philly Joe Jones.

Charlie's career with the Stones ran from the cramped clubs of Britain's early-'60s blues boom to the international stadium tours that became their metier, but through it all, he seemed determined to be as self-effacing as possible as a member of the world's highest-profile rock group. Nonetheless, the band fully understood his value to them, Keith Richards, in particular, often acknowledging how fundamental Watts was to the Rolling Stones' sound, perhaps because Watts was prepared to make space for the churning rhythmic drive of his guitar. The crisp economy of his drumming, both swinging & muscular, was remarkable for its absence of frills or fuss, freeing the rest of the group to express themselves around it.

Charlie, a trained graphic designer, also contributed much to the Stones' marketing and presentation, which came to the fore as they evolved into a global brand & their performances grew increasingly spectacular. He created artwork for some early Stones releases and collaborated with Mick Jagger on the design of their elaborate stage sets for tours including Steel Wheels/Urban Jungle (1989-90), Bridges to Babylon (1997-98), Licks (2002-03) then A Bigger Bang (2005-07).

Any conversation with Watts was likely to range amiably across topics from Savile Row suits, cricket – having often attended Test matches at Lord's or the Oval – & the Arabian horses that he reared with his wife, Shirley, at their Halsdon Arabians farm in Devon, but he'd invariably return to jazz: "The first person whose playing I was aware of was the baritone saxophonist Gerry Mulligan, and the track was Walking Shoes, with Chico Hamilton playing drums. That's what made me want to play the drums. Before that I wanted to play alto sax, because I loved Earl Bostic", Charlie recalled during 2012.

Watts became lifelong friends with his neighbour Dave Green, who would become a jazz bass player. The young Charlie, dubbed 'Charlie Boy' by his parents, became fixated on hard bop & cool jazz in the '50s, having bought himself a banjo when he was 14, but rather than learn how to play it, converted it into a snare drum. Watts was given his 1st drum kit as a Christmas present during 1955, and while other kids were shaking a leg to Bill Haley or Elvis Presley, he dreamed of playing drums with Miles Davis, or stepping into Art Blakey's shoes with the Jazz Messengers. His first band was the jazz outfit the Jo Jones All Stars, which he & Green both joined in 1958.

In the small pool of the nascent British 'blues boom', the future Rolling Stones Mick Jagger and Brian Jones, who was then going by the stage name Elmo Lewis, made appearances with Alexis Korner's Blues Incorporated, before Jones branched off to form his own group that included the Stones' unsung but faithful pianist, Ian Stewart. A meeting with Jagger & Richards led to the formation of the Rolling Stones, although it was a few months before the cautious Charlie could be persuaded to leave Korner's band to join them during January 1963.

Watts watched the Rolling Stones' remarkable trajectory from his vantage point at the back of the stage, occasionally allowing himself a quizzical smile but remaining detached from the cavalcade of sex, drugs and spectacular headlines that followed the band around the world. Renowned as the quiet, sensible one, he never strayed into the limelight if he could help it, although the title of Peter Whitehead's documentary film Charlie Is My Darling, shot when the Stones visited Ireland in 1965, recognised that Watts projected his own quiet mystique. While Mick, Brian & Keith were out on the town in London, Charlie quietly wed Shirley Shepherd during 1964 without telling his band mates, their relationship staying close until his death.

Watts' natural self-reliance failed him or a brief period in the mid-'80s, during recording of the Stones' L.P. Dirty Work [1985], when Jagger and Richards were at loggerheads, the future of the group looking shaky. With Charlie's daughter Seraphina having been expelled from school for smoking dope, Watts began hitting the bottle and developed a heroin habit: "Maybe towards the end of 1986, I hit an all-time low in my personal life & in my relationship with Mick. I was mad on drink and drugs. I became a completely different person, not a nice one. I nearly lost my wife, family, everything".

However, the ever-practical Charlie weaned himself off drugs before his addiction had become public knowledge, concentrating on building his family life focused around horses & breeding sheepdogs at a country estate that he'd bought in Devon. Watts also distracted himself from the squabbles and struggles of the Stones by forming the Charlie Watts Big Band, which featured many top British jazz players, touring the US then recording an album, Live at Fulham Town Hall [1986].

This was followed by the Charlie Watts Quintet during 1991, which recorded a string of L.Ps, including From One Charlie, a tribute to Charlie Parker then during the year in 2000 he teamed up with fellow sticks-man Jim Keltner for the Charlie Watts/Jim Keltner Project, a tribute to the pair's favourite jazz drummers. The L.P. Watts at Scott's [2004], was a live recording of the Charlie Watts Tentet at Ronnie Scott's club in London, which was issued as it emerged that he'd been undergoing surgery and radiotherapy for throat cancer.

While touring & studio work with the Rolling Stones continued, Charlie began playing with the ABC&D of Boogie Woogie during 2009, taken from the 1st-name initials of its members, who were the pianists Axel Zwingenberger and Ben Waters & bassist Dave Green. Charlie was known for being all business when he was on-stage with The Rolling Stones, but when he was playing with the ABC&D of Boogie Woogie, he let loose and had fun. They cut albums The Magic of Boogie Woogie (2010) then

Live in Paris (2012) while 'Charlie Watts meets the Danish Radio Big Band' was recorded live in Copenhagen in 2010, before being belatedly released during 2017.

For his entire musical career, Charlie Watts was known as the cool one, being the guy that the other members of The Rolling Stones always wanted to be like. In Stephen Davis' Stones biography 'Old Gods Almost Dead', it was said that was because Charlie was 'genuinely hip', with 'innate good taste'. In his autobiography 'Life', Keith Richards called Watts 'the secret essence of the whole thing'.

When Watts sat behind his drum set at each Stones concert, he was the consummate professional, calm, cool & collected, unblinking in his demeanour. He had a knack for keeping the rhythm of the group together, absolutely nothing seeming to faze him while doing so, but as the drummer of the ABC&D of Boogie Woogie, Charlie did something he seldom had on-stage with the Stones, really enjoying himself, constantly smiling, at times laughing, his elation being clear as he revelled in the music.

Boogie pianist Ben Waters was 1st to initiate the formation of what became the ABC&D of Boogie Woogie, a band celebrating the near forgotten style of piano-based blues and jazz music, featuring the A (Axel Zwingenberger on piano), B (Ben Waters on piano), C (Charlie Watts on drums) & D (Dave Green on bass). Waters had called Watts c. 3 years earlier to ask if the Stones' drummer was interested in performing with him and Zwingenberger, it taking little to convince him, his only request being to get Dave Green to play bass, telling Ben, "If Dave does it, I'll do it".

A year later, the musicians recorded 'Live in Paris', the ABC&D of Boogie Woogie's debut, recorded over several nights in September 2010 at the Duc Des Lombards jazz club. The live L.P. encompassed all the charm of the group in a city that had always embraced jazz music. "I said, 'We should play in Paris. It's big on jazz. It's enthusiastically jazz-centred. All the great Americans either lived or went to Paris since the '20s, from Josephine Baker to Sidney Bechet. It's one of the few countries in the world where they have two 24-hr radio stations of jazz. It's fantastic", stated an impeccably dressed Charlie in his New York City hotel room.

The set on the 'Live in Paris' was a cocktail of improvisation, originality & salute to the standards, but it was really a message of devotion to the great boogie-woogie musicians of history: "I've only ever heard them on record, and you couldn't say they were bad records. I mean, they're the benchmark of how you play this music", said Watts, referring to iconic boogie-woogie piano players like Albert Ammons, Pete Johnson & Meade 'Lux' Lewis.

Charlie's true passion was traditional jazz music. Not only did he like playing jazz, he was a great collector of jazz memorabilia. While the stick-man recognized that his career was indebted to the rock 'n' roll of one of the most significant periods in its history, the 'British Invasion', Watts said that he'd rather have been a jazz drummer during the '40s in New York City: "I'd love to have been good enough to play here then. To listen to and play with all those guys that I love, oh, sure. Having said that, there are other eras, as well & my career, if you like, some things have happened to me that are just amazing, really".

At the time of the British Invasion, Charlie hadn't thought that the era was particularly amazing or unique, having been more interested in playing the drums or listening to other stick-men than being part of a musical movement. Watts still didn't fully understand the term 'rock 'n' roll', even though he was a long-time member of a group that had become known as 'the greatest rock 'n' roll band of all time': "I don't know what 'rock' is. It's like pop. Pop is from 'popular'. I've never been interested in that. I love being popular, I might add, but I'm not interested in popular or its culture.

I never thought it would last like it has. It's also become, to be honest with you, just a word now. To me, rock 'n' roll is Chuck Berry or Little Richard. I mean, there are no bands that play like that any more. All those people were of the '50s and that's rock 'n' roll to me. Since then, I don't think it is.

I mean, what the fc*k's a 'rock chick'? It's stupid. It's just a popular name the fashion designers have called up. It's nothing. In the '70s, it'd be called a groupie. Before that it was called a whore or a prostitute, so a 'rock chick' is a bastardized version of that.

Boogie woogie was a popular form of music for c.5 years in America. All the big bands did one boogie woogie record. The Andrew Sisters sang about boogie woogie. Tommy Dorsey ... all the big groups had a section of the show that featured the piano player playing 8 to the bar, they called it. 'Beat me Daddy, 8 to the bar' stuff. I mean, it just died out, really". Could Charlie's fame attract new listeners to boogie woogie? Would Rolling Stones fans be interested? Could a younger generation be turned on to such a lost genre?

"Whether it turns them on, I don't know. It's dance music. It's a dance beat. It died out, but it spawned New Orleans & rock 'n' roll. Most rock 'n' roll piano players played great blues, and they played boogie woogie with it, so it's a combination of them all. If a young kid was talented enough to play boogie woogie piano, he might become another Little Richard or something. When we loved Richard, he was a good-looking young man & had great records, as well. It has to have a lot of things going for it, and kids follow movements. They were the ones that got boogie woogie players in the big bands & all that, because they loved to dance to it."

If there's one thing that boogie woogie is, it's a live performance music, the liner notes for 'Live in Paris' emphasized: "Any music is, and any musician who's any good is much more exciting & thrilling to see live. You're seeing them at work, and you're hearing it as it comes from them. I learned to play from records & watching guys do it, watching it done live. The best way to see a drummer is live. Stand near him, watch him play, listen and if he's any good that's what you'll hear, how good he is. If you'd gone to see Roy Haynes play, he was phenomenal & I don't mean lots of drumming. I mean, just the sound of the man and the presence of him is as great as all the things he does. It's just him being there, doing it. It's live music".

Although the Stones were known for their great rehearsal efforts, The ABC&D of Boogie Woogie didn't put much importance on rehearsing or following a set list. A live performance was spontaneous by nature, with the group capitalizing on that. Piano players Zwingenberger and Waters sprang songs on the rest of the band, any given song being subject to an impromptu jam. Watts thought that the one difference in playing between 2 piano players rather than a couple of guitarists, was that the music was much more conversational, saying of the songs introduced by either Axel or Ben to be performed by the group:

"They come out different every time. We don't play them in any order & we don't play the same songs, so I don't know if we're going to do 'Route 66' until the intro. We never know what we're playing. It keeps it interesting. You have to get the right sticks and all that, but that's the only hard bit about it. You miss the intro sometimes, because you haven't been ready, but it's different. It doesn't need that rehearsed thing. In fact, it would lose a lot if it was rehearsed tightly".

One would imagine that it had to be quite a challenge, shifting from the strict, serious business of mainstream rock 'n' roll to the fun & loose spirit of boogie woogie, but Charlie didn't see it that way, in large part because he did both: "I mean, if I played jazz all my life then you suddenly said, 'You're playing rock 'n' roll with the Stones tomorrow,' it might be quite a jump, but I've played with jazz players while playing with the Stones, who supposedly play rock 'n' roll".

All of that uninhibited energy of the ABC&D of Boogie Woogie was on display during the band's engagement at The Iridium jazz club in mid-town Manhattan. The Iridium was an intimate, classy jazz venue with great acoustics, just the kind of New York City club one could see Watts sentimentalizing over. The audience was a mix of Iridium regulars, jazz aficionados and Rolling Stones fans, a few of whom were holding onto their copies of the group's classic albums, hoping that their vinyl would be consecrated by Watts' signature after the show.

However, one important person was missing, the 'B' of the outfit, pianist Waters, Ben being unable to make the performance for some unannounced reason. Earlier, Charlie had mentioned that Waters was "lost in the Adirondacks somewhere", so the gig had to go on without him. Bob Seeley filled the 'B' role of the group that evening, a renowned American boogie woogie pianist from Detroit, who turned out to be quite a treat. Bob introduced himself by telling the story of his lifelong friendship & close bond with legend Meade 'Lux' Lewis then led the band into Chicago Flyer, a Lewis gem from the Blue Note years.

On the other side of the stage, Zwingenberger was smooth and restrained compared with Seeley's emotive style. Watts, in the middle, waited for his cue with sticks under his arm. When he came into the song, he played it as if enjoying a dream. At times he rolled back his eyes, as if in a euphoric state. Charlie was in his element during the next series of songs, appearing to be playing on Cloud 9, with the music as his silver lining. The crowd, once subdued with an inner, intense anticipation, was now on every jam, clapping when a musician excelled. Watts at times let loose when a given song built to a crescendo. He liked to glance at his band-mates as an acknowledgement of respect, often looking over at Dave Green whenever the bassist had played a nice run.

One of the highlights of the night was guest vocalist Lila Ammons, granddaughter of Albert Ammons & niece of famed tenor saxophonist Gene 'Jug' Ammons, who sang to a boogie woogie arrangement of 'Oh, Lady Be Good'. Blessed with a slick voice, she then sassed through some 'Alley Boogie' as if she were Lucille Bogan herself. The performances were so pure that it was easy for audience members to close their eyes then picture themselves in a New York City nightclub during the '40s and in the heart of that fantasy setting, Charlie could picture the late Ian Stewart, a pianist, uncompromising boogie woogie practitioner & co-founder and inherent spirit of The Rolling Stones: "Oh, Stu would love it. That's what he did. That's what he was but he'd have had his own band here".

Charlie Watts had always had the reputation of being the coolest & quietest Rolling Stone, but ask the drummer about something he really cared about – the great bebop players or the timeless jazz standards that the Charlie Watts Quintet performed on their latest L.P., Long Ago and Far Away – then he waxed lyrical. In the 5 years since that project, the Stones' backing vocalist Bernard Fowler had joined the quintet, with the group having recorded 3 more albums, each a labour of love undertaken by Watts in between commitments to the Stones.

Why had Charlie chosen songs like I've Got a Crush on You & In a Sentimental Mood for their new L.P?

"My mother used to sing some of them when I was a kid, hence the title of the album. It's quite nice setting a singer up like that with the strings. If you're a drummer, and you sit & the strings just swell like that, it's a fantastic sound to just swish away to. I enjoy that because I play with guitar players all the time".

The quintet's 1st 3 L.Ps were on Continuum, but they were now recording for the Stones' label, Virgin.

"Originally I wanted to do solo things behind the scenes, just bring them out on a little label. I don't really like talking about these things. Given the choice, I'd sooner play to you than sit and talk to you but when you've got it finished, it's really nice for folk to be able to hear it. With the other albums, guys in the band would be saying, 'My girlfriend or my mum wants one. Where can I get it?'"

Had Watts considered creating another book like Ode to a High Flying Bird?

"I keep a diary of drawings. I've drawn every bed I've slept in on tour since 1967. It's a fantastic non-book. I used to take a lot of things that keep you awake & I'd have nothing to do, so I have all these hotel rooms recorded".

That sounded worse than Bill Wyman's book, Stone Alone, with its endless lists of the women he slept with and how much money he made.

"Well, it's more boring. What's nice about it is, it's visual & it just goes on and on, so you think, 'Is this ever gonna end?' You've got Washington in '67 then you've got Washington a couple of years ago and they're kind of the same".

Did Charlie miss playing with Wyman?

"I never miss playing with him, but I miss him as a person. He got to an age – a ripe old age – where he was fed up with it. Bill never had a desire to be Darryl Jones or Charlie Mingus. He's very happy now because he has 2 young children. He went through a hell of a time with that awful wife he had, the 2nd wife. He's been very lucky with girlfriends, but very unlucky with wives".

Had Watts ever felt like quitting?

"I've always wanted to be a drummer. I've always had this illusion of being in the Blue Note or Birdland with Charlie Parker in front of me. It didn't sound like that, but that was the illusion I had. As long as it's comfortable with my wife, I'll continue to do it. I don't know what I'd do if I didn't do it. The problem with being a drummer: It's not like you can write songs or tiddle about on a piano. There's nothing for me to do at home. My wife tells me to get out of the house".

What was Charlie's approach to the drums?

"The way I look at drumming is, it's backing somebody. If you think like that, you're quite happy backing Keith in whatever time he plays – musical time or length of time. There aren't many folk that play like the Stones do any more, although the playing band has become popular in Europe again – like Blur & Oasis. At least you can hear that they're really playing: The drums are there, and the cymbals are too loud. I love that. The problem with Oasis is that we've already heard that with the Beatles. They're not the Sex Pistols. When the Sex Pistols came on the scene, I thought, 'Nobody does noise like that'. They were the best at that time".

What did Watts think of the Sex Pistols reunion?

"Of all groups – what the Pistols stood for and the way they did it – I don't think it'll work at the age of 40. There have been gaps, but the Rolling Stones have never stopped doing what we do, which is trying to play Chicago blues. When you stop then start again, there's another thing that comes into it, which is age. It's not going to be the same with them saying, 'F*cking b*llocks' in the middle of a song. When you're 20, everybody's with you doing it".

Folk could say that about the Stones too.

"If Mick was overweight, a lot greyer & bald – I mean, I'm grey and bald, but I'm not sitting out in front – if he was all those things, he'd know that, so he wouldn't do it, but he's as good as he ever was, and folk still enjoy it as much. I think we'll probably do it again".

A lot of Stones fans were surprised by Jagger's revelation that Charlie had a drug & alcohol problem.

"I've said it myself, but people don't believe it. I nearly killed myself. At the end of 2 years on speed and heroin, I was very ill. My daughter used to tell me I looked like Dracula".

How had Charlie stopped?

"I just stopped cold – for me & for my wife. It was never me, really. I passed out in the studio once, and that to me was a blatant lack of professionalism. You might have been drunk in the studio, but you'd never f*ck up. I passed out then Keith picked me up – this is Keith, who I've seen in all sorts of states, doing all sorts of things – & he said to me, 'This is the sort of thing you do when you're 60', which stuck in my mind. I think I'm very lucky to be alive and to have made a very good living doing what I do".

'For years I never talked to the press. Somebody asked me why I didn't then I said, 'Well, I don't really feel like talking. I don't like it'. I still don't. I trust the others to say whatever they say on my behalf. They never say things I disagree with. I'm not very sociable. I'd rather be sitting listening to the radio'.

- Charlie Watts, 1998

'Musicians are the most selfish people in the world, actually. The world revolves around them & all you live for is that 2 hrs on stage and that's all they have... They're the most unwelcoming folk, really. I'm not saying that they're not nice people or intelligent, but it's what they do. They aren't the most open of folk. I think it's their attitude & I don't think it's ever going to change. So much for philosophy'.

- Charlie Watts, 1981

'I give the impression of being bored, but I'm not really. I've just got an incredibly boring face'.

- Charlie Watts

'We all thought Charlie was very kind of hip when we 1st met him, because of his jackets and shirts. Because he was working in an advertising agency, he was very different. It was good for the band to have someone who was sort of sharp'.

- Mick Jagger, 1979

'With Charlie we were thinking about the atmosphere in the group. In the early days I thought Keith might be an awkward person to get to know. I'd watch Keith with other folk, and he always seemed to back away a bit, but he & Charlie were a f*ckin' comedy team. They had a dual sense of humour'.

- Ian Stewart, 1979

'We had the advantage that Keith and I both get along very well with Charlie. The fact that there's 3 of us who get along so well is very important'.

- Mick Jagger, 1979

'I always wanted to be a drummer. I always wanted to play with Charlie Parker. When I was 13 I wanted to do that'.

  - Charlie Watts, 1994

'I'm the sort of player that needs to be kicked up the arse, i.e. he needs somebody around him that's that brilliant it sends him along. I couldn't turn music round personally. There are certain people that think they can, and certainly do turn it round. I'm not that sort of player. I sit there, I hear what's going on & if I can make it, that's fine. I'm not that sort of player - I'm not that sort of person, anyway'.

- Charlie Watts, 1973

'To me, how an American plays the drums is how you should play the drums. That's how I play. I mean, I play regular snare drum, I don't play tympani style, although I know guys who play fantastically like that. I play march-drum style. Most rock drummers play like Ringo; a bastard version of tympani style. In reality, that's what it is, because tympani style is fingers and most rock drummers play like that because it's heavy offbeat'.

  - Charlie Watts, 1981

'Charlie's always there, but he doesn't want to let everybody know. There's very few drummers like that. Everybody thinks Mick & Keith are the Rolling Stones. If Charlie wasn't doing what he's doing on drums, that wouldn't be true at all. You'd find out that Charlie Watts is the Stones'.

- Keith Richards, 1979

'White drummers don't swing, except for Charlie Watts'.

- Keith Richards, 1977

'I don't know how the hell that old sucker got to be so good. He'd be the last one to agree, but to me he's the drummer. There's not many rock 'n' roll drummers that actually swing. Most of 'em don't even know what the word means. It's the difference between something that trundles down the highway but never takes off and something that actually flies. It's got nothing to do with the technicalities, the flash fills, the solos & the power - although, I'll tell you, I would hate to be on the end of his fist and like all good players he's a modest, self-effacing person. Like Stu (Ian Stewart), the good ones don't need to be flash. They don't need to blow their own trumpet. Only folk who are unsure of themselves mouth off'.

- Keith Richards, 1985

'Charlie never says anything. He just stands there with his arms folded, holding his cup of coffee. If you ask him what he thinks of something, he'll just say, 'I don't know', but he listens & when the time comes, he's right there. Having a drummer like that, who can play rock 'n' roll, make it swing and so many other things - he plays reggae great, which not many non-Jamaicans can - that's all the difference'.

- Ron Wood, 1977

'There's nothing forced about Charlie, least of all his modesty. It's totally real. He can't understand what folk see in his drumming'.

- Keith Richards, 1981

'Charlie, after 20 years, still can't stand the thought of having to do even the slightest thing that strikes a false note, like smiling at somebody if you don't want to. He'd rather give them a scowl, so at least it's honest'.

- Keith Richards, 1983

'Charlie is incredibly honest, brutally honest. Lying bores him. He just sees right through you to start with & he's not even that interested in knowing, he just does. That's Charlie Watts. He just knows you immediately. If he likes you, he'll tell you things, give you things, and you'll leave feeling like you've been talking to Jesus Christ. They say he's a dying breed, but with folk like Charlie, they must always have been rare. Genuinely eccentric in the sense of having his own way of doing things.

Just to put it on a very physical plane: At the end of the show, he'll leave the stage, when the sirens will be going, limousines waiting then Charlie will walk back to his drum-kit to change the position of his drumsticks by 2 mm. He'll look at it then if it looks good, he'll leave. He has this preoccupation with aesthetics, this vision of how things should be that nobody will ever know about except Charlie. The drums are about to be stripped down then put in the back of a truck, but he can't leave if he's got it in his mind that he's left his sticks in a displeasing way. It's so Zen. So you see what I mean about who the hell can I possibly play with after this guy with such a sense of space & touch. The only word I can use for Charlie is deep'.

- Keith Richards, 1988

'The only time I love attention is when I walk on-stage, but when I walk off, I don't want it. For the band, I want everyone to love us and go crazy, but when I walk off, I don't want it. I guess I want both worlds. I never could deal with it & still can't'.

- Charlie Watts, 1981

'I collect anything, not only drums. I do. I collect anything'.

- Charlie Watts, 1994

'I don't sleep on tours, 'cos I got no one to sleep with, so I talk to folk and I draw'.

- Charlie Watts, 1979

'I get bored anywhere. The only time I'm not bored is when I'm drawing, playing the drums or talking. I talk a lot, about nothing usually, and all contradictory. Shirley always accuses me of having no beliefs. Maybe that's why I can talk to anyone'.

- Charlie Watts

'I make a sketch of every bedroom I sleep in. If you're in place for 2 or 3 days, it's comfortable to complete. When you're in & out it's hard, but I've sketched every bed I've slept in on tour since about 1968. It's a visual diary that doesn't mean anything to anyone. I never look through them once I've done them, to be honest. It's more a record, to know I've got it... I'll look at them all one day'.

- Charlie Watts, 1998

'He's such fun to play with, he's so on right now. I do believe the guy keeps on getting better and better & better, with less and less effort. That's what I've always admired about musicians is that when it's slamming a bit and you look at the guy then he says (flip with the finger), as if he's having a cup of tea or something, that effortlessness. He's always been elitist & arrogant and I admire that'.

- Keith Richards, 1997

'I got off the plane in '72 then said 'No f*cking more!' because I don't actually like touring and I don't like living out of suitcases. I hate being away from home. I always do tours thinking they're the last one then at the end of them I always leave the band. Because of what I do I can't play the drums at home, so to play the drums I have to go on the road & to go on the road I have to leave home, which is like a terribly vicious circle that's always been my life'.

- Charlie Watts, 1989

'It's very difficult to keep a marriage together when you're on the road. Not so much now as earlier, because the nice thing about now is that one can dictate what you're doing. Then, you couldn't. It's harder on folk around. It's a very lonely life'.

- Charlie Watts, 1989

'Mick's taste in music... isn't as airy-fairy as mine. He's blues-and-R&B-oriented... Visually, it's the same. I'll veer to the right colour and Mick will put an edgy stamp to it. If I go too pink or chartreuse, he'll bring it back to bright red, which I find hideous'.

- Charlie Watts, 2005

'Maybe I'd have been a better person if I'd gone through all that drug taking... Part of it is that I never was a teenager, man. I'd be off in the corner talking about Kierkegaard. I always took myself seriously & thought Buddy Holly was a great joke'.

- Charlie Watts, 1970s

'My drug and alcohol problems were my way of dealing with family issues. Looking back on it, I think it was a mid-life crisis. All I know is that I became totally another person c. 1983 then came out of it c. 1986. I nearly lost my wife and everything over my behaviour. I wasn't particularly fun to live with. I would've died... I just stopped everything. I barely ate for 2 months, because I'd started to get fat from the drinking'.

- Charlie Watts, 2000

'Drugs are very hard to give up. For me, anyway. I didn't even take that many. I wasn't that badly affected, I wasn't a junkie, but giving up amphetamines & heroin was very, very hard. Much, much harder than the rest of it... I stopped after I slipped down the steps when I was in the cellar getting a bottle of wine. It really brought it home to me how far down I'd gone. I just stopped everything - drinking, smoking, taking drugs, everything, all at once. I just thought, 'enough is enough''.

- Charlie Watts, 2000

'It's genuinely enjoyable what I do. It's a lot of fun. Being in this band is a lot of fun. It's bloody hard work, but it's a lot of fun... We're very lucky. We have a huge crowd of folk who like us and they just love looking at Keith Richards & at Mick wiggling his arms. They've been doing it for 30 years'.

- Charlie Watts, 1998

'You don't get the accolades if you're crap, so that's what I mean about this group - they're damn good and I don't care if folk say they're noisy. They are noisy. They make my ears hurt, but they're bloody good at being noisy & they're bloody good at whatever they do. What I try to do is make it better and I try to help out the best that I can'.

- Charlie Watts, 1981

'You have to be a good drummer to play with the Stones & I try to be as good as I can. It's terribly simple what I do, actually. It's what I like, the way I like it. I'm not a para-diddle man. I play songs. It's not technical, it's emotional. One of the hardest things of all is to get that feeling across'.

- Charlie Watts, 2000

'It's a drug. It's something that for some reason people do. Count Basie's done it for 50 years, working round the world. I know it's a living, money, obvious explanations, but still there's that thing - he has to do it. He goes out and does it. The same thing I think applies to us. It's something you have to do if you're a band - that's what I was saying earlier about the Rolling Stones, to me they're a group. It's work, fun, everything, it's a lifestyle & I think most bands are a lifestyle. I like that - you make a way of life and I don't know any other, that's what mucks you up. For me, there's no other way of life. If tomorrow it packs up, fine. C'est la vie, as they say in Germany'.

- Charlie Watts, 1973

'I'd be scared of stopping. What I do is play the drums. I've never found anything to take its place. I don't know what I'd do if I didn't do it. As you get older, you suddenly have this number in front of you & you haven't got a great deal of time left. You panic a bit. Two years' touring out of that is prime time'.

- Charlie Watts, 2000

'Charlie is a great English eccentric. I mean, how else can you describe a guy who buys a 1936 Alfa Romeo just to look at the dashboard? Can't drive - just sits there and looks at it. He's an original, and he happens to be one of the best drummers in the world. Without a drummer as sharp as Charlie, playing would be a drag. He's very quiet - but persuasive. It's very rare that Charlie offers an opinion. If he does, you listen. Mick & I fall back on Charlie more than would be apparent. Many times, if there's something between Mick and I, it's Charlie I've got to talk to. It could be as simple as whether to play a certain song, or I'll say, 'Charlie, should I go to Mick's room & hang him?' and he'll say 'No'. His opinion counts'.

- Keith Richards, 2002

'It's been a long time since curtains went up. I get very nervous. If you didn't you'd toss it off - you'd take it for granted & I don't take the Rolling Stones for granted, or anything they do. I wish I could relax and enjoy the show more, instead of thinking, 'Where are we now?' Keith always gives the impression that he's happy with whatever bar he's playing in a song. He's never worried about the next one & those couple of hours are over in a flash. You think, 'God, that was Chicago done, and all I did was worry about where the ending of a song was'.

- Charlie Watts, August 2005

'I want to be buried next to Charlie Watts'.

- Keith Richards, June 2016

'I really play to please Keith & Mick and then the audience & if you get all 3 you're laughing'.

- Charlie Watts, September 2016

'I love this group, but it doesn't mean everything to me. I always think this band is going to fold up all the time - I really do. I never thought it would last 5 mins, but I figured I'd live that 5 mins to the hilt, because I love them. They're bigger than I am if you really want to know. I admire them, I like them as friends, I argue with them and I love them. They're part of my life & they've been part of my life for a lot of years now. I don't really care if it stops though, quite honestly. I don't care if I retire now, but I don't know what I'd do if I stopped doing this. I'd go mad'.

- Charlie Watts, 1981

Charlie Watts, aged 63, was being treated for throat cancer, undergoing radiotherapy at the Royal Marsden hospital near his home in Chelsea, west London. Watts was diagnosed with the disease after going into hospital during June 2004. The musician, who hadn't smoked since the '60s, was said to be in 'good form' having walked to the hospital to be treated. His band-mates had been informed and he'd been supported by his wife, Shirley, during the 6-week course of treatment, of which he'd completed 4 weeks.

A spokesman for Watts said: 'Having been diagnosed with throat cancer following a minor operation in June, Charlie Watts is reaching the end of radiotherapy treatment. He's expecting to make a full recovery then start work with the rest of the group later in the year'. He said Charlie's treatment had not interfered with any touring or recording plans for the band who'd been 'relaxing between work commitments'.

Watts, who once said that his time with the Rolling Stones was '5 years of playing & 25 years of hanging around', toured with the group from September 2002 to October 2003. An accomplished jazz musician, as well as the most laid-back member of the Stones, he'd returned to his 1st passion earlier in 2004 when he'd spent some time that April with his 'tentet' performing nightly at the world-famous at Ronnie Scott's jazz club in the West End of London. Charlie had regularly performed at jazz clubs during quieter spells of his career with the band.

Ronnie Wood, a guitarist with the group, was told earlier that year to give up smoking by doctors after traces of emphysema were found during a routine scan. The Stones were expected to return to the recording studio that October to begin working on a new L.P., before embarking on another world tour believed to be starting during 2005.

Rolling Stones drummer Charlie Watts was thought likely miss the band's latest U.S. tour, scheduled to start again in September '21, to allow him to recover from an unspecified medical procedure. A spokesperson for the sticks-man stated that the procedure was 'completely successful' but that Watts needed time to recuperate. The Stones were set to resume their No Filter tour with a stadium show on Sept. 26th in St. Louis.

"With rehearsals starting in a couple of weeks it's very disappointing to say the least, but it's also fair to say no one saw this coming," a spokesperson for Charlie said in a statement. Watts, 80, said that he did 't want his recovery to further delay the tour, which was scheduled to visit several U.S. cities including Dallas, Atlanta, Los Angeles and Las Vegas. "For once my timing has been a little off. I'm working hard to get fully fit but I've today accepted on the advice of the experts that this will take a while", he said. Watts would be replaced by understudy Steve Jordan, who'd played with Keith Richards for years.

Sir Mick Jagger & Keith Richards paid tribute to their band-mate Charlie Watts, following the death of the Rolling Stones drummer in a London hospital on Tuesday 24th August '21. In posts on Twitter and Instagram, vocalist Sir Mick shared a photograph of Charlie smiling while seated behind a drum kit. Lead guitarist Richards also took to social media to share a picture of a set of drums with a 'closed' sign on them.

The news came weeks after it was announced that he'd miss the Rolling Stones' US No Filter tour the following month to recover from an unspecified medical procedure. Watts had helped the group become one of those who took rock 'n' roll to the masses during the '60s with classics including (I Can't Get No) Satisfaction, Jumpin' Jack Flash, Get Off My Cloud & Sympathy for the Devil.

The photograph posted by Jagger on his social media, which didn't have a caption, showed Charlie performing with his own jazz band, The ABC&D of Boogie Woogie, at the Casino in Herisau, Switzerland in January 2010. Sir Paul McCartney and Sir Ringo Starr of the Beatles were among the other stars from the world of rock to remember Watts. McCartney described Watts as 'a lovely guy' & 'a fantastic drummer', who was 'steady as a rock', while Fab Four sticks-man Starr wrote on Twitter: 'God bless Charlie Watts, we're going to miss you man'.

Sir Elton John Tweeted: 'A very sad day. Charlie Watts was the ultimate drummer. The most stylish of men, and such brilliant company'. Other top drummers paid homage, with Stewart Copeland of The Police telling BBC Radio 5 Live that Charlie had an 'unique rhythmic personality' that set him apart. 'He's unique, he's irreplaceable. There's only one guy with that sound. You can try to figure it out on paper, what made that sound. You could say his kick drum was leading the charge but his back-beat snare was just a little hair behind the beat & that combination... You can describe that, but there was only one guy who could do it'.

The Doors' John Densmore remembered him on Twitter as 'an early mentor, a fellow jazz fan'.

US drummer and singer Sheila E said Watts had 'done so much for us musically & as a drummer' having been 'one of the best'. Kenney Jones, sticks-man for The Who and the Small Faces, told the BBC that Charlie was the 'heart & soul of The Rolling Stones'. Also paying tribute, The Who front-man Roger Daltrey said that Watts was the 'perfect gentleman, as sharp in his manner of dress as he was on the drums'. Folk singer Joan Baez remembered him as 'A prince among thieves' and 'a gentleman through & through'.

Charlie Watts wasn't ever the most flashy of drummers, not being known for the frenzied solos of Ginger Baker of Cream, or for his explosive kick drum like Keith Moon of The Who. Charlie was the subtle, stoic heartbeat of The Rolling Stones for 58 years. A jazz aficionado, he was attracted to the drums after listening to Chico Hamilton play brushes on Walking Shoes, only being introduced to the dark arts of rock 'n' roll by Mick Jagger and Keith Richards during the early '60s.

Watts joined the Stones in January 1963 after the group had dismissed several other sticks-men then they never looked back. 'Charlie Watts gives me the freedom to fly on stage', Keith later observed. His jazz-inflected swing gave the Stones' songs their swagger, pushing & pulling at the groove, creating room for Mick's lascivious drawl. Charlie was at his best on the cowbell-driven Honky Tonk Women plus the locked-down groove Gimme Shelter, when he threw in some uncharacteristically showy fills.

On and off the stage, he was quiet & reserved, staying in the shadows while letting the rest of the band bask in the limelight. 'I've actually never been interested in all that stuff and still am not. I don't know what showbiz is & I've never watched MTV. There are folk who just play instruments, and I'm pleased to know that I'm one of them", Watts stated in 1991. His passing was announced in a statement from the Rolling Stones' publicist Bernard Doherty, which described him as 'a cherished husband, father & grandfather, who was one of the greatest drummers of his generation. He passed away peacefully in a London hospital earlier today surrounded by his family'.

Bill Wyman gave a heartfelt tribute to his former Rolling Stones band-mate Charlie Watts the day after the drummer died. Wyman was the group's bassist from their formation until his departure was announced during 1993, although he'd already quit following their 'Steel Wheels/Urban Jungle' tours of 1989–90. Posting on Instagram, Bill shared a picture of the sticks-man with the caption: 'Charlie, you were like a brother to me. In the band and in life. Rest in peace'. Rolling Stones Mick Jagger, Keith Richards & Ronnie Wood all paid tribute on social media, with the latter simply writing: 'I love you my fellow Gemini ~ I will dearly miss you ~ you are the best'.

Paul McCartney posted a video on social media in which he said 'a huge blow, so sad to hear about Charlie Watts – Stones drummer – dying. He was a lovely guy. I knew he was ill, but I didn't know he was this ill, so lots of love to his family, his wife, kids and extended family & condolences to the Stones. It'll be a huge blow to them because Charlie was a rock, and a fantastic drummer, steady as a rock. Love you Charlie, I've always loved you. Beautiful man, great condolences & sympathies to his family'. Fellow former Beatle, Ringo Starr also paid tribute to Watts on social media, posting: 'God bless Charlie Watts, we're going to miss you man, peace and love to the family, Ringo".

Charlie was one of 3 Stones members, alongside Mick Jagger & Keith Richards to have featured on all of their studio albums to date, the last being the covers L.P. 'Blue & Lonesome' [2016]. Watts' last performance with the group took place in Florida on August 30th, 2019 as part of their No Filter tour. Brian Wilson of the Beach Boys said 'I'm just shocked to hear about Charlie Watts. I don't know what to say, I feel terrible for Charlie's family. Charlie was a great drummer and I loved the Stones music, they made great records. Love & Mercy'.

The Who's Pete Townshend wrote, 'Full Moon. Rainbow. Always a sign. Charlie Watts wept at Keith Moon's funeral. I wish I was capable of such tears today. Instead I just want to say goodbye. Not a rock drummer, a jazz drummer really, and that's why the Stones swung like the Basie band! Such a lovely man. God bless his wife & daughter, and I'll bet the horses will miss him too'.

E Street Band drummer Max Weinberg posted 'A monumentally sad day learning my personal hero Charlie Watts has died. I'm devastated & my soul aches for Shirley, Serafina, the extended Watts family and of course his band mates. I don't know what to say really. Charlie Watts, rest In peace my friend'.

'Charlie's drumming is powerful and unique. His approach is entirely his own & helped shape the sound of rock 'n' roll. Blessings, Charlie Watts', wrote Robbie Robertson. Questlove said Watts was 'The heartbeat of rock 'n' roll', Paul Stanley of KISS called him one of the 'true timeless icons', and Michael Des Barres described him as 'The debonair brilliance, the rhythm of the Rolling Stones'.

Robyn Hitchcock said Charlie was 'the motor in Britain's sexiest beat group', while Sheryl Crow thought the loss had left 'A huge gaping hole in the universe'. Lars Ulrich of Metallica wrote, Thank you for paving the way. Thank you for setting the standard. Thank you for making it swing. Thank you for being cool as f*ck. Thank you for literally inspiring every single rock 'n' roll drummer on this planet'.

'A very sad day. Charlie Watts was the ultimate drummer. The most stylish of men & such brilliant company. My deepest condolences to Shirley, Seraphina, Charlotte and of course, The Rolling Stones', posted Elton John. Others who paid tribute to Watts included John Fogerty, Nile Rodgers, Carl Palmer, Bootsy Collins, Perry Farrell, Nancy Sinatra, Sonic Youth, Dave Davies of The Kinks, Bill Kreutzmann of the Grateful Dead, Hall & Oates, Jason Isbell, Chuck D, Jon Wurster, Sloan, Sleater-Kinney, Dinosaur Jr, Tom Morello, Liz Phair, Michael McKean, Axl Rose, Slash, Joan Jett and Billy Corgan.

'Drummers are bonded together by virtue of their instrument & I'm saddened that today we lost a brother. The last time I saw the Rolling Stones was in the arena in Oakland where the Grateful Dead had performed many times before'. — Bill Kreutzmann   August 24th, 2021

'Very sorry to hear of the passing of The Rolling Stones drummer Charlie Watts. My deepest condolences to his family, the band and the fans'. — Axl Rose   August 24th, 2021

'The countenance of rock 'n' roll is forever changed this day. Devastating loss, RIP'. — Slash

Charlie Watts truly knew what was called for in Rolling Stones songs, not just the Captain Obvious super hits, but also those that weren't get celebrated enough, including his groove on Almost Hear You Sigh from Steel Wheels & their rendition of Harlem Shuffle on Dirty Work. There'd been debate over what was the perfect bracket between the Stones' work - where did it start and where did it end? but Charlie had always been a solid foundational drummer. Watts was the anti-drummer, who wasn't performing to let one know how hard he was working, giving one the basic foundation.

What I really felt akin to, as far as Charlie's & my drumming was concerned, was that my reputation was as stoic as Watts' reputation — like the serious face that he nearly always had. I came to the world when the temptation to show off was at a high, and it was a mighty task to check one's ego in at the door when you were a drummer, to not beg for attention or to do anything to distract from the team mentality. During those first 5 - 6 years in the Roots, to maintain that discipline, especially in a genre that wanted complete flash & trickery, the motivation in the back of my mind was always that Charlie became a legend, not because of who he was associated with, but because he was providing the foundation.

A solid foundation is more important to me than the size of one's drum set or how fast one drums or how loud you drum. Only real sticks-men know the value of Charlie Watts and that he was the world's greatest metronome. His serious drumming & stoic drumming was kind of my blueprint with the Roots. Because Charlie did less, that made him more.

It was weird that all the incorrect Stones records were what attracted me to them then when I reached my 30s, c. '98 - '99, especially when all these reissues were coming out, suddenly I saw the magic in Can't You Hear Me Knocking or any of the material in Exile on Main St., Watts work on 'I Just Want to See His Face', where the drums really weren't defined or the bluesy, Shake Your Hips. I studied him a lot.

The producer Don Was told me a really fantastic story that I refuse to believe to this day. He said that he'd play 'The Seed' by the Roots for the Rolling Stones, kind of taunting them with, 'This is who y'all need to be sounding like'. I believe he was working on A Bigger Bang at the time and I was like, 'Wait, you what?' & he's like, 'Yeah'." He told me how many times he played it for them.

In my mind, when I tracked that song on our Phrenology record, there was a certain raw sound that I wanted to that drum tone of The Seed and in my mind to get raw, I felt like I had to pretend I was my younger self & undo the things that I learned during the past 10 years of drumming. I kind of just put myself in sort of Sticky Fingers-era Watts or his drumming on Exile, just kind of a very loose drumming. I definitely remember spending a lot of time with Exile on Main St., trying to channel that feeling or that rawness before I tracked The Seed. There was a certain texture that I wanted to achieve with that song.

Often, when hip-hoppers or rappers try to approximate rock music, the 1st thing in their mind is the Smoke on the Water riff or Iron Man or Smells Like Teen Spirit. Like, whatever will make Beavis and Butt-Head want to head-bash, that's the rock they think of but for me, I wanted to approximate something closer to Exile on Main St.

Charlie's greatest trademark was probably that he never hit the hi-hat when he hit the snare, which was very unusual, because drummers were programmed to hit everything at the same time. I've never seen a drummer just individually hit them the way he did. His hi-hat hand never played when the snare hand played & the same with how he applied his rolls, his kicks and what not. Like, again, a rare moment of him just rolling his ass off was the end of Start Me Up, which was sort of like, 'Ooh, he's getting loose tonight', but I realize that that's more mastery than it is not being advanced enough.

The average amateur or newbie will probably think, 'The less that I do, the more it will reveal that I'm not as skilled as the next guy', but that was absolutely, positively not the case with Charlie Watts. With his level of drumming, especially it being so unorthodox, I could definitely hear a difference in my drumming once I stopped, depending on the hi-hat for a lot. Like with Brown Sugar, that's a great example, where his concentration on the kick & the snare, not so much on the hi-hat, actually makes it bigger, the same with the 4-on-the-floor — or in this case, the 8-on-the-floor — for Satisfaction. Just the fact that Watts does less, which makes it sound heavier.

I've pretty much had real face time with every member of the Stones, except for Charlie, but I got to see a couple of Stones shows. I saw the 'theatre show' in 2002, which was small considering that I also saw one of those Voodoo Lounge stadium shows, about which I thought, 'This is way too much to take in'. For me, my appetite was absolutely satisfied with what I saw. I walked away wondering, 'Wow! I wonder if I'll be this powerful in my '70s, still drumming'.

The Stones have been around for nearly 6 decades, and I'm sure that those guys have been committed to each other for longer than the longest relationship that any of those gentlemen have had in their domestic lives. That screams volumes about the importance of legacy & how well it worked, because I know folk that have committed time to each other but the wheels have fallen off, they've run out of ideas and don't know how much further they can go. I just truly admire the Stones' tenacity and willingness to still reach further & dig further.

Outside of the Stones, Watts was an accomplished jazz drummer, and I think creativity is transferable. Charlie knew what was called for when he went back to the Rolling Stones. That, to me, is what made him even better & even more of a genius. Trust me, his 'less is more' technique is probably some of the most genius playing that you'll ever hear.

E Street Band drummer Max Weinberg had one inspiration in mind as he prepared to record his part for 'Born in the U.S.A'. back in 1982: the late Charlie Watts' crisp playing on the Rolling Stones' 'Street Fighting Man'. "When Bruce pulled out that riff, I went right to 'Street Fighting Man'. When I was laying down that drum part, I'm thinking, 'OK, I'm Charlie Watts — I'm going to do my best Charlie Watts'", stated Max. Shortly after learning of Watts' passing, Weinberg, who interviewed him for his book The Big Beat [1984], shared some memories of a long-time hero who became a friend.

"It's hard to imagine a world without Charlie Watts. I'm just stunned. The first thing I flashed on was November 1965, at the Mosque Theater in Newark, me in the 2nd row, when Get Off of My Cloud had just come out. I used to sing that in my group, badly, and there I was, really close, seeing the Rolling Stones live & of course, focusing on Charlie.

I have a beautiful note from Keith Richards that he wrote after he read The Big Beat, where he references Charlie, and I'm feeling for Keith, because there are many would-be Charlie Watts–type drummers, myself included. You'd always see wanted ads for 'Charlie Watts–type drummers', but there was only one Charlie Watts. I can't express what Watts meant to me as an individual & certainly as an icon of music, not just in rock.

Apart from his drumming, his musicality, and his droll sense of humour, he was just the ultimate gentleman. He was so meticulous in his attire. That was one of the most impressive things about him, and his drumming tied into his personality. When you look at the amassed work, whether it was with the Stones, Rocket 88, or anything else he did, the quintet, the orchestra, he was immaculate.

I was once in his hotel room on 52nd Street. Charlie had just arrived. The Stones were playing Madison Square Garden that night. I was with a friend of mine, and we were both interviewing him for Modern Drummer magazine. Watts invited me in, because he had to unpack. He had these leather suitcases, which he opened up & everything in them was immaculately folded, which is quite the opposite of mine when I'm on tour, so I was most impressed with that but he took everything out, refolded everything then put it in the drawers. I've never seen any rock 'n' roller, ever, put anything in the drawers, but he was very precise about where everything had to go, which kind of reflected his drumming.

One of the things that we connected on was that I knew a lot of the sticks-men that he admired. The night of the day the E Street Street Band broke up, October 18th, 1989, I got a call from Charlie Watts. The juxtaposition was freaky. He asked, 'You're friends with Joe Morello, right?' I said, 'Yes'. Joe was the legendary drummer for the Dave Brubeck Quartet. Charlie said, 'And you also know Mel Lewis?' Mel was a very famous bebop drummer.

I replied, 'Yeah, I met Mel when I was a teenager'. Mel, famously, for 40 years, railed against rock 'n' roll. He hated rock. Watts said, 'I don't see any reason why they would, but do you think you might let Joe & Mel know that it would be such an honour for me to meet them. They're such heroes of mine'. I replied, 'Charlie, if I can get that together for you, it would be my honour'.

That was hours after the E Street Band broke up and my high school reunion was the night before, so my head was spinning, but I had a mission by then. Mel was in the last stages of cancer, he passed away c. 6 months later and Joe was blind, but I called both of them. I said, 'My friend, Charlie Watts, of the Rolling Stones, would love to just say hello to you & the Stones are playing in New York'.

We ended up going, Charlie having arranged everything. I was met at the outer gate, they let me drive down the ramp right to the backstage area, where each of the Stones have a sort of tented area then we were ushered in to see Watts, whose face lit up like it was Christmas. He literally grabbed both of their hands, said 'Gentlemen, it's such an honour for me to meet you' then he began talking about obscure records that they played on. By then it was like, 'Wow! This kid really knows our work'. I was standing there, so depressed because the group had broken up, but I'd just pulled off this summit meeting.

I was planning to go to law school, and Charlie started talking about Micky Waller, who when he got fired from Rod Stewart's band, became an attorney. In any case, we took a picture, the 5 of us; there's Mel Lewis, Joe Morello, our mutual friend, the great drummer Danny Gottlieb, who came with us, with Charlie in the middle, arms around Joe & Mel's waists, beaming like a 12-year-old. Then we went to the show, and Mel Lewis, who'd spent years railing about how rock 'n' roll music showed the decline of Western civilization, got it. He loved it. He said, 'Charlie is a hell of a drummer. He's solid as a rock'".

Old rockers make too many promises they can't keep, so one could bet the life & lightness of the Rolling Stones' 23rd studio album would be regarded as a miracle. Without playing 'best since' games, it ranked near the top of the 8 that they'd made since 1980. However, there were only 8, most of which dragged or sucked. Not even the most propulsive songs on Voodoo Lounge [1994] or Bridges to Babylon[1997'], approached the driving interlock of Rough Justice: Mick Jagger's high-energy drawl powered by Keith Richards's rude precision and Charlie Watts's uncommonly ecstatic beat, although if A Bigger Bang's lead track was worthy of Exile on Main Street, it would fall in line somewhere to the rear. 'Best since' was a tough game with these guys.

Although Ron Wood's slide & Darryl Jones' bass were also major positives on Rough Justice, it was the 3 original Stones who made the L.P. go--Jagger played bass on 5 tracks, although not the strongest ones. Apparently, Watts's recovery from throat cancer had both inspired rock's greatest drummer to top the high standards he'd seldom slipped below and given his old comrades spiritual space to renew what had once been one of rock's most fruitful partnerships. Mick was leaner & less phlegmy throughout, while Richards hadn't come up with a guitar part as addictive as the one on Rain Fall Down since the days when he was running on his own blood.

The lyrics weren't bad either: 'Once upon a time I was your little rooster/Now I'm just one of your cocks' was only the 1st of many vernacular twists that showed Jagger was trying. There was a decent George W. Bush-bashing song but one puzzle remained: why anyone should care about the ideas and travails, much less effort level, of the fabulously wealthy, monumentally self-involved roué who said that he couldn't keep a woman & probably deserved no better. Mick remained an A-list celebrity, so some would care, and rock aesthetes would be piqued by his resurrection, but where once he was a generation's reality principle, his emotional distance had long since degenerated into cynicism. Coming back from that would be the real miracle.

Charlie Watts was earning good money performing in jazz outfits around London, so it took no little effort for the Rolling Stones to recruit him. Charlie didn't agree to join until they could guarantee him a salary of £5 / week. 'We went shoplifting to get Charlie Watts. We cut down on our rations, we wanted him so bad, man', Keith Richards later wrote in his memoir, Life. Rock 'n' roll was still a relatively new music—it had been only a decade or so since black musicians from Mississippi & Tennessee had started mixing up elements of rhythm 'n' blues, gospel, country, and jazz, performing with a kind of lunatic urgency— & Watts wasn't particularly well acquainted with its particularities. It didn't matter. He and the Stones rapidly became foundational to the genre.

Charlie had little interest in celebrity & though he struggled with addiction to heroin, alcohol and amphetamines in his '40s, he didn't want to lead a life of debauchery. He wed the sculptor Shirley Ann Shepherd during 1964, the couple having a daughter, Seraphina, in 1968 then bred Arabian horses on a farm in Devon, SW England. On-stage, Watts provided a staid counterpoint to Mick Jagger, who squirmed around in jewellery, leather, and fur, being magnetic, flamboyant, electric.

Following a night out partying in Amsterdam, a drunken Jagger once called Watts's hotel room demanding, 'Where's my drummer?' Charlie rose from bed, shaved, changed into a sharp Savile Row suit, slapped on some cologne then knocked on Mick's door. When Keith opened it, Watts walked past him then spat at Jagger, 'Never call me your drummer again', before punching him in the face. Richards described the aftermath of the event in Life: 'Mick fell back onto a silver platter of smoked salmon then began to slide toward the open window & the canal below it'. Keith grabbed Jagger by the lapel of his jacket before he fell out of the window, it apparently taking him 24 hrs to talk Watts out of punching Mick again. Charlie wasn't anyone's hired hand, and he knew it.

Drumming is often ugly—belligerent & combative, all jerky elbows, exaggerated grimaces, and sweat-soaked shorts—but Watts looked beautiful when he played. His style wasn't animalistic, being almost pointedly reserved, with his posture suggesting a preternatural elegance. He soon became known for his effortlessness & discipline, the way he never did too much, there being poetry in restraint, Charlie's playing attracting little attention to itself.

His isolated drum tracks have become available on-line, not always being perfect in the technical sense, but they are in other, unquantifiable ways. A favourite is from Sympathy for the Devil, the opening track from Beggars Banquet [1968], the samba inspired beat being constant, hypnotic, and vaguely malevolent, feeling as though a spirit is being conjured up, with something very dangerous or exciting about to happen.

Making sense of Watts's virtuosity, involved observing the way that he made contact with the snare, Bruce Springsteen having once written 'Charlie Watts's snare sound is the Rolling Stones'. He was influenced by radical jazzmen including Charlie Parker & Mingus, but to dwell on that felt evasive, shirking the essential mystery at the centre of his work: Why did Charlie Watts sound so much better than everyone else?

Charlie gave a solo interview to Matt Lauer during 1993, who was filling in on Later with Bob Costas, a late-night talk show. Lauer asked if he thought the Stones were the world's greatest rock-'n'-roll band, Watts responding 'That's the sort of thing that critics, those people… It's better than being the worst, innit?' The pure vitriol he applied to the word 'critics' was comic, although it made sense that Charlie would've regarded them with scepticism. What made him so incredible was his 'feel', something that can't really be explained. Watching Watts play was one of the best ways to check in with the riddle and thrill of art—to see something miraculous but not to understand it.

Charlie Watts was rearranging chairs around a giant strategically placed TV screen at The Hospital Club in London before discussing his latest project, The ABC & D Of Boogie, the drummer, along with life-long friend, bassist Dave Green, having teamed up with a pair of the world's leading boogie woogie pianists: German veteran Axel Zwingenberger, and the prodigious Ben Waters. 'Rolling Stones: 50', a weighty, career spanning compendium of compelling photography sat on the table but for Watts, the heady days of touring in the '60s paled into insignificance when compared to the unfolding events at Nottingham's Trent Bridge cricket ground, the test match playing out on the TV explaining why he'd been rearranging the furniture.

Looking at the book, did Charlie feel lucky to have had his life documented so closely?

"I'd never thought of that. I've never seen half of those things. It was a revelation, because you never see half the stuff".

As the book progressed, there was less candid material, giving the impression that for the last 3 decades, the group hadn't spent much time together other than on stage.

"As you reach the end, the tours are 2 years long. I'm living with Ronnie Wood for a couple of years, so I don't need to see him for another 2 years. In the early days, the tours went from one to the other... Oh sh*t, he's out! [the cricket was still showing on the muted TV]... Er... Er... Where was I up to?"

Watts was talking about touring.

"During the mid-'60s the tours would be a trip around England, then a trip around the US, recording in America, back to Europe, UK to US. You were living together the whole time & we used to get a month off, at the most. You were younger, though and also you were more photogenic, to be honest. I don't think Keith would want you photographing him at 2 in the morning now".

Brian Jones was the first Stone that Charlie met. Did it feel like he was joining Jones' band?

"It was his group, really. He was the one with the passion. Brian also played slide & steel, things that folk didn't play. He'd play like Elmore James. We used to go to dances and he'd be playing [James'] Dust My Broom. Nobody'd heard of this stuff".

Did Watts think Jones would've been happy just to keep it like that – a purist R&B band?

"No. One of the things that f*cked Brian up was wanting, and desperately trying, to be a star. He was a star, but he couldn't cope with it, physically or mentally".

How had Charlie felt when Sam Cutler started introducing them as 'The Greatest Rock 'n' Roll Band In The World' in 1969?

"I didn't believe it. What about Little Richard? Then you have Dave Bartholomew & Fats Domino, Chuck Berry's studio group - there isn't a better rock 'n' roll band. That's where we got it from. Roll Over Beethoven by everybody else is a joke. We came close sometimes with Little Queenie or Around And Around".

Maybe they were better than they thought.

"I can't hear them like you, so I don't listen to them. A lot of white groups to me are vastly overrated. I say white bands, because most of the music I like to play on record is by black American musicians, '40s & '50s stuff. When white musicians did get hold of the blues, they seemed compelled to expand it in all directions: Led Zeppelin, Cream, 15-min. versions of Crossroads. The Stones never did. Zeppelin were amazing. Just the sound of Bonham and Jimmy Page was an amazing sound in itself, without anything else then you had the fact that they were bloody good players".

Had Watts read Keith's book?

"No. I don't have to. I know him. He very kindly sent me a signed copy, because I like signed books – I collect them – but that was it for me".

Had Charlie considered writing a similar one?

"No. I wouldn't know what to say. I'm very private. I wouldn't want to talk about half the things, and I forget a lot. I'm not really that interested in talking about me... me & the Rolling Stones, actually".

Watts was in Vanity Fair's Best Dressed Hall Of Fame, and was wearing a suit on a swelteringly hot day – sartorial matters were clearly very important to him. Did clothes maketh the man?

"No, they don't, but they help make the man look great. Not everybody has it, not many folk are interested, for a start & the general public don't care any more, so it's all out the window, really".

A wardrobe of bespoke clothes must've been a good incentive to keep in trim.

"Blimey, are you kidding? Not half. During the early to mid-'80s I took drugs and that but then by the mid-'80s I'd stopped that but I drank rather heavily. I ballooned a bit & God, I couldn't get some of my trousers done up! That was it. I stopped everything. I lived on nuts, peanuts and sultanas. That's all I ate for months".

That'd be a marvellous incentive to clean up your act though.

"Oh yeah, a well-made suit that you try to keep fitting you for 30 years is the incentive. I still wear clothes I bought 30 years ago. They cost so much money I refuse to let them go".

Charlie Watts is a jazz drummer. He'd drummed with band-leader Alexis Korner in London's blues scene, which the Stones emerged from, but always saw himself playing jazz. Keith Richards has said he regards the Rolling Stones to be a jazz band, at least on-stage, because of Charlie. It was Richards, Watts said, who taught him new ways to hear rock 'n' roll: 'While they were all going on about John Lee Hooker & all these other marvellous people like Muddy Waters, I'd be putting Charlie Parker and Sonny Rollins in. That's what I was into when I joined the Rolling Stones, that's what I used to listen to. Keith taught me to listen to Elvis Presley, because Elvis was someone I never bloody liked or listened to. Obviously, I'd heard 'Hound Dog' & all that, but to listen to him properly, Keith was the one who taught me".

Charlie also began listening to New Orleans musicians who played rock 'n' roll and R&B, as well as jazz.

"Like Earl Phillips, Jimmy Reed's drummer. Earl Phillips kind of played like a jazz drummer. Another New Orleans drummer, Earl Palmer [who played with Dave Bartholomew, Fats Domino, Professor Longhair, and Little Richard], always thought of himself as a jazz player, which he was; he played for King Pleasure".

Watts came to see how jazz and rock 'n roll emerged from similar backgrounds, sometimes played by the same players.

"It's quite a normal mixture in New Orleans for the drummers — somebody like Zigaboo [Joseph Modeliste, drummer for the Meters]. He could play bebop but could also play 2nd-line rhythms. Ed Blackwell was a revolutionary drummer with Ornette Coleman's quartet & he was what we'd call a jazz player, that's what he did, that's what he was, but he could play a New Orleans second line, because he was from New Orleans".

Charlie had recorded 10 jazz albums without the Stones, in a wide variety of styles, beginning in 1986 with Live at Fulham Town Hall, by the Charlie Watts Orchestra — an oversized orchestra that included 7 trumpeters, 4 trombones, 3 altoists, 6 tenors, a baritone, a clarinetist, 2 vibraphonists, piano, 2 basses, Jack Bruce on cello, and 3 drummers. 'Lester Leaps In' featured a massive tenor conflagration, being played at breakneck clips.

Watts had also issued recordings with a tentet, a quintet & a big band, which played versions of You Can't Always Get What You Want and Paint It, Black, having recorded 2 Charlie Parker tributes & had released a couple of luxuriantly scored sets of American Songbook standards — Warm & Tender and Long Ago & Far Away, both featuring long-time Rolling Stones backing vocalist Bernard Fowler. On the vocal L.Ps, Watts muted his rhythms into a faded heartbeat, guiding songs of longing and loss.

However, his most adventurous work was a sweeping tribute to jazz drummers, in collaboration with sticks-man Jim Keltner, who'd played with Eric Clapton, Ry Cooder, Delaney & Bonnie, Bob Dylan, George Harrison, John Lennon, Ringo Starr, and Gábor Szabó. On the sprawling, ambitious Charlie Watts-Jim Keltner Project, the pair played a series of 9 tributes with titles including Kenny Clarke, Roy Haynes, Max Roach, & The Elvin Suite.

They didn't try to copy the drummers they were recognizing, though on Airto, they fairly reconstructed the sound that the Brazilian percussionist evoked in Miles Davis' ensembles of the '70s. Charlie and Keltner's dedications were mostly impressionistic constructions that caught something of the essence of the 9 sticks-men they paid homage to, using unusual instrumentation as well as occasional loops and electronics, plus West African-sounding rhythmic undertows. The tracks named after Art Blakey & Tony Williams were especially enjoyable.

Watts' jazz recordings stood on their own yet also deepened an understanding of his place in the Rolling Stones. When one heard him drum with his stunning tentet on Watts at Scott's, it was as if all the beats withheld over the years from his work in an electric-blues and pop band had suddenly fallen into place. One could imagine superimposing one perspective over the other & there you had it: A picture of the history of drumming emerged in the recordings, as it developed in the blues-based formations of Blakey, Max Roach, and — a major touchstone for Charlie — Elvin Jones, finally informing the razor-edged swing that Watts instilled in the Rolling Stones, then wound up some place altogether different in his epic with Keltner.

Charlie was in a Beverly Hills hotel's small, comfortable conference room, dressed in a fine grey suit, a couple of shades darker than his swept back hair, sitting with his legs crossed & his hands crossed at his wrists above them. He spoke about seeing Tony Williams in the young drummer's early years with Miles Davis, saying that 'He was so unlike anybody else'. When informed that Williams had once said that the single influence who'd really opened him up to drumming was Keith Moon, Watts' eyes grew wide, as he tilted his head backwards, as if taken aback: "Blimey".

Did that make sense? "Not to me. Keith Moon, there was a character. Loved him. There's only one of him. I miss him a lot. He was a very charming bloke, a lovely guy, really quite...whew, but he could be a difficult guy, really. Actually, there wasn't only one of him. He was more like 3 people in one. He used to live here in Los Angeles for a while, in some of his madder days. God, I remember being here once with him when he tried to turn me on to chocolate ants; he was walking about with tins of chocolate ants. That's what I mean. He wasn't your regular guy, in that way, but he was, in his heart, a nice guy. I always got on well with him".

Watts shook his head and smiled at the memory. "He was an amazing drummer with Pete Townshend. I don't know if he was a very good drummer outside of Pete. A lot of guys, I don't think, would've liked playing with him. He didn't play real time or anything. He wasn't funky or anything. He was a whole other thing. He was on top of everything & maybe that's what Tony liked, but you'd never think that Tony was like ... I would've thought Roy Haynes was his big influence.

Tony Williams was a lovely man too, and he was writing some great stuff at the time he died. He was getting out, writing more than just playing. Brilliantly, he was writing brilliantly. He was very young when he joined Miles & became this iconic figure. I saw him when he was 18, I think, in London, the 1st time, when he had the black kit, nobody played like that. Years later, when Williams died, I saw the brilliant Roy Haynes perform his gig at Catalina's, and I suddenly thought of Tony as an extension of Roy, which I'd never realized before. When Williams came to London in the '60s with Davis, like I said before, he completely blew everybody away, because nobody played like that. They didn't ride that way or do things like that. Then I saw his band Lifetime with Larry Young & John McLaughlin. I went with Mick Taylor to see that. It was fantastic. The 3 of them were incredible".

What Charlie mostly talked about that afternoon was durability, no other well-known drummer having played in a group for 50 years, maybe the only other one that had lasted that long having been the Duke Ellington Band, from 1924 to 1974. Watts seemed rather surprised as he pondered being the longest-lasting group drummer in history. "Many guys have drummed 50 years, but I guess it's true, what you say. When we were going along through the years and people would say, 'God, you've been going for 20 years,' or something, my stock answer in those days was, 'Yeah, but Duke Ellington has been going 40-something years'. Of course, he never had the same band, really. He had a lot of the same guys in & out. The wonderful Sonny Greer was with him for, blimey, from when he was in his 20s; he must've been 30 years with him, easy, up to the '50s. Then Ellington swapped a lot of drummers around, so, no, there haven't been … I don't know what that means, actually, 50 years with one group".

That Charlie really liked it.

"Well, yeah. Also, I prefer bands to … I'm not Buddy Rich, I've never been a jazz musician that's in a book that you ring up to do a gig. That would worry the life out of me, turning up and playing with folk for the 1st time. I've never had that virtuosity. It takes about 3 or 4 gigs before I feel comfortable. Most of the drummers I like, really, are group guys, like Sonny. They've been in units for a while. It doesn't happen so much nowadays. Roy Haynes, he's been in so many great, great bands. Or the groups have been great with him in them, under great leaders — Lester Young, Charlie Parker, Gary Burton.

Stan Getz had one of the great bands with him. There's also a great record with Monk that he did, I think it's one of the Five Spots. It's amazing, really. There's a great album he did with Coltrane called To the Beat of a Different Drum. Roy is an amazing guy who plays now as well as he's ever played. If any young person asked me who they should follow in one's life, I'd say Roy Haynes. He's eternally young — there's absolutely nothing wayward about him.

He's at an age where most guys aren't even bothering with it, really, but you put your arm around him, he's solid. He's a fantastic man & a very, very charming guy, beautiful man. When the Rolling Stones started, all those other groups were obviously going — they were big — and now we've gone past them in years, in longevity. This is nothing to do with fame and fortune or greatness. It's just longevity, actually & suddenly we've gone past them."

Probably nobody had drummed so hard, so relentlessly and fiercely as Watts over a lifetime. "That's a drummer's lot. When you'd see Otis Redding, that band live, those tempos…. He was entertaining, doing it all, but he could stop during a sax solo or something. That drummer though, was going the whole bloody time. It's what you do. The drummer is the engine. It's worse when you get tired & have a lot of the show still to do.

There's nothing worse than being out of breath or your hands are killing you, but you still have a quarter of the show to go. That's the worst one. When you were young, you'd have a drink to get through that, but now I couldn't do that. I like to be over-ready for things. That's really one of the reasons why I started to play jazz — the love of it was another — but it was to do other things while we weren't on the road, because we'd work for a couple of years, you'd be great at the end of it then you wouldn't work for another year or so. I like to do something to keep my hands going, really".

There'd been reports about tensions between Mick Jagger and Keith Richards. Had there been any doubts about the 50th-anniversary tour happening?

"Not to me, but to many folk there was a doubt. The 2 big offenders of that virtually lived together when they were kids, didn't they? They lived down the road from each other. It comes from all that. They're like brothers, arguing about the rent, but then if you get between it, forget it. They leave you high & dry. I think it's part of being together for 50 years. Keith couldn't say things in his book without knowing Mick that well. I haven't read it, actually. I just heard things he'd said, and it's what he felt.

I always thought we should do something for the 50th year, which Bill Wyman told me actually is this year — it wasn't last year. I was very in favour of playing a show, or a few of them. It's all right to perform 3 numbers, but by the time you've rehearsed, paid for everybody, it's like a juggernaut, our thing. It's not just me & Keith turning up then having fun, although that really is what it is, but the whole thing of it turns into a production, so you generally have to put on 2 or 3 shows to pay for thinking about getting it together.

The shows in London and New York were good & sort of spurred this on. I hope this is as comfortable as that was, because that was really comfortable to do. I like it when you can see the end of it. When you have an endless list of dates — 50 shows in America or something — you just look at it then go, 'Oh, Christ', but it's very tempting to carry on, once you've started that. As Keith would say, 'Why don't we do more?' It's logically the thing to do, because the start-up is the hard thing on your body, so obviously, non-stop is the best thing. We'll see".

Were the Rolling Stones the best at being the Rolling Stones when they were on tour or on-stage?

"Yeah. Yeah. Yeah. Yeah, we're a live group. We always have been, even in the early days. The Beatles were fabulous in a studio, getting their songs together, but we were much better at entertaining — we were more raucous. I think we're a better live band than a lot. For your ego, there's nothing nicer than driving down Santa Monica while hearing yourself on the radio, especially if it's a new record, but the real fun is on the stage.

That's why I like jazz and why I prefer playing in clubs, because it's more immediate. It's just what I like. I think everybody does probably, apart from Mick, who's more about song-writing, that sort of thing. I'm sure Keith prefers playing live to the other stuff. Folk would look at us, hear the music then think, 'God, why do you bother to rehearse for that?' but we always do & we always have."

Every night it seemed like there was breathing room, there was a chance of something a little different.

"A lot of that comes from Keith, really. Keith's very much like playing with a jazz guy, very loose. He can go anywhere, and if you follow him & it's right, it's something special, which is kind of what happens with jazz in its moments, really. He's very much like that. It's very easy to play with him. You can go anywhere really, sometimes. Roy Haynes told me you had to be quick with Bird [Charlie Parker], because he was so quick thinking, his little inflections and that. Keith's kind of like that. I don't mean Keith's like Charlie Parker, but it's the same feeling. It can go somewhere quickly & if you go with it where he thinks it should go, it's a lot of fun. That's why it's loose. Sometimes we don't go with it, so it falls apart".

Was "going with it" more difficult on large stages in arenas?

"You can hear better in a smaller room, except now the stage equipment is so advanced. In the early days, Keith used to have his Vox amplifier on a chair, tilted up so I could hear him. He still does, actually — he has it right by my hi-hat, so I can hear him. In the early days, when it was what I call the Beatle period, which was all screaming girls, you couldn't hear a bloody thing, but I had to really hear him to know where the song was, because in those days, you didn't have very good PA. I couldn't hear what Mick was singing, really. Now, it's quite sophisticated, but it's also incredibly loud. When a band like ours goes into a small club, it carries half of that with it, and it's miles too loud for me in a club. We never used to be like that. It's very difficult to suddenly jump from that huge stage down to that. It's pretty hard".

Richards said that Watts was essentially the reason that he still played with Mick Jagger & the reason that the Rolling Stones endured so well and renewed so effectively. Mick had said that he couldn't imagine the group continuing without Charlie. The band survived the loss of guitarists Brian Jones & Mick Taylor then the departure of bassist Bill Wyman. They withstood years of a world's distance apart from one another, but they couldn't imagine truly being the Rolling Stones without Charlie Watts, who was like-minded: "They're the only people I want to play rock 'n' roll with".

Much of that was to say that when the Rolling Stones played music together, when they walked on-stage together, they were an interesting coalition of history, musicianship, personality, pain, loss, joy, daring, change and most importantly, rough-hewn fellowship. The longevity of the Rolling Stones had become as distinguishing a characteristic of the group's history as their blues-indebtedness & all the notoriety and rebelliousness that put them on the map in the first place. That longevity had taken its toll, at times their union seeming strained beyond repair, but they knew there was an alchemy at work between them, a collective mystery that was beyond their individual talents or reputations. Beyond that, none of the 3 original members — Charlie, Mick, Keith — were at ease offering insight into why their legend & appeal survived so potently, but they realized that it endured when they were together, especially in the presence of an audience.

"We're very, very fortunate. I've always felt that folks have liked this combination of people. Mick, Keith, Brian, and Bill: People turned up to see them. First it was 100 attending then it was 200 then it was a lot. Folk like looking at Mick Jagger and watching what Keith's doing. I don't know why, but they do. I mean, I do know, I know how good Keith is & I know Mick is the best front-man going now that James Brown and Michael Jackson have gone. Being out there, he's the best. He takes it deadly seriously, as well; he keeps himself together. He looks great — everything you could want. You wouldn't expect them to turn up to see me — it's like, 200 people — but the Rolling Stones say they're doing something then we get more folk standing outside, listening to our rehearsals, than I do in a club listening to me do a set. It's something that I've got no idea why".

The Rolling Stones announced a raft of UK live dates for 2018 that year. How would the tour be bigger than the others?

"I've got no idea. I never knew about the others when they got bigger & better. It's usually how you set them up – the stage and that. The problem is, we're not doing enough shows to go as berserk as we used to. It's still a good thing to do though. Maybe folk are fed up with the big stage, I don't know".

Would it be the last Rolling Stones tour?

"I've got absolutely no idea. I'm looking forward to Sunday 8th July, which is the last show. That's as far as I can think ahead with The Rolling Stones. They said we'd finish in 1965 but…"

Had Watts ever thought about retiring?

"No. I've thought that the band might stop a lot of times. I used to think that at the end of every tour. I'd had enough of it – that was it, but no, not really. I hope when it ends that everyone says, 'That'll be it'. I'd hate for it to be a bloody big argument. That would be a real sad moment, but to say 'This is the last show', wouldn't be a particularly sad moment, not to me anyway. I'll just carry on as I was yesterday or today".

Would that be the end of the group?

"I think if Mick or Keith retired then it would be, but they could get another drummer, another guitar player. If Daryl didn't want to do it any more we'd have a nightmare finding another bass player but Mick & Keith would or could carry on. If Mick said 'I'm retiring' I don't know how we'd do a show without him, or Keith".

Would they play Glastonbury again?

"Well, yeah! I think we would. It was a great day. Mind you we were very lucky with the weather. We did Glastonbury and 2 Hyde Parks & it was glorious."

Were the Stones working on a new L.P.?

"When we did the blues album 'Blue and Lonesome', that was in the middle of the second lot of sessions for the L.P. We've done another lot since then, so we've done 3 or 4 sets of sessions, but I don't write the songs so I don't have the final say. Once we've played them I'm not interested really, but Mick has to live with them & put his voice on them. Keith will sit for hours listening. I don't know where we are with them to be honest. Every time we go in to the studio I think, 'Well that was the one', but it's whether they're happy with it and I don't know if they are yet".

What were the new songs sounding like?

"I've got no idea. I could say they sound very much like Stax Records but when they come out they sound like Motown".

What was Jagger & Richard's relationship like lately?

"Very good. They were like brothers when they argued. That's why they argue. They're fine. We did this type of tour in the middle of last year. The problem with time now is it's all become very short. I mean the 'Blue and Lonesome' album feels like a while ago but it's actually a year ago now. It's quite difficult".

Had Charlie ever come close to quitting?

"Yeah, all the time. I used to leave at the end of every tour. We'd do 6 months work in America then I'd say, 'That's it, I'm going home'. A fortnight later, you're fidgeting then your wife says: 'Why don't you go back to work? You're a nightmare'".

Watts once punched Mick Jagger for calling him 'his drummer'...

"I was drunk. It was in Amsterdam, because there was a canal nearby".

Did Mick ever do it again?

"I don't think so. I actually said 'You're my singer', but I was drunk".

Charlie had been married for 54 years, which was unusual for a rock-star. What was his secret?

"Because I'm not really a rock-star, I don't have all the trappings of that. Having said that, I do have 4 vintage cars but I can't drive the bloody things. I've never been interested in doing interviews or being seen. I love it & I do interviews because I want folk to come to see the band. The Rolling Stones exist because fans come to the shows. There's nothing worse than playing in a club with 3 people sitting in the front – one's your girlfriend, the other's your mate – and that's the audience. If you want to play Old Trafford you've got to fill the place up. For 20 years I never did an interview. I did one with Ray Connolly & I didn't like the quote. I did say it, it wasn't Ray's fault, but I thought 'That's it!' I never did another interview but then Mick got fed up with having to do all of them, so I was roped in".

Did Watts ever get sick of talking about The Rolling Stones?

"I don't really talk about them much. They don't really enter my life to be honest. If Mick rings up it's not The Rolling Stones. Obviously there's a bit of me that thinks it's work, but he usually rings to ask my opinion on a design or something. He gets very annoyed with me, because I don't have a mobile, so he can't get an instant reply – he's a real speed freak. It has to go via the postman then I have to ring him and hope he's in. He gets a bit pissed off nowadays with that. Years ago that's how we used to design the stage, but now it's a bit quicker. It's easier to do it when we're altogether, but other than that, they don't really enter my life to be honest".

It'd be the 50th anniversary of Brian Jones passing the following year- would he be proud of what they'd achieved?

"I think so. He would've loved to be a part of it. I don't think he would've coped with it though. He didn't cope with it for the last year of his life. Brian initially was the one who everybody spoke to, 'cos none of us wanted to talk to anyone. Mick was very much in the background during those early times. Brian very much pushed this group to be a band. He pushed us to get work. All the clubs we used to play in London were because Brian was on the phone annoying owners, asking 'Can you squeeze us in?'

We usually played in between jazz bands, because most of the clubs in London were run by jazz musicians or their managers. Alexis Korner conned Bill Pemberton into having the worst night for Jazz – which was Thursday night – as a try-out for his R'n' B group, which I was in. Then it became the biggest night of the week. Before that it was Sundays at the Marquee Club with Johnny Dankworth's Orchestra – a bloody marvellous band. Dudley Moore was the piano player, it was a fantastic band. Great bloke, Johnny Dankworth".

How was the Boogie Woogie group The A, B, C & D born?

"It's an atypical formation, with 2 pianists. One of the 2 asked me if I wanted to join them, I agreed and I suggested hiring David Green, my childhood friend, a wonderful jazz bassist. We played music that was popular during the late '30s in America, boogie-woogie. It's a more cheerful genre than jazz. When it rocks, it becomes incredibly contagious. They all dance".

What did Charlie do apart from those concerts & his activities with the Rolling Stones?

"I own a country house in Devon, I go there. I also live in London and travel to Paris a lot, so I don't really do anything … other than sit behind a drum set from time to time".

Why had he joined the Rolling Stones in the early '60s, instead of continuing to practice jazz at the weekends?

"I already used to participate in jazz concerts with David Green. He was much better than me at that, so I turned to another musician, Alexis Korner. He organized sessions at the Marquee that at the time were called rhythm 'n' blues. Brian Jones was there, Mick & Keith too. I met them there, because Mick was singing in Alexis's line-up. When they started rehearsing together, they asked me to join them. At the time, I was in between jobs when I started playing with the Rolling Stones. We'd become increasingly popular, so I never thought of looking for another job in graphic design".

Had Watts tried to influence the musical style of The Rolling Stones?

"No. Mick and Keith would find a riff then we'd improvise on it. They said to Bill & me, 'good', or 'faster, stronger'.

Why did Charlie always have that distant air?

"I'm shy. I could never have been at the front, I'd rather be behind".

Who were the musicians Watts most admired?

"There are so many. First Duke Ellington, such a graceful, talented man. If there's one drummer I admire above all else, it's Roy Haynes, who's 85 years old now, his 1st recording dating from 1948. He accompanied Lester Young, Charlie Parker, Stan Getz … I saw him on New Morning 3 years ago, he was as fantastic as during 1965".

Was that an influence on Charlie?

"In the way that I play? No, I'm not that good".

What's a good drummer?

"The one that sets the rhythm and makes you dance. I learned my craft by watching folk on stage. I've never taken a lesson & can barely read music. I used to go to dance halls and nightclubs to see the musicians. I don't recommend that method to young people: it's a lot of work if you only know how to listen".

Watts references were quite 'old-fashioned', while the Stones were associated with youth, pop & debauchery. Had he felt schizophrenic with them?

"No. I liked Chicago blues, as did Brian and Keith. They constantly listened to Jimmy Reed on his old gramophone".

Although the band had evolved.

"It evolved in the sense that Keith infused his musical style and Mick spoke his words, but we still played the blues. When they started writing their songs, the group took it to another level, it grew. I played the same things. Before it was Little Richard then it was Mick Jagger & Keith Richards. I copied Little Richard's drummer a lot".

Charlie was very humble.

"What could I boast of? I was afraid of exploding"

Mick and Keith said that without Watts the band would no longer exist.

"They're nice to me, but that's not true. You can record albums with anyone, as long as you have the songs. That's what matters. Perhaps they mean by that that it's good to belong to a group".

Had Charlie wanted to leave at some point, like Bill Wyman?

"No. Bill only left because he was having a difficult time with his former wife, Mandy. He didn't understand what he was going through, although it was difficult then he met Suzanne & decided it was enough, but we gave him a year to think about it".

Did Watts still like touring?

"It's hard. Conditions have certainly changed since the '60s, we're no longer on top of each other and we're not so young any more. Today we have space, thank God, but every day you see the same faces & some go crazy in contact with the Rolling Stones. They're losing their minds. We use folk or share the poster with some who drowned in drugs, alcohol, whatever. Flattery and this way of life called 'rock 'n' roll' are very harmful".

Was Charlie afraid that the band would blow up in the '80s?

"I was especially afraid of exploding! I went through the mid-life crisis & it was also a fun time for the band. Nothing helped, the L.Ps weren't great, Mick and Keith weren't getting along, I wasn't doing well at all, but it was never a question of firing me".

Jagger wanted to be successful on his own …

"Could be, but that wasn't the case!"

Did Watts have a favourite Rolling Stones album?

"No".

A song ?

"No. You keep asking me about the Rolling Stones, but they don't mean to me what they mean to you. It's just one activity among many, with folk I know, of course I love, but who I work with. We don't talk about this among ourselves!"

Had Charlie read Keith Richards' autobiography, due out the following month?

"No. He wrote it with a guy who accompanied us on tour. That must've been going on for 5 years. I won't read it. I haven't read Bill or Ronnie's. I'm not interested".

Didn't the legend concern Watts?

"What legend? All I want is this: That the Rolling Stones get it right. The rest … 'rock 'n' roll' doesn't mean much to me. It doesn't occupy my days. My wife is different, she listens to rock 'n' roll, she gets records, I never have, even during the '70s. It's work. As for the 'debauchery' we see in 'Exile on Main Street', it didn't appeal to me. I played then I'd go to bed. I'm not the right person. My wife plays songs & says, 'This is great!' I hear Mick Taylor's guitar then I say 'Yes'. I'm not going back to that".

It was a great adventure, the Rolling Stones …

"My life is a great adventure".

I'm not a journalist; I'm a drummer.

"Yeah, so I heard".

I've been trying to do some research and write some notes, but hopefully we can just sort of let it go, do some talking. I've been listening to the new record, which I think is really great. To me, it's a real late night record.

"Oh, that's okay".

Sort of along the lines of 'Frank Sinatra, Sings for Only The Lonely' or Dinah Washington.

"Yeah, right".

I was wondering about the recording of this L.P. Did you record it sort of old style or was it very modern techniques that you used?

"Oh, I don't know anything about modern techniques. We were all in the same room & played it live".

That's what I was wondering. If it were live —

"Some of the solos are overdubbed 'cos of leakage, but mostly, yeah, all the orchestration of the rhythm section is live, but the singing on this one was all overdubbed, because Bernard Fowler got snowed in in New York. He couldn't get there, but on the last one, Warm and Tender, most of that is live. We like to do them live. Some of these are live, but most of them are overdubbed 'cos he couldn't get there in time. It took a fortnight to do & he got there on the 2nd week".

That's not long to spend on an album, which is good.

"We cut it, mixed it and everything in 2 weeks. Well, 2 and a bit weeks.

When Charlie was in London during the late '50s or early '60s, was he seeing and hearing much live jazz?

"Yes, lots. There were loads of clubs in London".

Was there anything that particularly stood out from that time?

"Loads, loads of things. I mean, I saw all American bands in the '60s. I still have all the programs. It was all very new then because in Britain they'd had a huge ban, a musicians union ban of all American artists, so during 1930-something, I think Duke Ellington was the last person to play here then I saw him in the early '60s when they all came back. Most of the guys I saw play were British guys in clubs, but I can't talk about them 'cos you don't know any of them".

Probably not many of them.

"None of them".

Probably. Did Watts ever have much interest in things like Sun Ra, Albert Ayler, recordings of that style?

"Yeah. I've got loads of his records".

Had Charlie ever seen him live?

"No, I never saw Ayler in New York either".

Was Watts familiar with some of the jazz music that was going on in New York City lately?

"Not really".

The sort of music that's inspired by more free & out recordings. Musicians like Charles Gayle and John Zorn.

"Not really, no".

Were there other folk making jazz records that Charlie enjoyed?

"No, I don't buy many records. I mean, I buy older records. Quite difficult to keep up with lots of records".

Watts was mainly interested in vintage recordings.

"Yeah, I suppose, the stuff I hear I get but now I'm trying to think... Oh God, I can't remember the last new record I bought. I can't remember what it's called".

The 1st time I'd seen Charlie play was in Detroit, Michigan at the Pontiac Silverdome. I think it was 1981 or 1982. I was just out of high school. I guess they were touring with Tattoo You around that time. Iggy Pop was the opening act.

"Yeah. He's great, isn't he?"

Did Watts have any thoughts about what it was like when punk came along, being in the Stones?

"Punk?"

Aye, during the late '70s.

"The best group at being punks were the Sex Pistols".

Who were reforming that year.

"Well, they're going out again. I don't think, I mean they haven't got one of the leading players in it, so...".

They went back to an original player who was in the band before Sid Vicious was. A guy named Glen Matlock.

"Well, let's hope they're good. I kinda think it's being dumb. I mean, they've never pretended it's anything more than just going out, earning some money & that's it, but I think they're the best band to come out of that whole thing by far. Their records certainly are".

Had Charlie ever see them perform?

"No".

I guess not many folk did. They didn't really perform for that long. Was Watts familiar with Devo's cover of Satisfaction? Had he ever got a chance to hear that?

"I've heard the record. I never saw them. The best group at being punks were the Sex Pistols".

Did Charlie have any thoughts about their recording of Satisfaction?

"No. It's very interesting when other artists do something. I know Mick loves it, but then he would. He's the songwriter. No, not really any thoughts. Just interesting, but they were a very interesting band, actually, Devo".

They sort of paved the way for some of the video things that are going on.

"Yeah. Oh yeah".

I wanted to ask Watts about one of the Stones' recordings that stood out, the recording on Sticky Fingers of Moonlight Mile. Did he have any recollections of recording that?

"Me, Mick Taylor and Mick played it in Jagger's front entrance hall in Stargroves. That's all I remember".

That's the song that was started out without Keith. Could Charlie say anything about playing with Howlin' Wolf on his recording that he made in London?

"Well that record was made next door to where I made Long Ago and Far Away".

It was made in the studio next to it?

"Yeah, the little studio. It's where Jimi Hendrix used to play when we were in the big one then we'd play in the little one & he'd play in the big one.

That was at Olympic Sound.

"Yeah, Olympic Studio. Howlin' Wolf was very easy to work with, but we had a good band. I mean it was Bill Wyman, Eric Clapton and Stevie Winwood. I mean, you can't get better than that. Well, unless you have Steve Cropper & Booker T. They're as good as that. That's how good they are, so it was really a lot of fun".

Had it seemed strange to perform with Howlin' Wolf or did it just feel great?

"Aw, it felt very good. I mean, I've played most of those songs anyway, but when you play with the artist who wrote them and originally recorded them, there's always a twist in them that you never realize is there".

Something that's inside.

"Well, just the way they make it lay, but it was very interesting. Well, I mean the stuff that he did at Chess is the stuff. What we didn't get in London was any edge on it, but he was an older man then. He had a stupid bugger of a producer with him, a college boy".

I wanted to ask you about the recording of a Godard movie that you appeared in.

"Which film?"

Jean-Luc Godard. Which I think had a different title originally. Now they're calling it Sympathy For The Devil.

"Right, right, it's actually called something else".

It was pretty great to document how that song had come together.

"Yeah. It's very good. That's Olympic Studio, the big studio. That's where we cut this record in May, except it's better now than it was then & it was good then.

Which song on the new album did Louis Armstrong compose?

"Some Day You'll Be Sorry".

Had Watts ever seen him perform?

"Yeah. A lot of times, but only from the '60s through. I didn't see him before that, but I wish I had. He came to England in the '30s.

There'd been a lot of the recordings from that time issued lately.

"He went to Paris as well. He spent quite a while in Paris, I think".

Hadn't Charlie lived in France for awhile?

"Yeah, I still have a house out there. Going out there next week. Not Paris, but in the south".

Was Watts familiar with a French singer/songwriter Serge Gainsbourg?

"Yeah".

Had Charlie ever meet him?

"No. I don't really like him".

Could Charlie speak French?

"No, not really. My wife and daughter do. I think Serge Gainsbourg is a bit, like many French singers, terribly pretentious".

Really?

"Yes, I don't think he's very good. I don't, I'm sorry. I don't think he's at all a talent".

I've been enjoying some of his records lately that were made during the late '60s to early '70s, which were influenced by rock 'n' roll.

"Well, I think he's very minor. I always have done. I just don't think he's very... there's a lot of French singers like him. They get away with being French".

"Rock 'n' Roll Circus was going to be issued that year, a video and a CD. Was Watts aware of that?

"Somebody mentioned it, yeah".

I've been curious about seeing that ever since I was a teenager. It was always one of the Stones' performances that you were sort of never allowed to see.

"Well, I don't know why it was never released. I know Mick never liked it. That's probably why it was never issued. I think it was very good from what I remember. Doing it was great, because there were wonderful moments on it. The Who were great on it".

Aye, that's the only clip that I've ever seen.

"Yeah, I think some of the stuff we did was good, although Mick never liked it, but some of it was great".

Aye, that's what I'm really curious about.

"We got it together though, so it's a lot more honest than just appearing in it. It was our thing. It was great. There's a great sequence of Jethro Tull. It's all live as well".

I've never seen them live in anything.

"Oh no. With the original group, with this wonderful drummer on it, his name I've forgotten at the moment, but marvellous. It was really good. They opened the show, I think. It's really good. I mean, I'm saying really good; I remember it being very good. I remember standing there watching 'em, being very impressed. Oh God, Bunker, I think his name is, the drummer. I just remember him being very good".

I'm very curious to see this whole tape.

"Well, so am I. I haven't seen it for 20 or 30 years or whatever it is".

Had Charlie ever spent any time in Memphis, Tennessee?

"On this tour?"

When Stax was on the go.

"No, no. I mean, I went there. We played there on this tour, that's all really. A couple of days, I suppose".

Had Watts got a chance to look around at all?

"In Memphis? Yeah, but when you're on tour you do 3 streets & you think you've seen it, but Memphis is just that Beale Street and that other bit & I don't know".

I think there's a bit more.

"Well, I'm sure there is for folk that live there, but I mean, I just saw the Mississippi and the thing... it was great. For me, I love all that, but you're whisked off to some other place. I suppose we were there for 4 days at the most".

I spent some time recording there last spring & summer and really enjoyed the city itself.

"Well, I love the South. Wonderful, I think. You working?"

I just finished a tour with Sonic Youth.

"I was in New York. I was supposed to ring you or something?"

I was in London finishing our tour out there.

"Where did you play?"

We played 3 nights at the Forum.

"Oh yeah. Did you have a good time?"

We had a great time.

"Aw good. Okay, well, come and see me if you're around or whatever".

I'd like to very much.

"Yeah do".

The Rolling Stones were playing Glastonbury! Was Charlie excited?

"I don't want to do it. Everyone else does. I don't like playing outdoors, and I certainly don't like festivals. I've always thought they're nothing to do with playing. Playing is what I'm doing at the weekend. That's how I was brought up, but that's me, personally. When you're a band ... you do anything & everything, but Glastonbury, it's old hat really. I never liked the hippy thing to start with. It's not what I'd like to do for a weekend, I can tell you. The worst thing about playing outdoors is when the wind blows if you're a drummer, because the cymbals move ... it really is hard to play then".

The Stones were also playing Hyde Park that summer. What could Watts recall about their famous gig there in 1969?

"Oh, quite a lot. The Dorchester! That was our dressing room, and Allen Klein walking about like Napoleon. He was the same kind of shape & the armoured van going into the crowd. I had to rush around and get my silver trousers done for it. Then Mick Taylor, of course, it was his 1st big gig & my wife got hit with a stale sandwich. I remember her going mad about that. I don't blame her. She got hit on the back. She reckoned it was stale, because it obviously hurt a lot. The butterflies. I didn't like that, because the casualty rate was worse than the Somme. Half of them went 'Woosh' & the other half of them were dead".

Was Charlie still in shock from Brian Jones' death?

"Shock? Brian dying? No. It was very sad but it wasn't unexpected. We'd carried him for a few tours and he was quite ill. We were young, we didn't know what was wrong with him. I still don't really. He always suffered from terrible asthma, he drank heavily on the road & he got into drugs before anyone else in the group. It was a question of, 'Do we carry on?'"

Mick Taylor joined the band ...

"Amazing player. I think we made our best music with Mick".

Was Hyde Park the height of the hippy thing ...

"Altamont was more hippy than that I thought. That was a very peculiar one that was".

With a lot of big stadium groups nowadays, it feels like the staging of the show is the most important thing, whereas the Stones still strike one as being a real group. Sometimes they were good but sometimes not so much.

"Jagger is the show really. We back him, but Mick wouldn't dance well if the sound was bad. It doesn't come into it with a lot of bands, because the lead singer just stands there. We've always been about playing it properly. I don't mean technically brilliant ... The rest is candy-floss, it's froth. The costumes you're wearing, that' ... What you're really doing is playing the drums or the guitar".

What did Watts think of drum machines?

"They're great for songwriters and producers. Recording is a very precise thing – it's playing it dead right every time & it can be fun, but if you're writing a song, it's great to be able to tell the machine you'd like it louder, rather than having to tell the drummer. It's not what I'm interested in. I like the drum kit sound and somebody playing it – preferably me, but it could be anyone".

Given Charlie's jazz background, was it a bit of a comedown when he joined the Stones?

"It was more of a shock joining Alexis Korner. I'd never played with a harmonica player before – I couldn't believe Cyril Davies when he started playing. We only played out of London once, in Birmingham. Cyril got £1, because he was a professional musician; so did sax player Dick Heckstall-Smith & bassist Jack Bruce. I wasn't, so I got half a crown. Fantastic, isn't it? Half a crown! The Stones were just another gig, but then we started touring around England ... I was waiting to start another job, but I never went back to it. I was a bit out of sync with all of them, Brian, Mick and Keith, but Keith taught me to listen to Buddy Holly, things like that. Mick taught me a lot about playing with songs really, the melodies & that".

Was part of the Stones' success down to each of them having really done their homework?

"I sort of agree with that. Everything is easier and quicker now. I wanted to be Max Roach or Kenny Clarke playing in New York with Charlie Parker in the front line. Not a bad aspiration. It actually meant a lot of bloody playing, a lot of work. I don't think kids are interested in that, but that may be true of every generation, I don't know. When I was what you'd call a young musician, jazz was very fashionable. It was very hip to know there was a new Miles Davis L.P. out. Now no one knows what records come out. Especially me, because of this thing [the iPhone] ... but in those days ... an album: you kept it, you treasured it".

Watts must've really studied the records that he had.

"Oh, we did. I remember a Duke Ellington L.P. that we played for ever".

Charlie must've had to save up for them.

"I'd swap things: a cymbal for a certain record ... Then I'd go to Ray's Jazz Shop. That's when it was in New Oxford Street, in the basement of Collet's. God bless him! He was green, he was never allowed to see daylight, they used to keep him in the cellar. Then I'd sell the record & go and buy the cymbal back".

What was Watts' big problem with the hippies when that all started?

"I wasn't a great one for the philosophy and I thought the clothes were horrendous, even then".

What did Charlie think of the rest of the Stones in their Satanic Majesties phase?

"I didn't mind them doing it. Brian was the first one at it. I remember him playing the London Palladium with his bloody hat on & his pipe and sitar ... fantastic. Brian was the first one to know and meet Bob Dylan as a friend & Jimi Hendrix. He used to be fun in those days".

At the height of the Stones' success during the 60s, did Watts have a sense that they were making history?

"No. It was just a case of keeping up with everyone else. It's still the same now".

Charlie said the band did its best work with Mick Taylor. What was his favourite Stones song?

"God, I don't really have one to be honest, I don't really listen to them that much".

Did Watts think Bill Wyman had made a mistake in leaving the group?

"No, not a mistake, because he was in the middle of a terrible marriage that he should never have got into. He had a horrendous time with the Mandy girl then wed a very good woman, had 3 kids very quickly and he was very, very happy, but it was a shame he left because a) it was great having him & b) I think he missed out on a very lucrative period in our existence. There were very sparse periods you went through building the band, and he didn't really reap the rewards that we do now".

What did Charlie spend his dough on?

"Me? I collect things".

Old records?

"Yeah. There's a great place in Vienna. I collect jazz mostly. Drum kits as well. I've got one of Kenny Clarke's drum kits that he gave to Max Roach – I bought it off his widow. I have Duke Ellington's, the famous Sonny Greer's drum kit, it's fantastic. Big Sid Catlett, one of the great '30s swing drummers ... & books, not antiquarian books, signed 1st editions of mostly 20th-century writers. Agatha Christie: I've got every book she wrote in paperback. Graham Greene, I have all of them. Evelyn Waugh, he's another one. P.J. Wodehouse: everything he wrote".

It sounded like a healthy addiction.

"Well, I'm old. It's not the sort of thing a boy of 20 would be keen on".

Had there been times when Watts had thought about knocking it on the head?

"I thought that before the O2, but it was actually very comfortable to do. It was good fun, is what I meant to say".

Charlie had misgivings.

"Misgivings? Yeah, oh yeah, I always do. It's a young person's game. The thing I find difficult is that 50% of it is image, not my side of it, but it is, and as you get a bit older you think, 'Oh gawd'. I don't like looking at the pictures. I think Bowie looks all right. For some reason everyone's talking about

David Bowie at the moment, but he does look good. Some others haven't weathered so well & some guys who were really on fire haven't made it. It can take its toll on you, without you knowing or caring at the time, because you don't care when you're in your 30s or 40s".

Was it fun playing with Mick Taylor and Bill again at the O2 show?

"It was great! I loved it".

What about their guests, there & in the States?

"It was really good. We were lucky we had Jeff Beck. He's a phenomenal player".

What about the younger bunch, like Florence and the Machine?

"Florence, she was all right. Lady Gaga was a really good sport, but they hung about with my granddaughter more than they did with me. We're silly old farts! I think Mick tries to keep up with them".

As well as Hyde Park, they'd also announced a US tour.

"It's a very short tour for us. It's only 18 shows. It's nothing".

Who was the driving force in putting the Stones back on the road?

"Well, you wouldn't do it if Mick didn't want to do it. You've got to have Mick & Keith, but the driving force is Mick. If he's enthusiastic, he'll push everyone along. Keith's much more laid-back about it".

Were they getting on well? Keith was quite rude about Mick in his book.

"Oh yeah. Oh, that. Brothers, innit? Brothers in arms. You just let it take its course, really, things like that".

Was there any more new music in the offing?

"There's nothing yet. I've lost track with the record industry world, I don't get it any more. It's gone beyond me. The last single I thought was very good, but things don't mean anything any more. They're just tacked on the end of a reissue – and that ends up selling more than a new album. It's not like when Sgt Pepper came out then you thought, 'Blimey! We'd better do one better ...'. Folk say you need a new L.P. out when you go on tour. Well, we did that on our last tour, but I don't know if the record sold. I suppose, as Mick says, it gives us something different to play on stage. It's not Brown Sugar again".

Did it ever feel like they were just going through the motions on stage?

"Sometimes you're pot-boiling. Sometimes you're on song".

Would Watts get to a point where he said, 'That's it, no more?'"

"You seriously do now have to look at your age, because if this goes on for another couple of years, I'll be 73, but I say that at the end of every tour then you have a fortnight off before your wife says, 'Aren't you going to work?'"

Despite being the drummer of the most enduring rock group in history, Charlie Watts was really a jazz drummer, with all his idols & role models coming from the world of jazz. For a long time Charlie led his own traditional swing band in the UK. Among his favourite jazz drummers was New York City-born Sheldon 'Shelly' Manne, who played all styles of jazz but was best known for his work with the West Coast movement. Shelly once recorded an album titled My Son the Jazz Drummer! which featured hard-bop and soul-jazz versions of Yiddish & Israeli songs, including Bay Mir Bistu Sheyn, Di Grine Kuzine and Yossel! Yossel!

Watts attended art school then for a brief period worked as a graphic designer, his 1st job being with Brooklyn-born Bob Gill, who was co-founder of a design firm in London. Before Bob became a well-known designer, responsible for logos including one for a public radio series about 'The Jewish Experience', he played piano at summer resorts in the Catskills. Later in his career, Gill and an old army pal, Robert Rabinowitz, a painter, were asked to write & design a multimedia history of the '60s, using Beatles music for the score. The result was Beatlemania, which ran for 3 years on Broadway, producing several offshoot tours over the years.

Charlie never turned his back on art, designing several Stones L.P. covers and being heavily involved in the design element of their stage shows, but music exerted a stronger pull on the sticks-man. Alan Clayson's biography of Watts [2011], stated that his 'first public engagements were with a so-so semi-professional unit, whose principal stock-in-trade was Jewish wedding receptions'. "I never knew what the hell was going on, as I'm not Jewish"', said Charlie.

Like some of his band-mates in the Rolling Stones, Watts served an apprenticeship in Blues Incorporated, a group led by English blues guitarist Alexis Korner, who was born in Paris to an Austrian-Jewish father & a Turkish-Greek mother. The band played hardcore blues clubs in London, acting as a training ground for a generation of English rock musicians whose work was based on electric blues.

Charlie was also known as one of the most stylish dressers in rock, The Daily Telegraph naming him as one of the World's Best Dressed Men, while Vanity Fair magazine inducted him into the International Best Dressed List Hall of Fame in 2006. Like Leonard Cohen, Watts wore classic, traditional suits when not drumming, crediting his dad for taking him to his tailor: "In those days you'd have a little Jewish guy in the East End of London, who made you things". He also paid tribute to Bronx-born clothes designer Ralph Lifshitz, better known as Lauren: "Ol' Ralph Lauren does some lovely things. His stuff is the sort I love — old English and Waspish Boston". On June 3rd, 2014, the day before the Rolling Stones performed in Tel Aviv, Charlie visited the Western Wall in Jerusalem's Old City with guitarist Ron Wood.

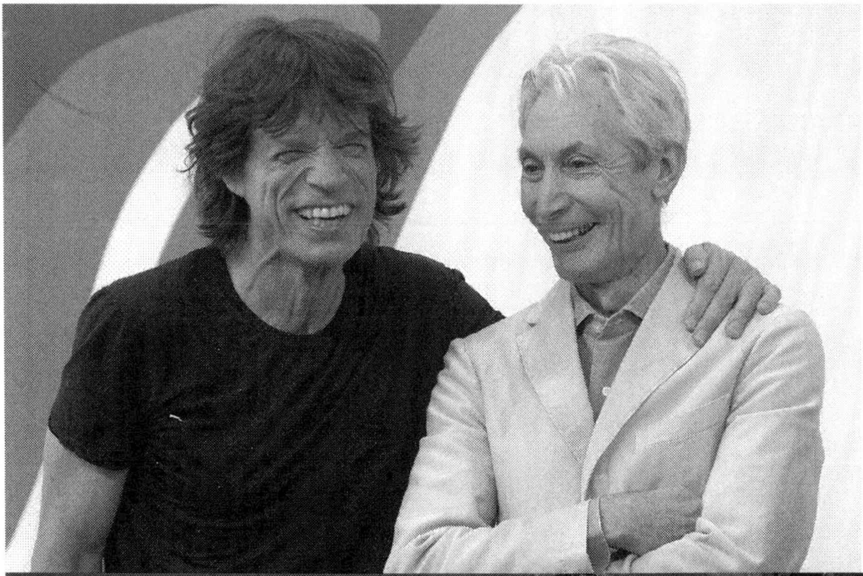

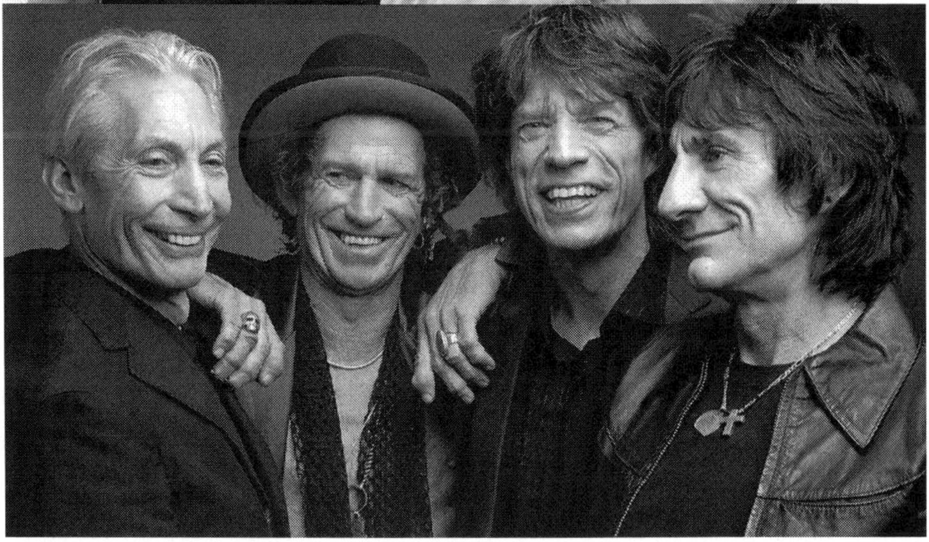

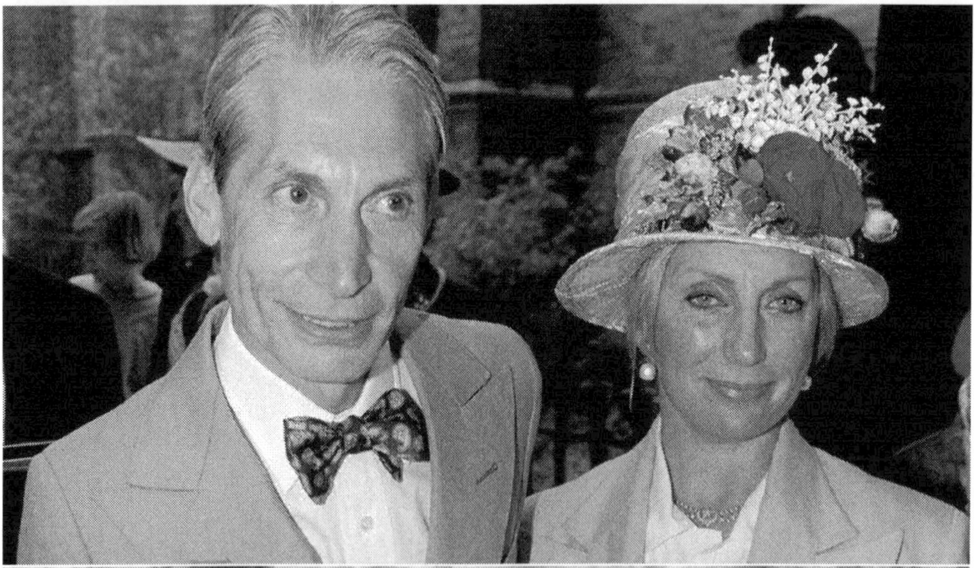

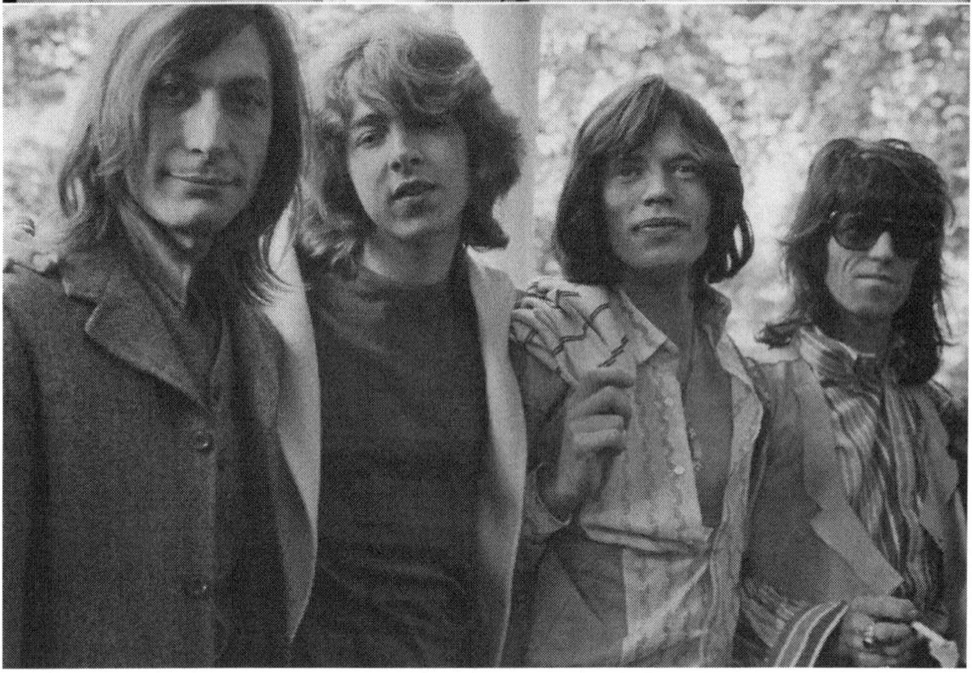

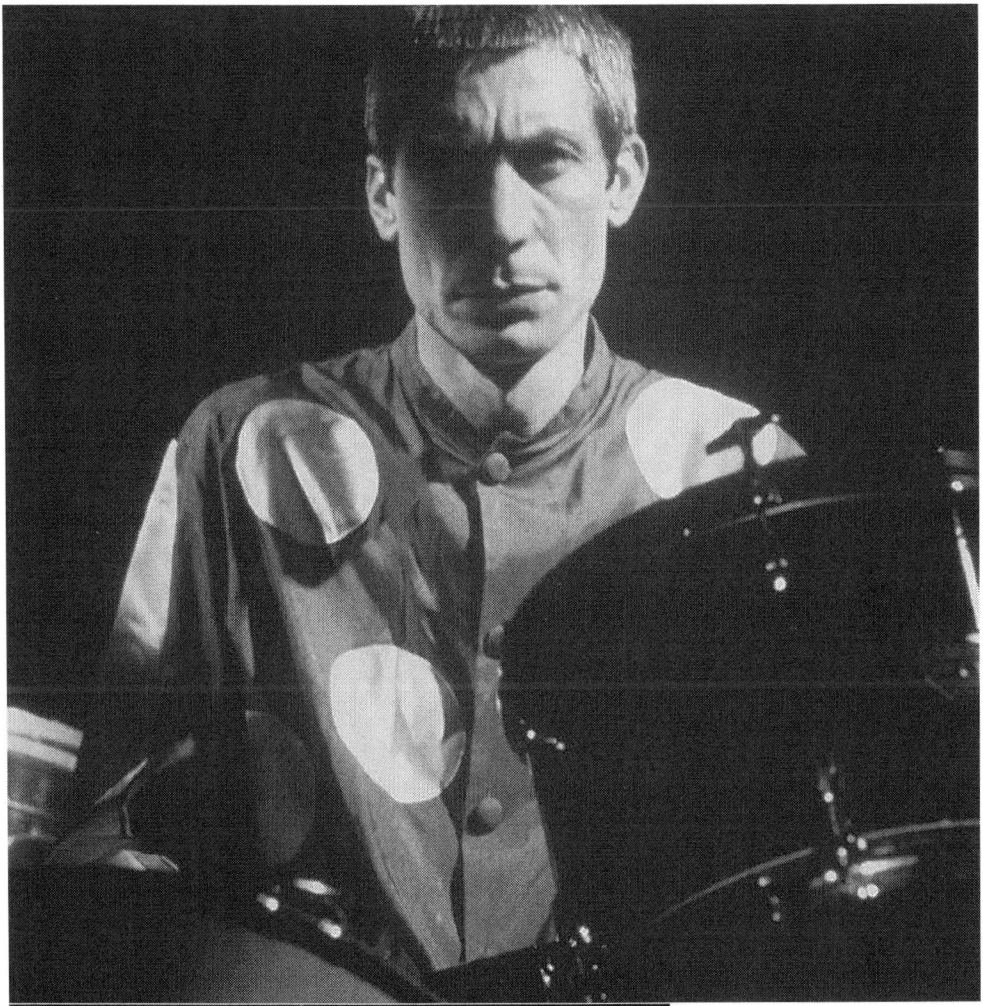

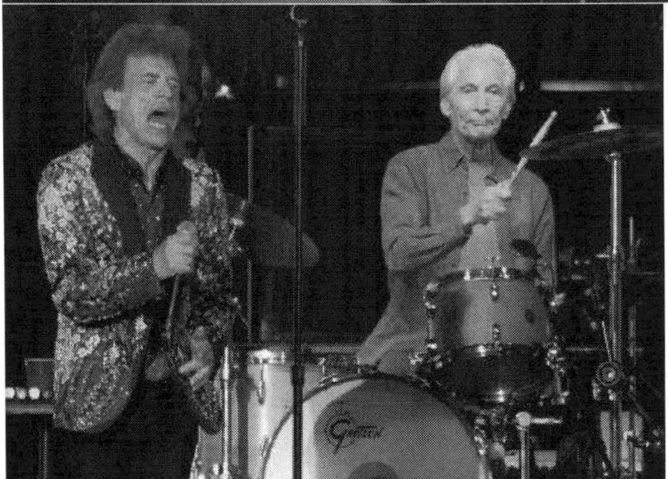

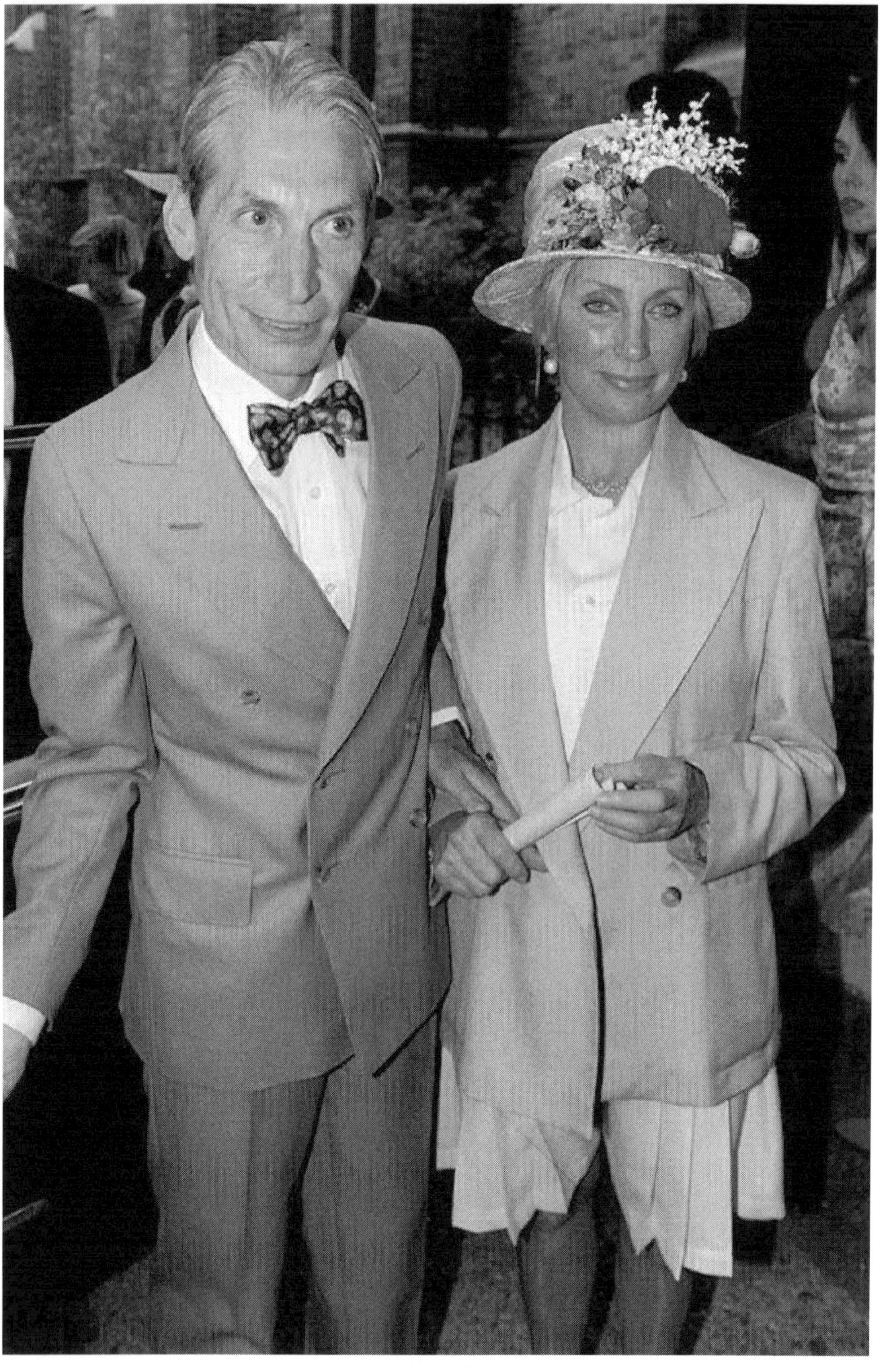

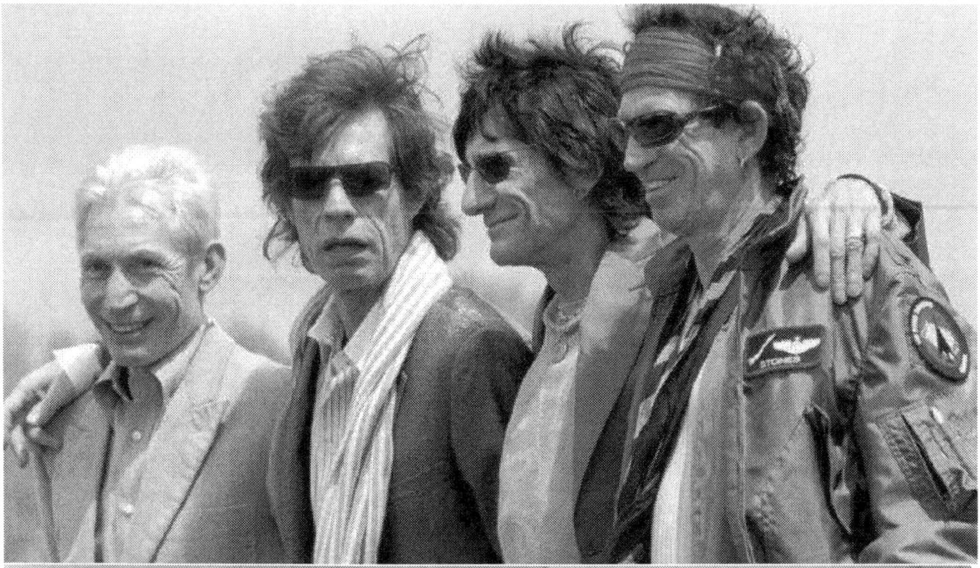

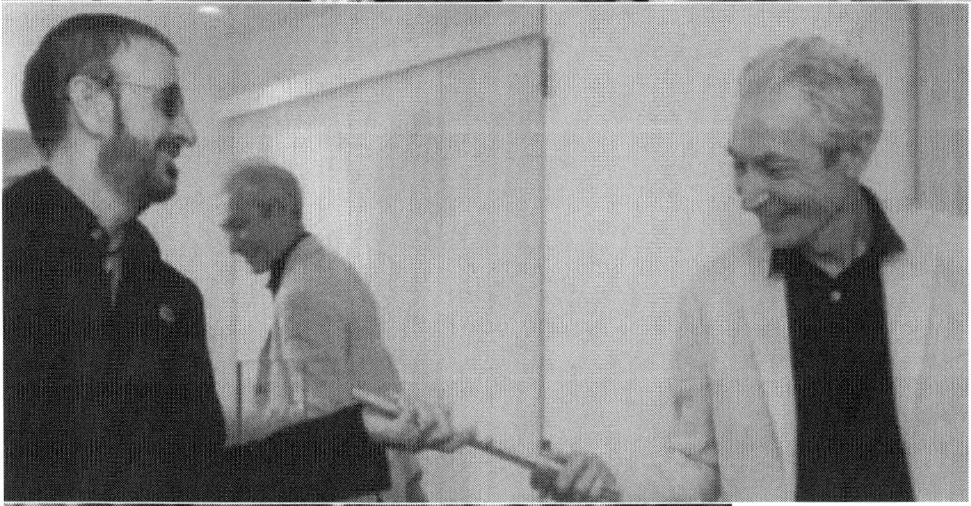

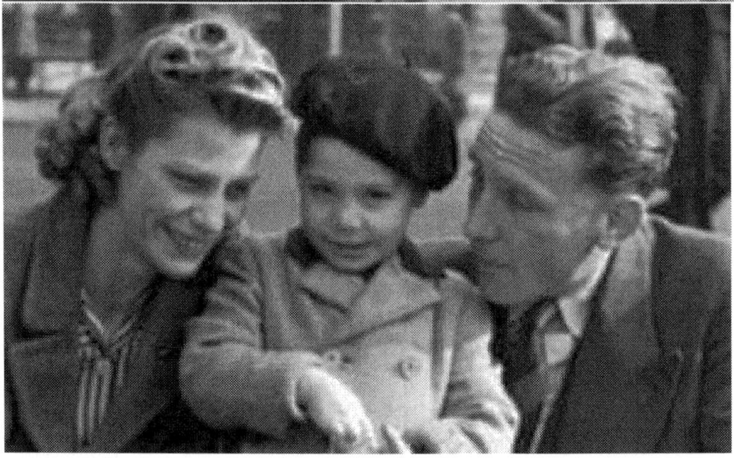

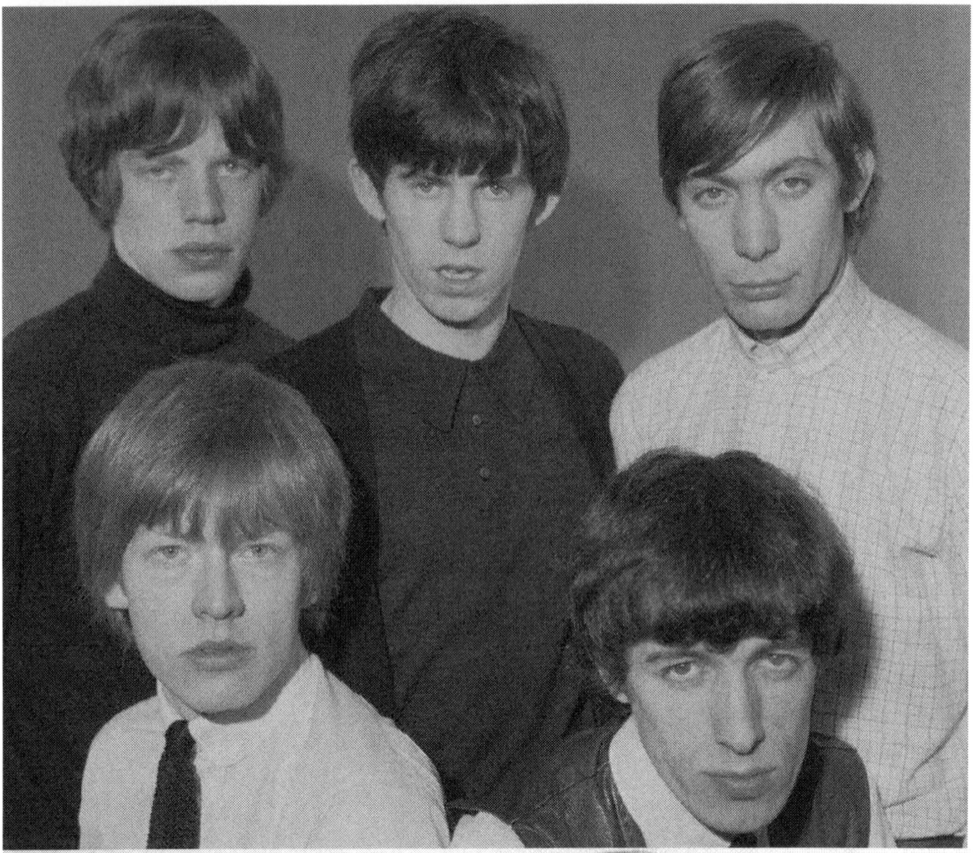

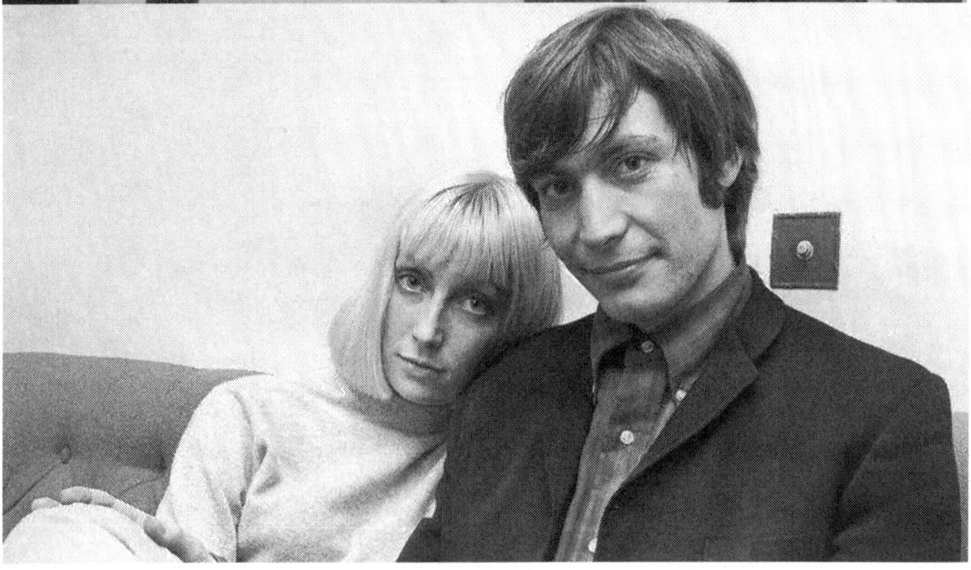

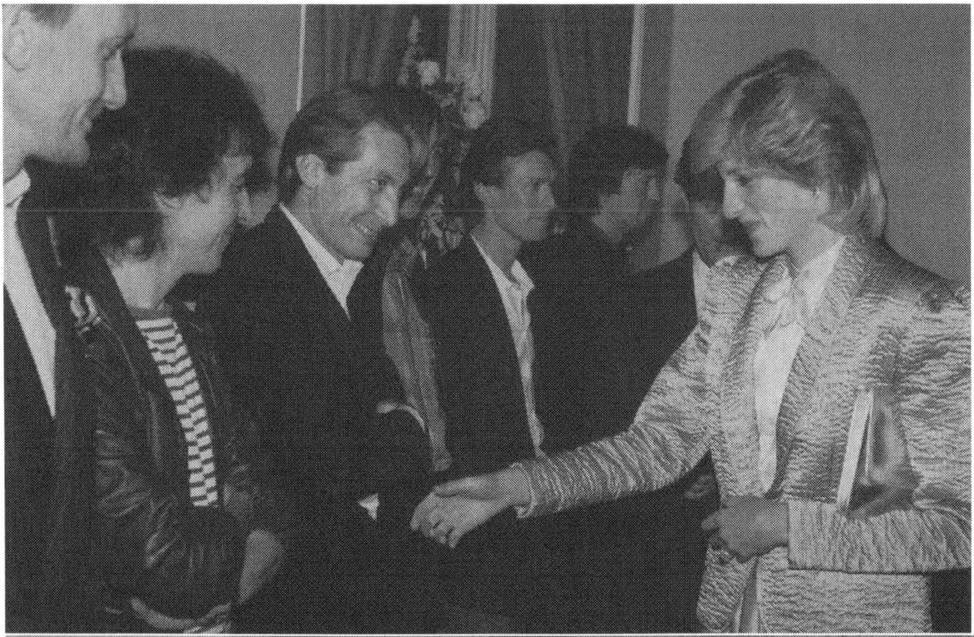

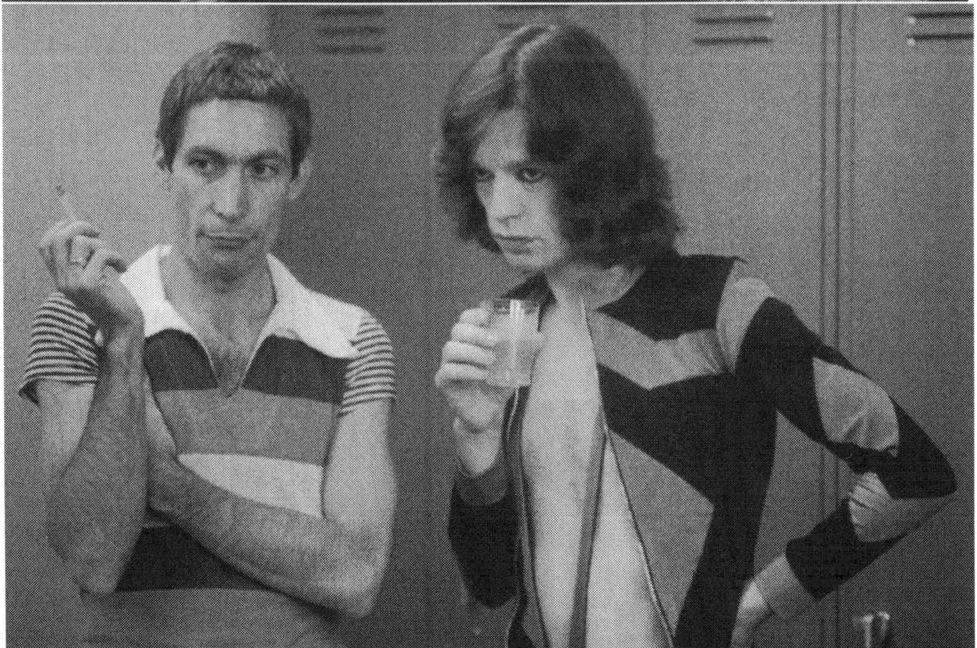

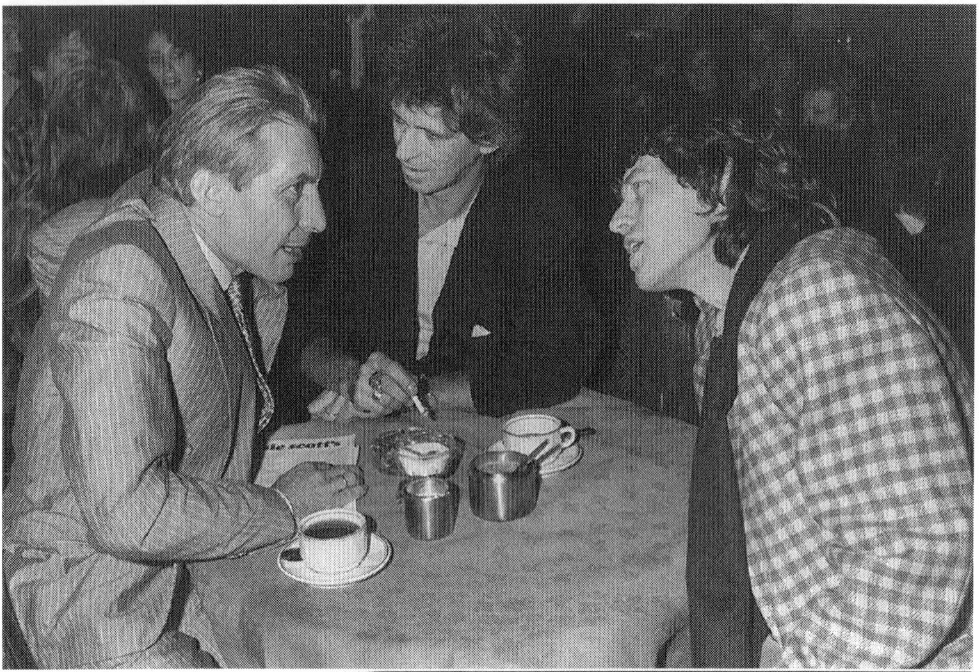
ie scott's

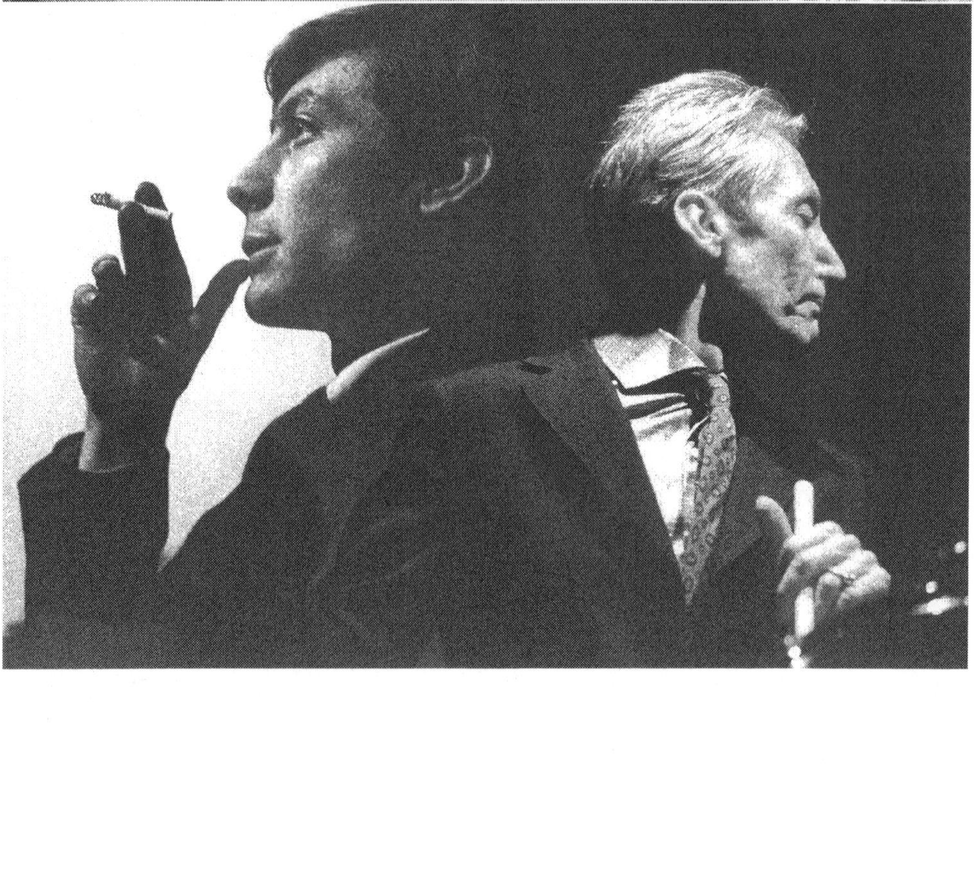

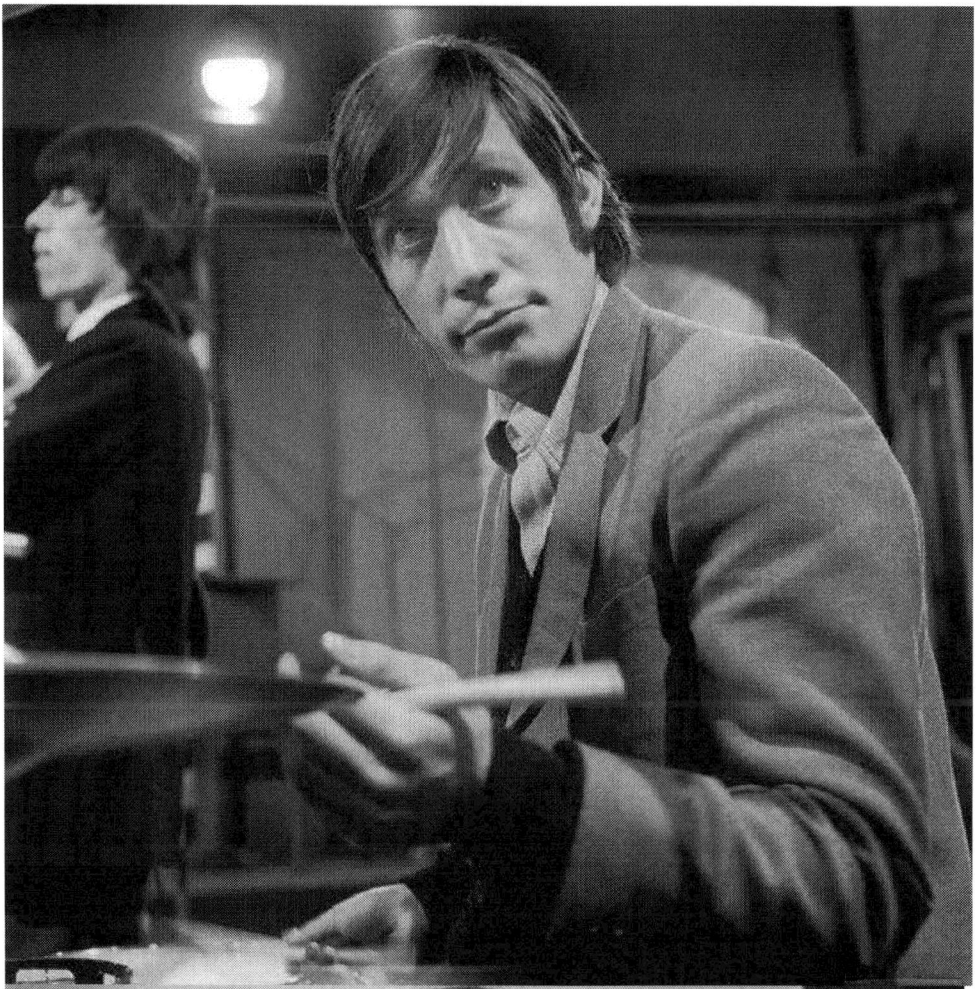

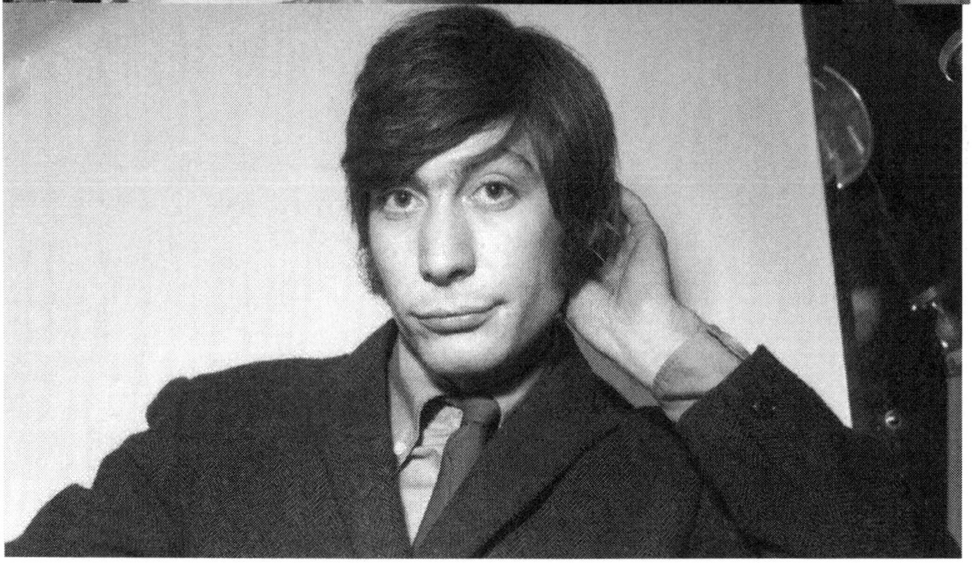

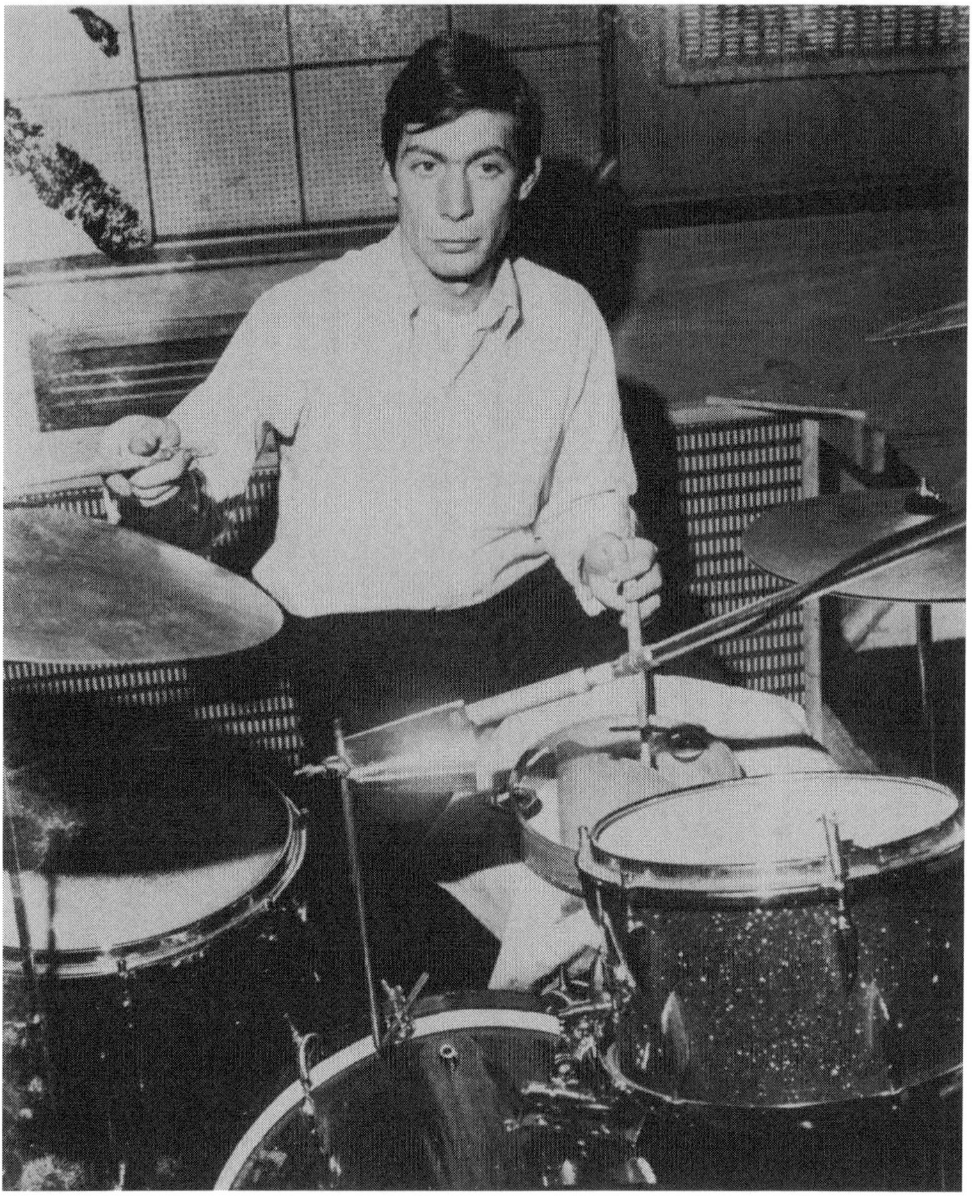

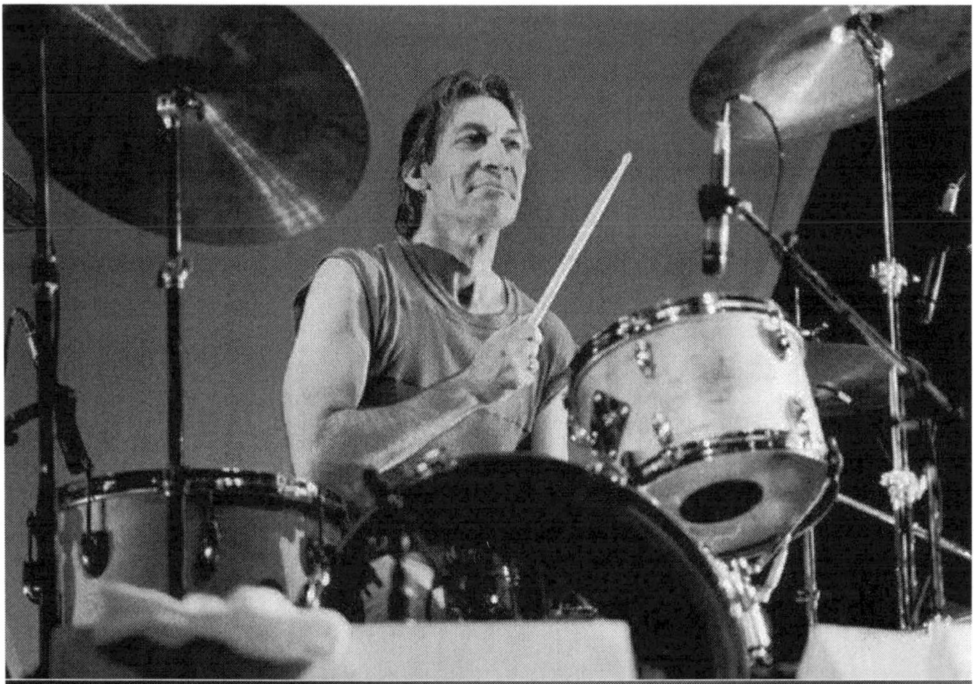

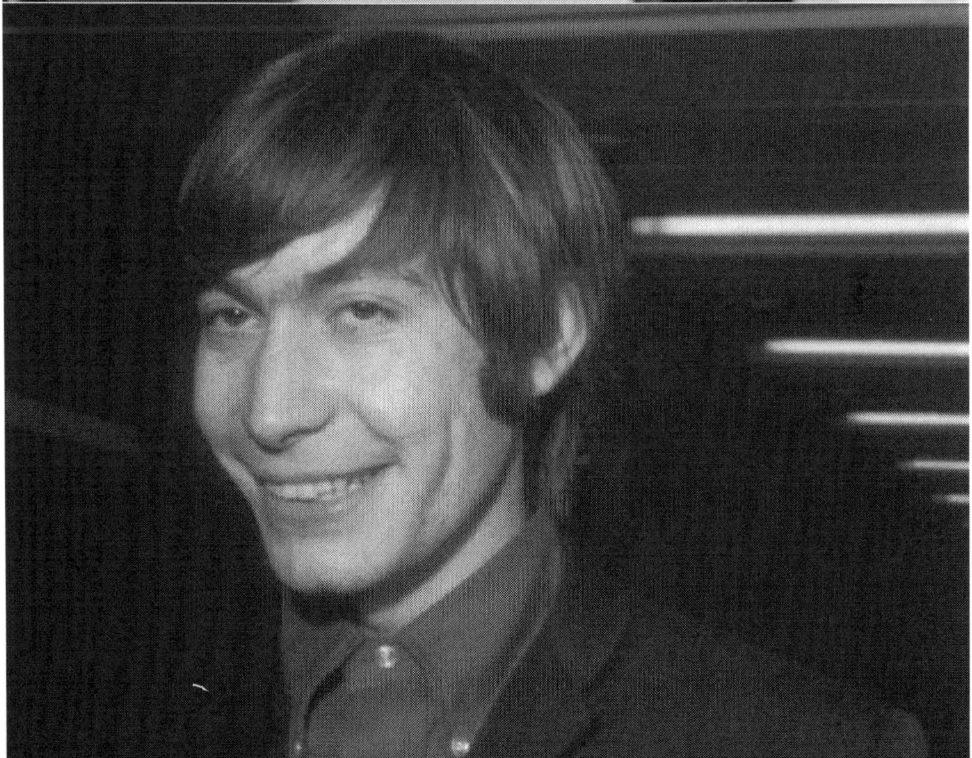

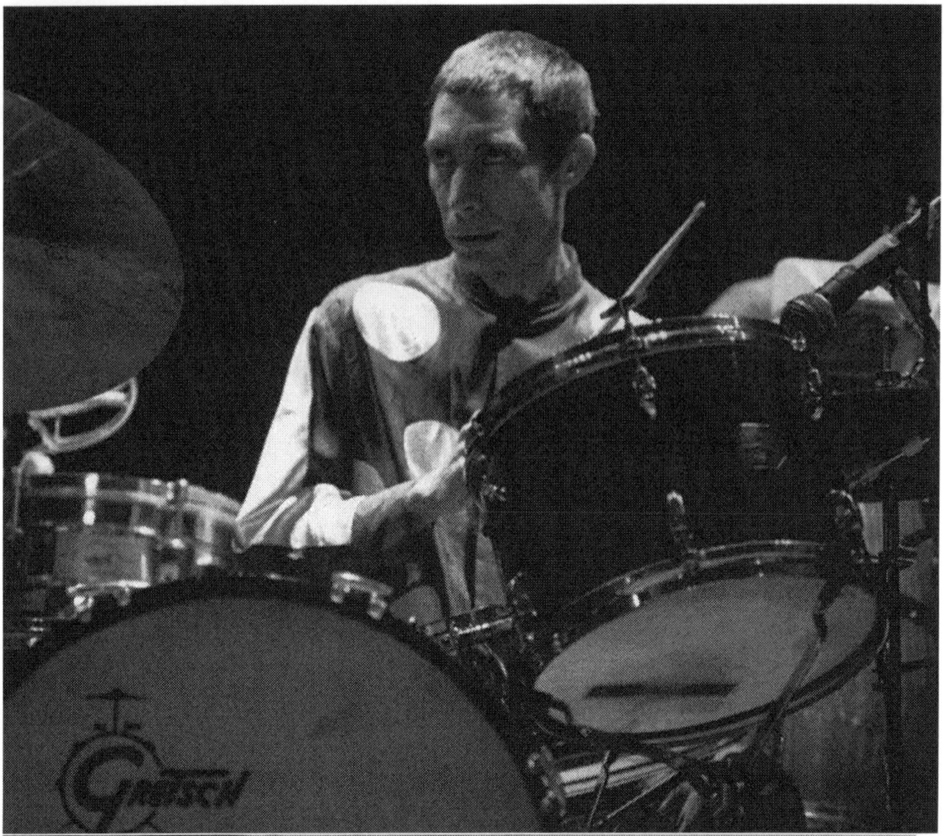
GRETSCH

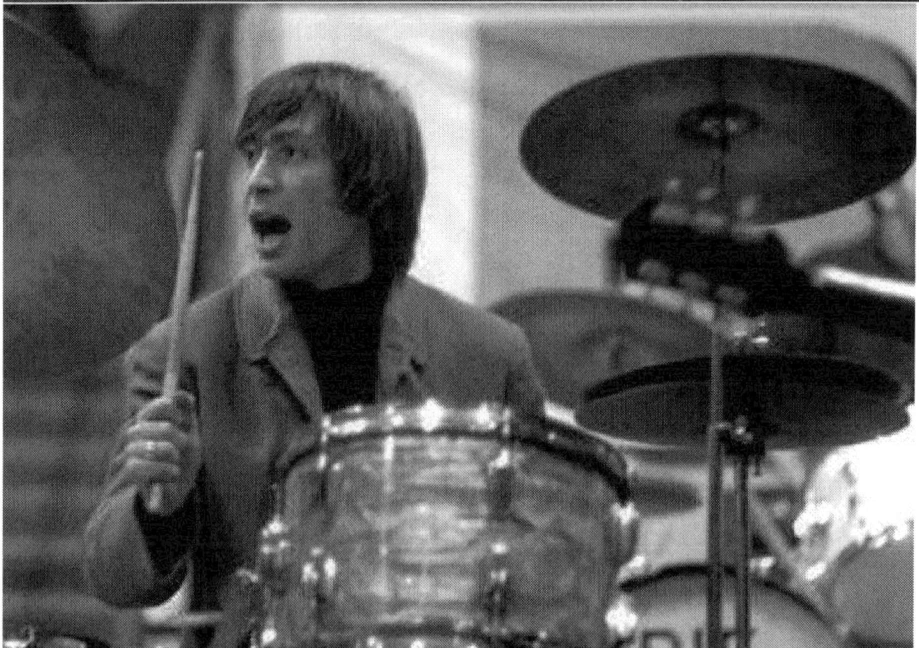

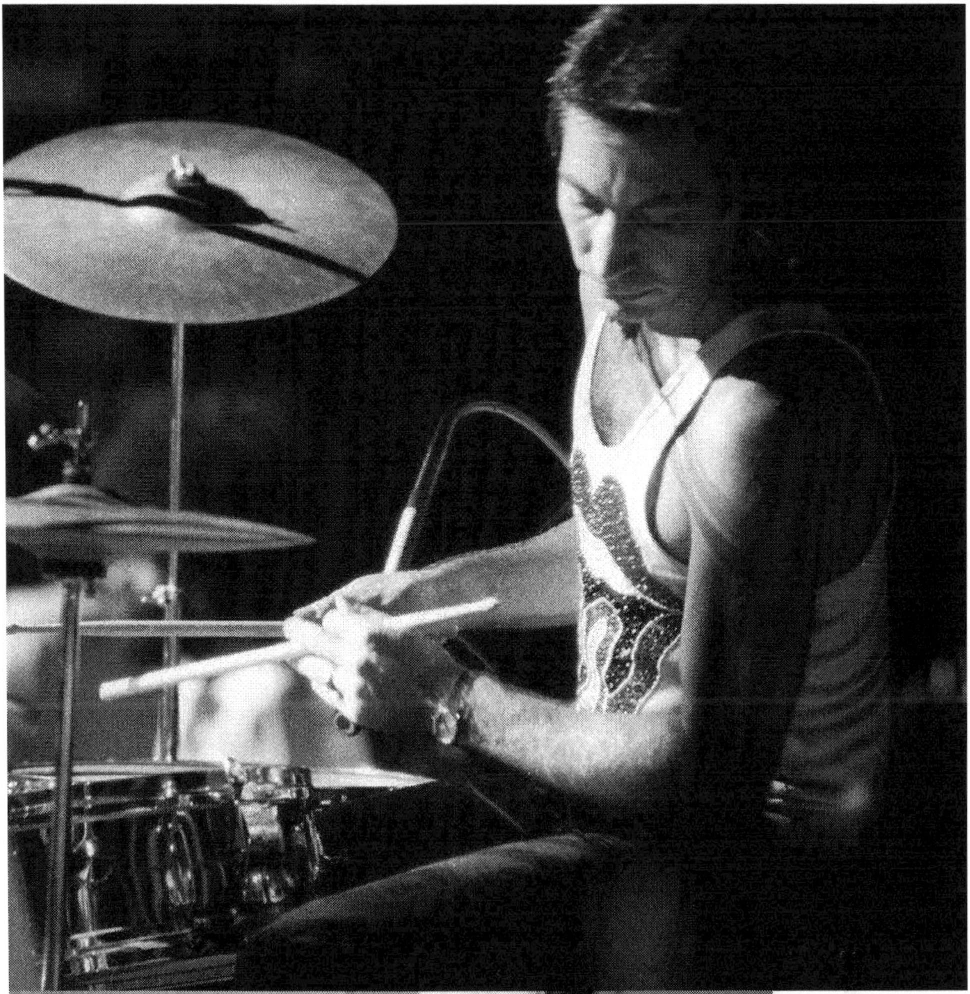

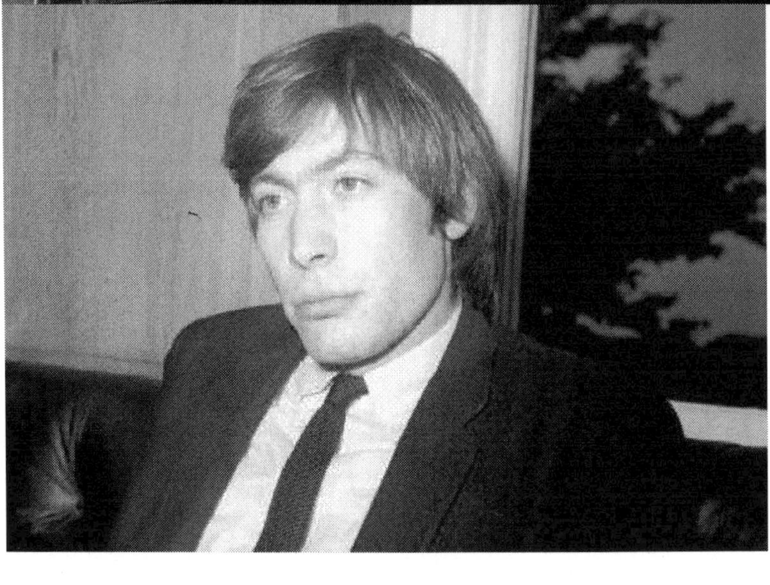

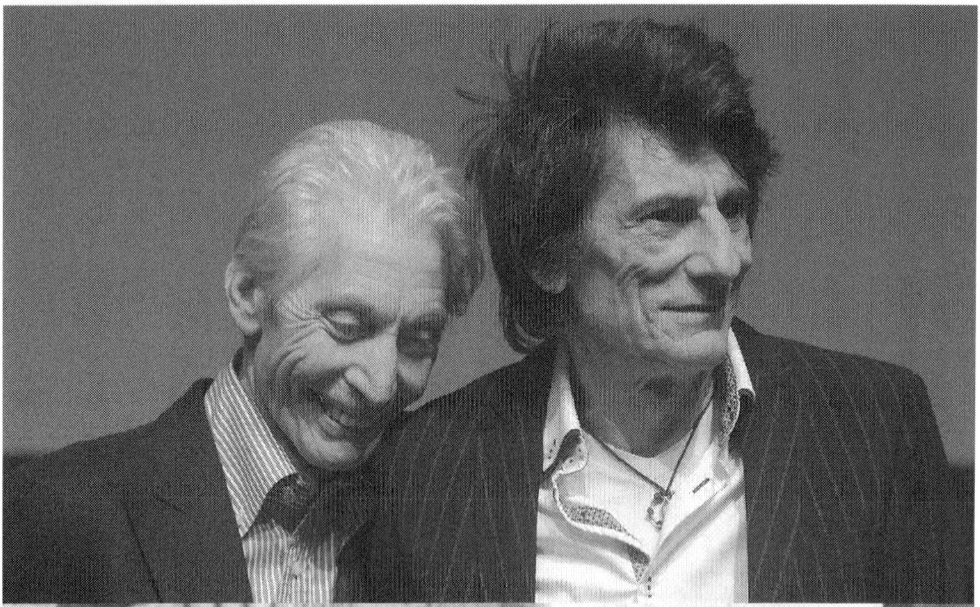

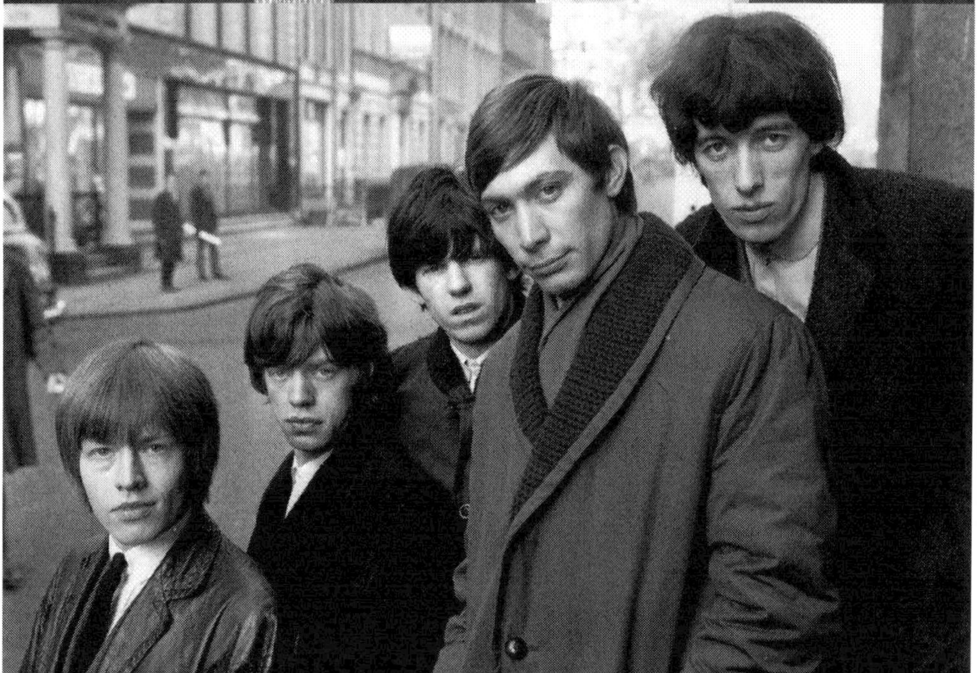

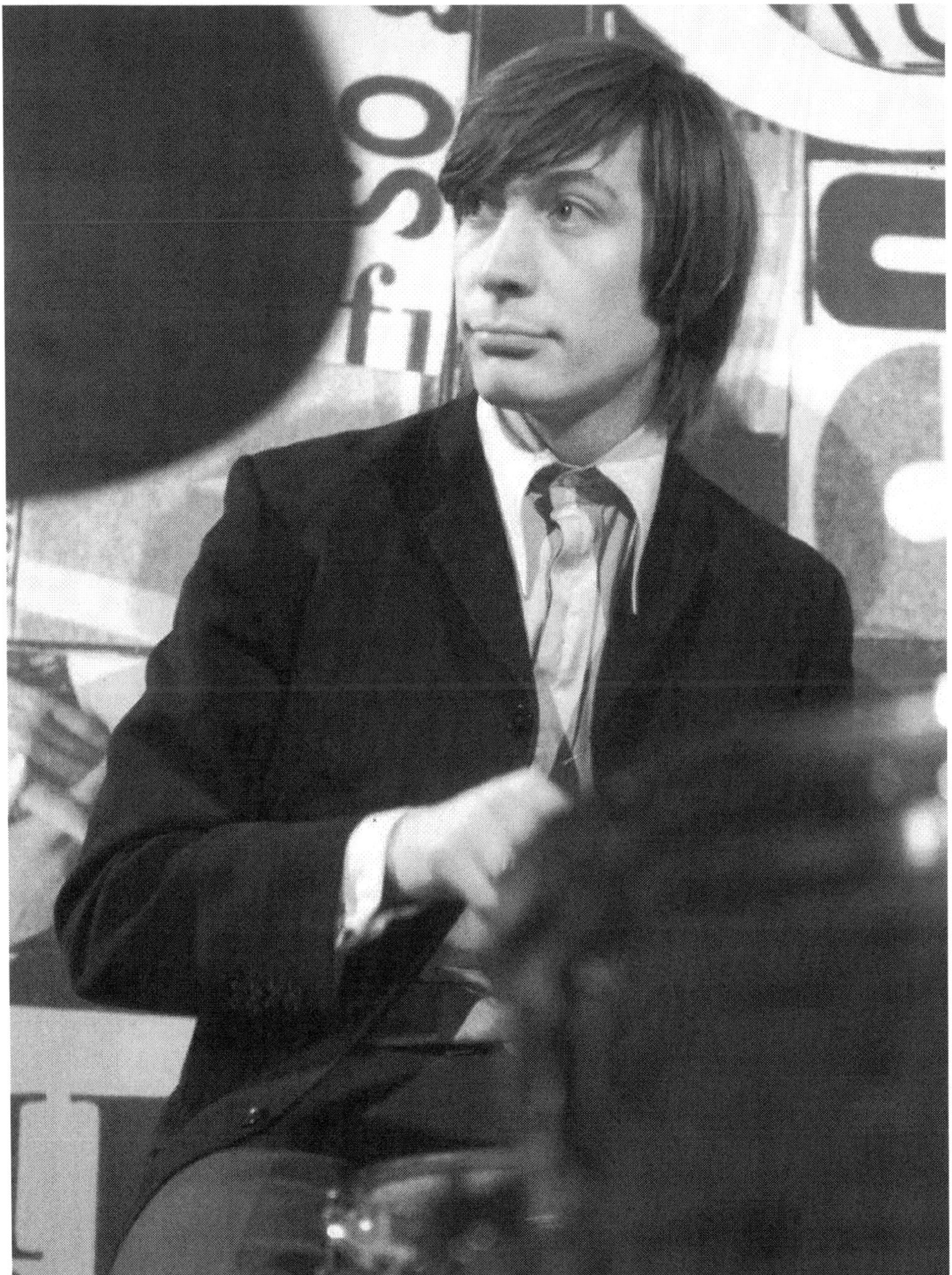

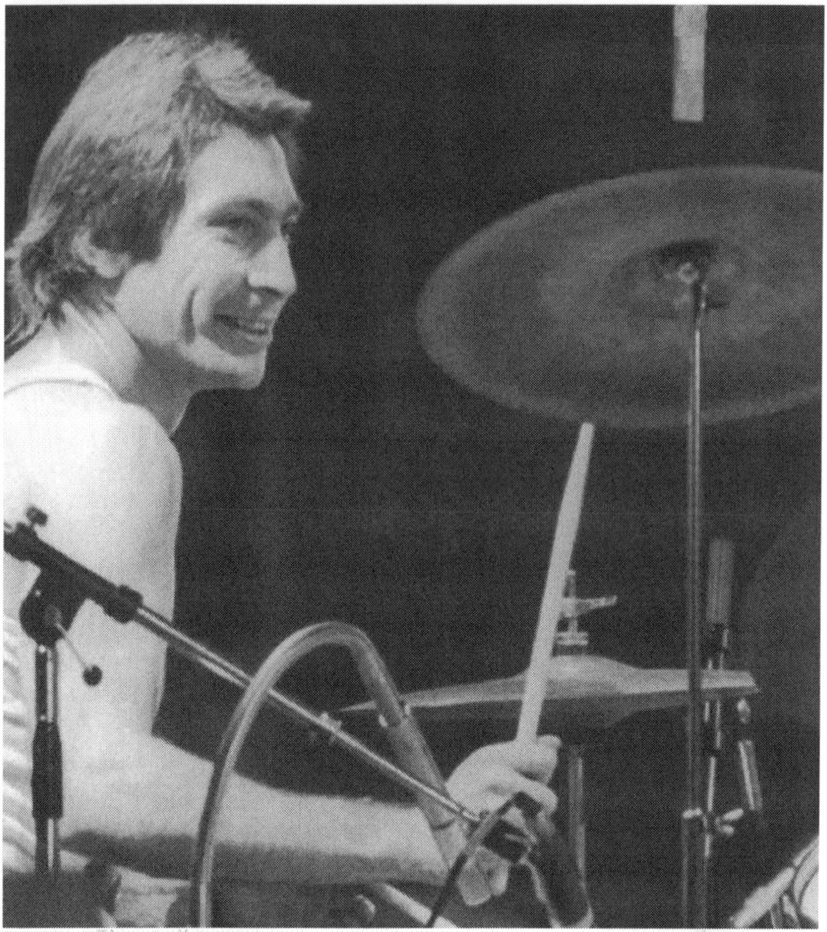

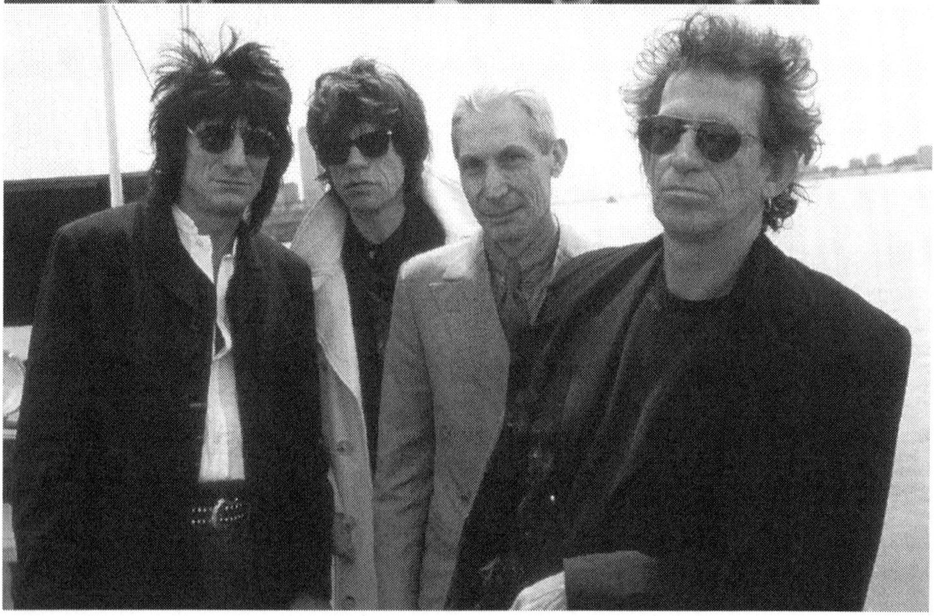

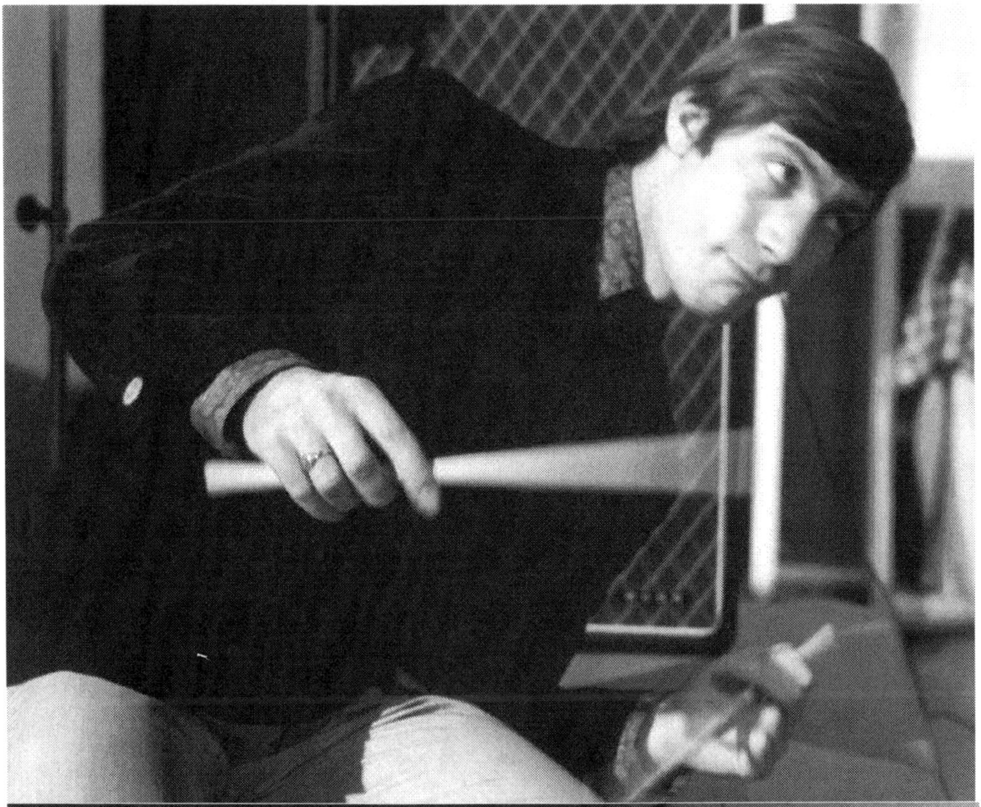

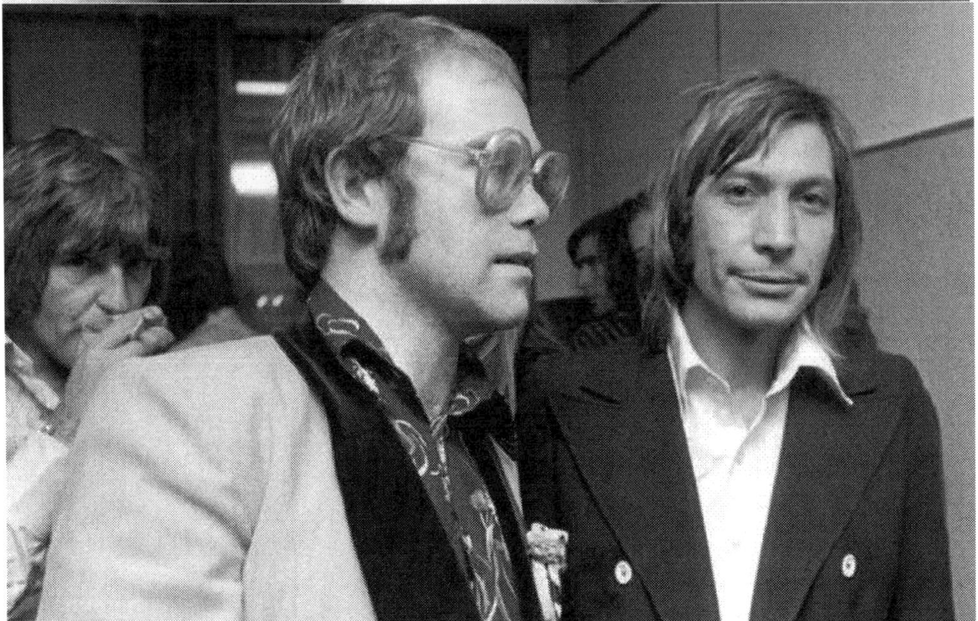

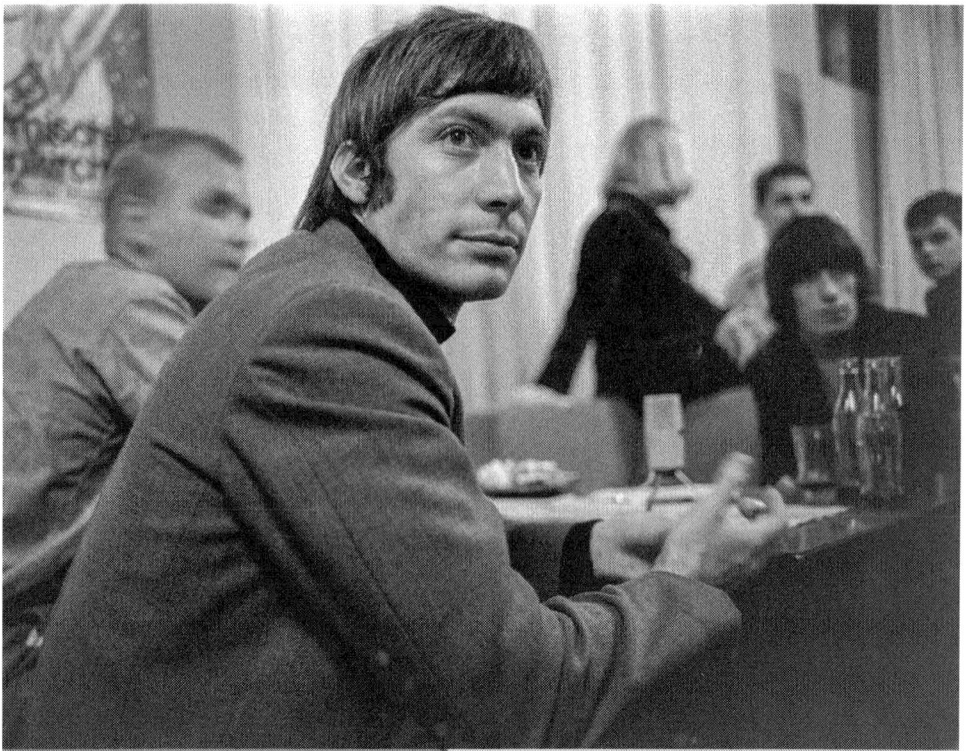

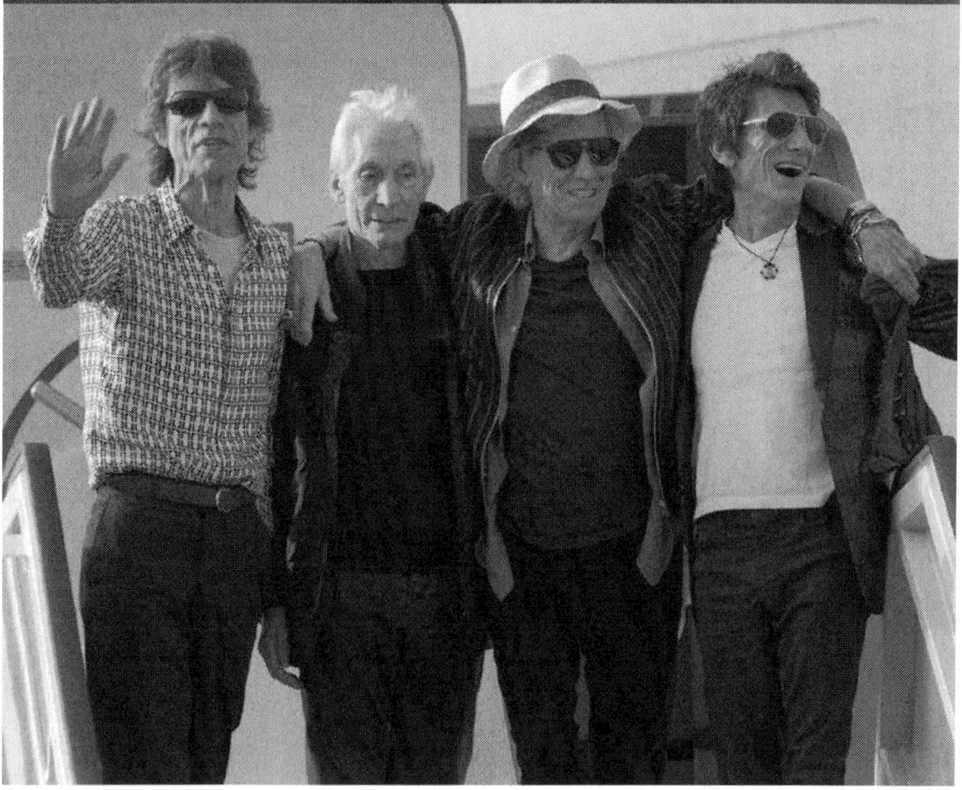

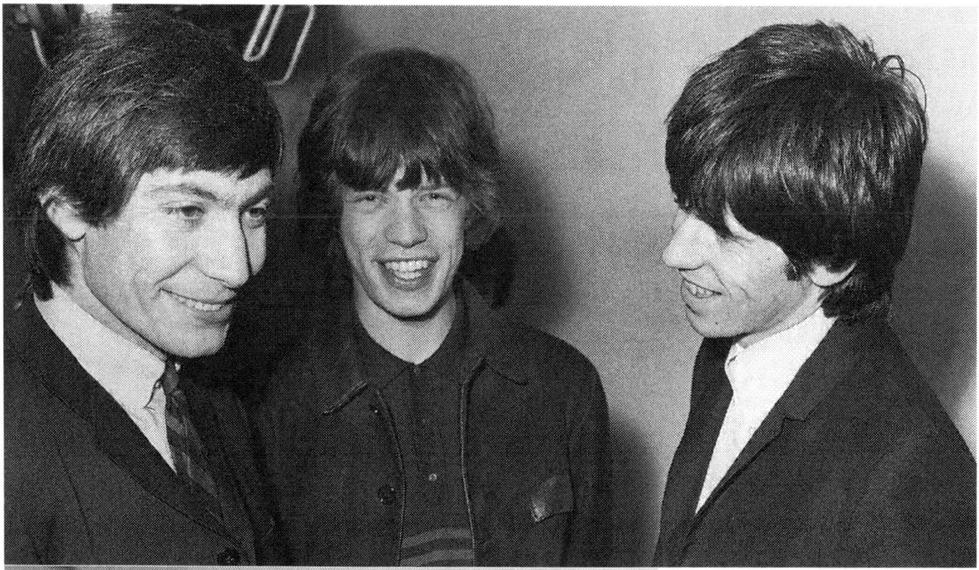

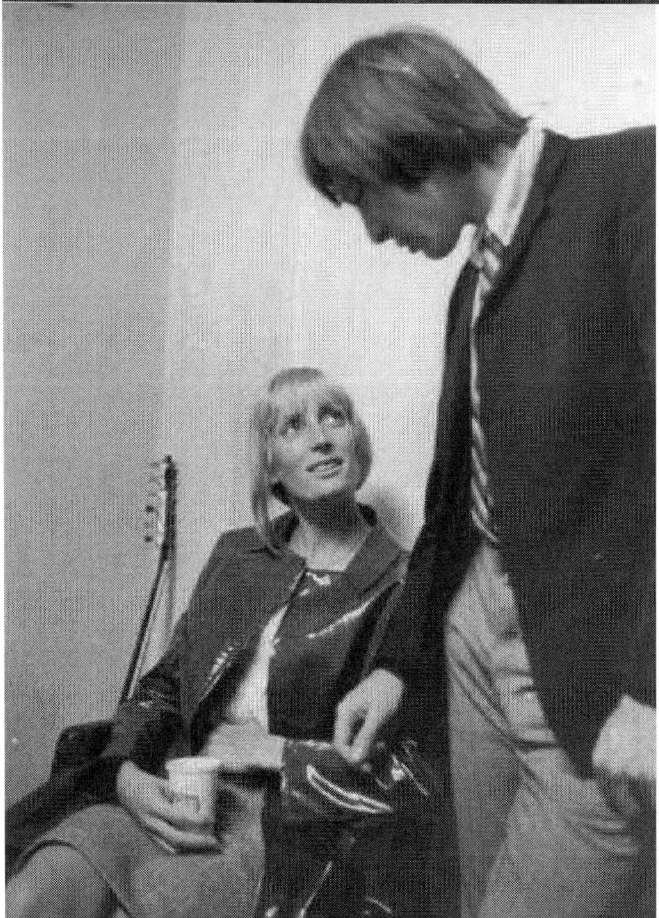

66

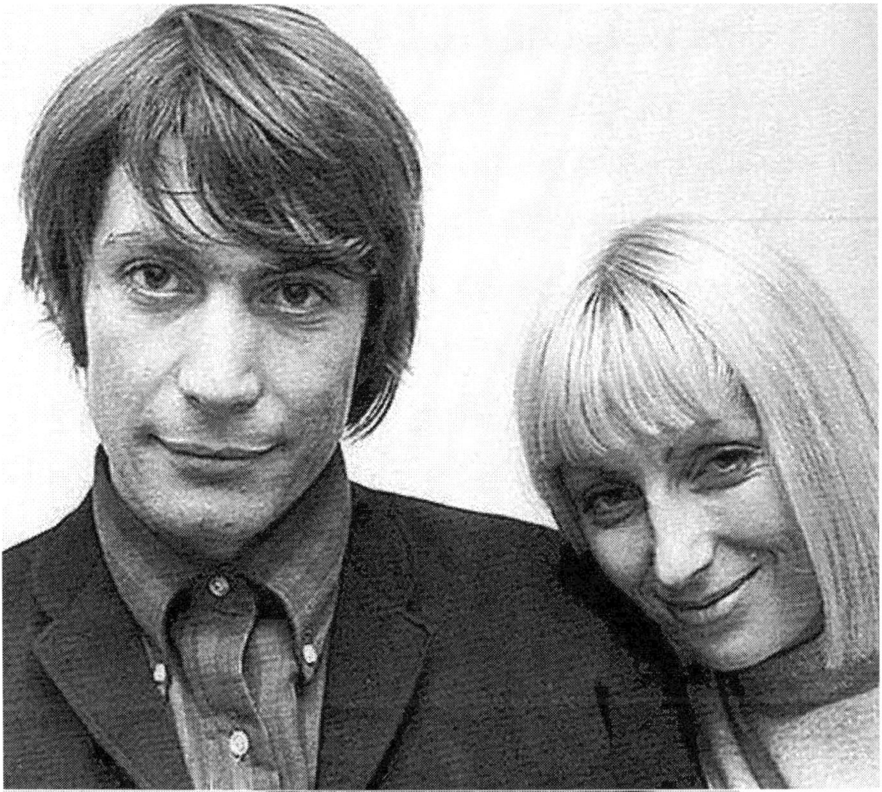
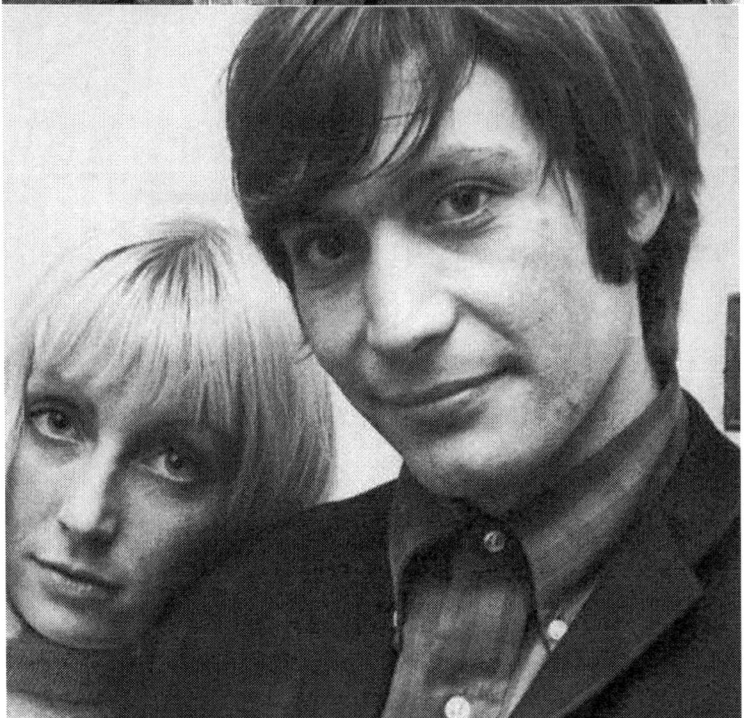

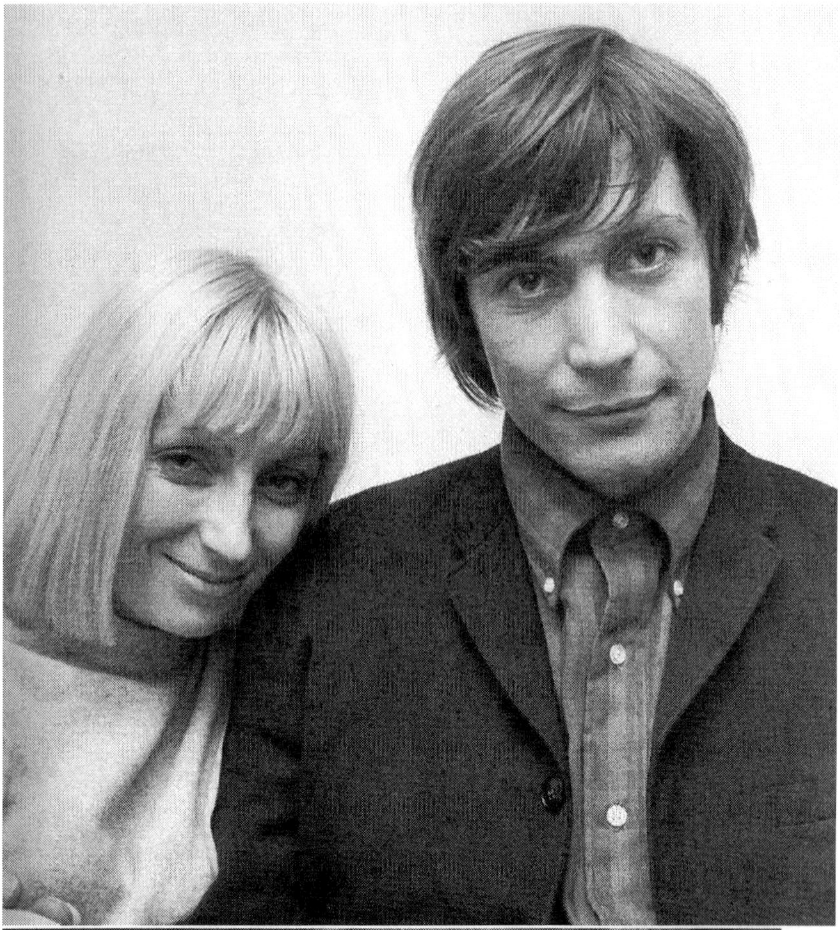

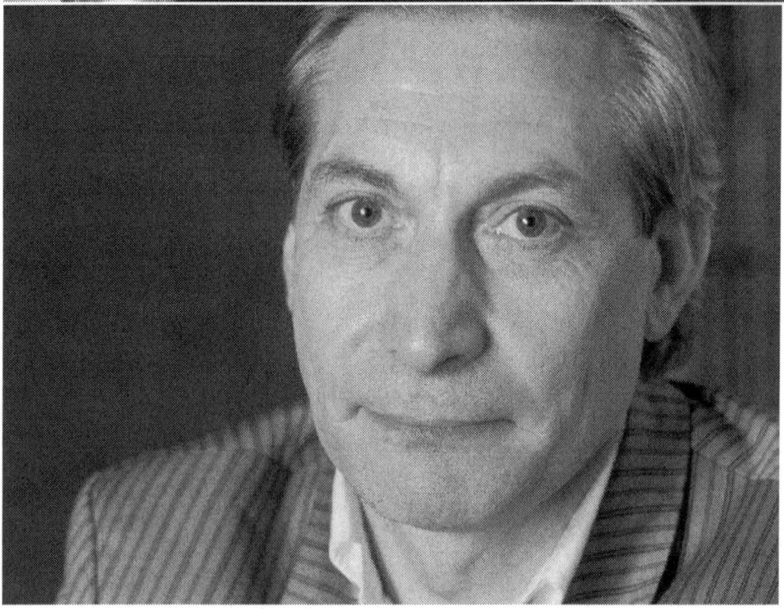

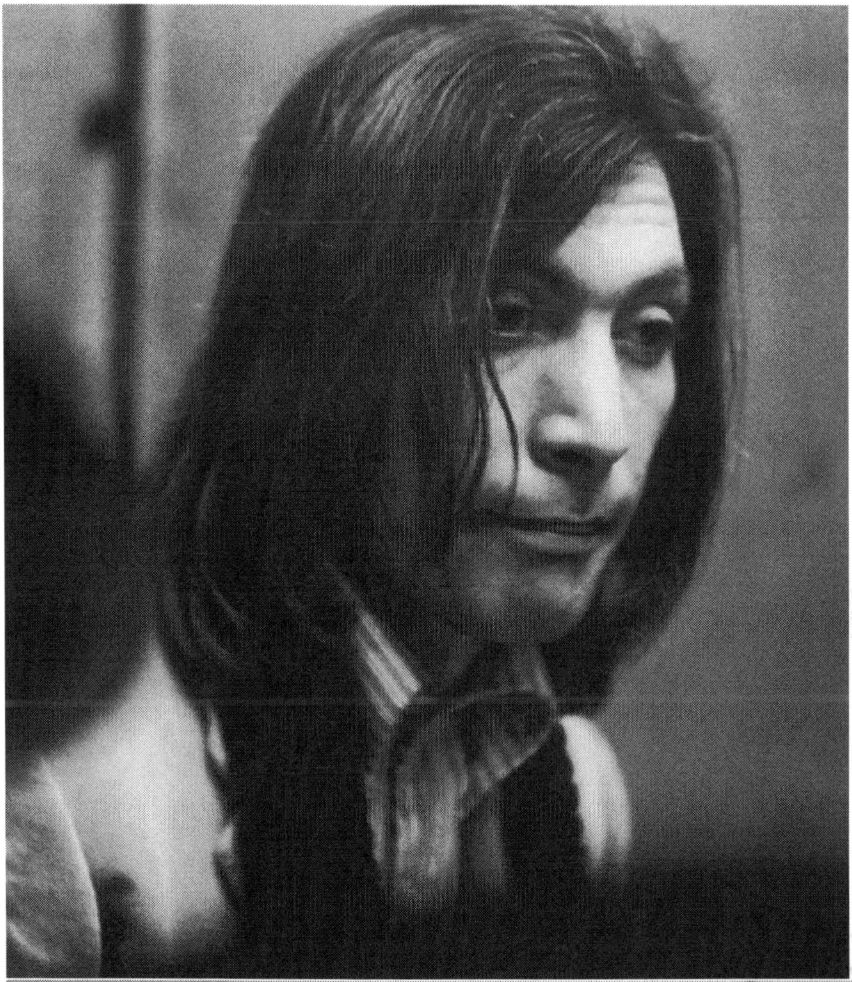

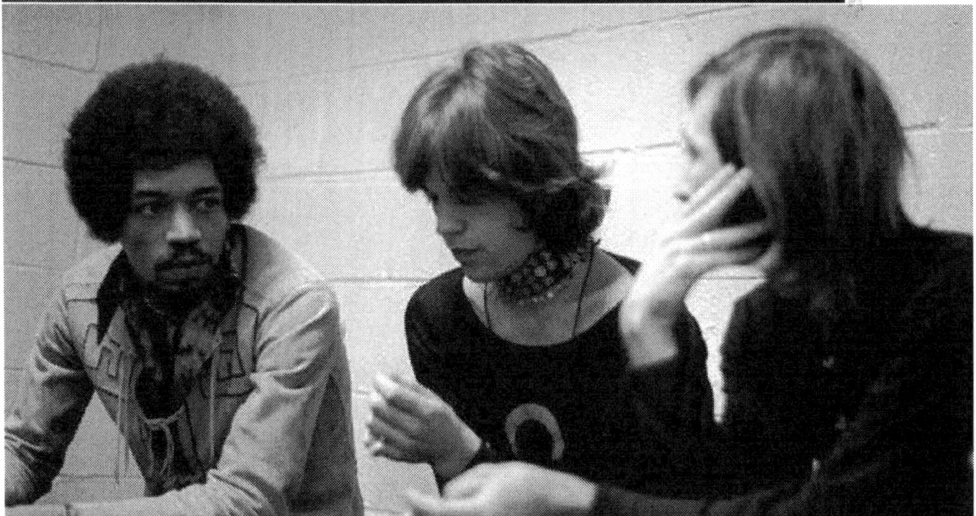

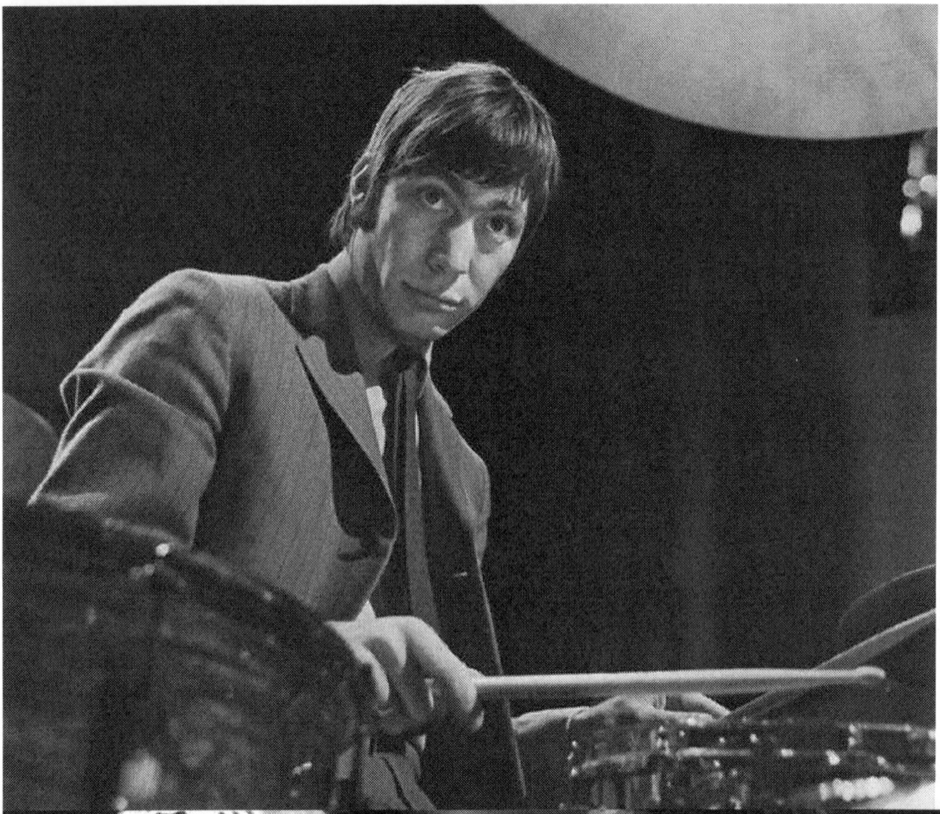

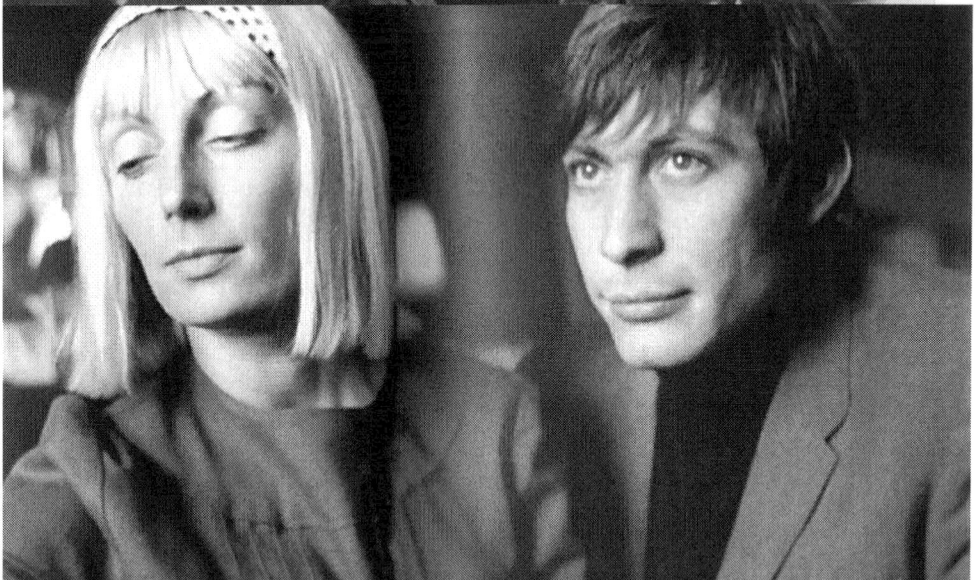

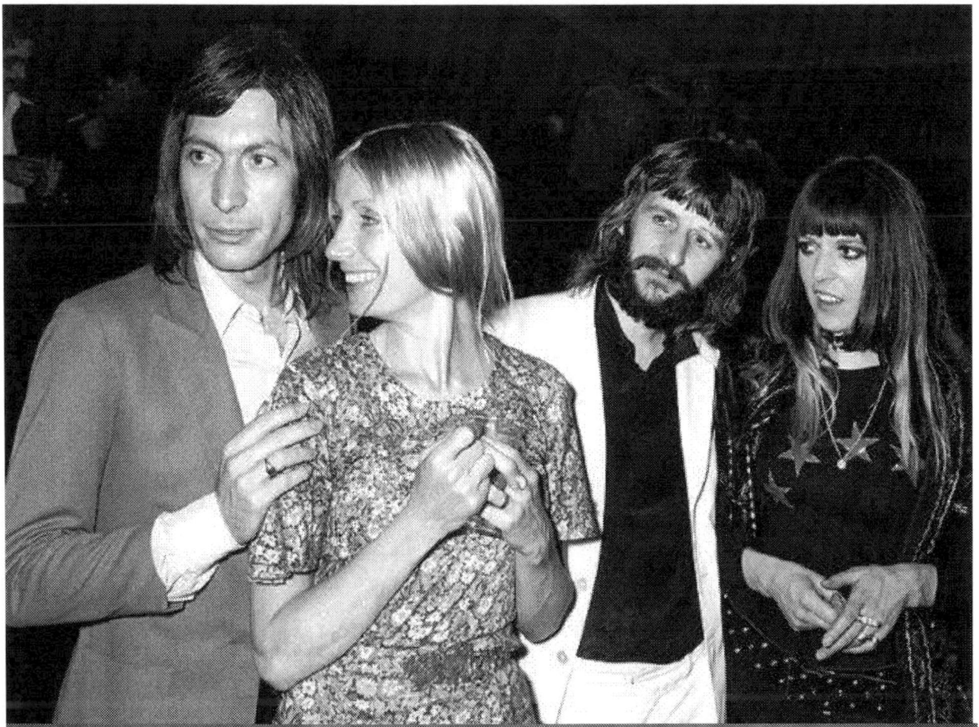

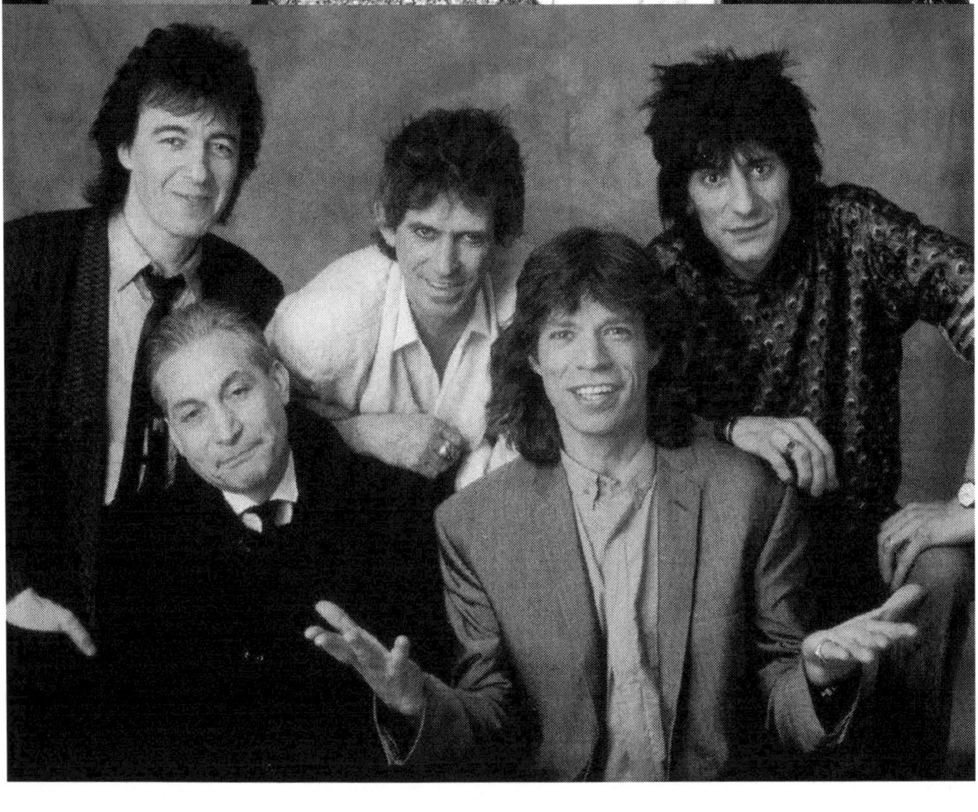

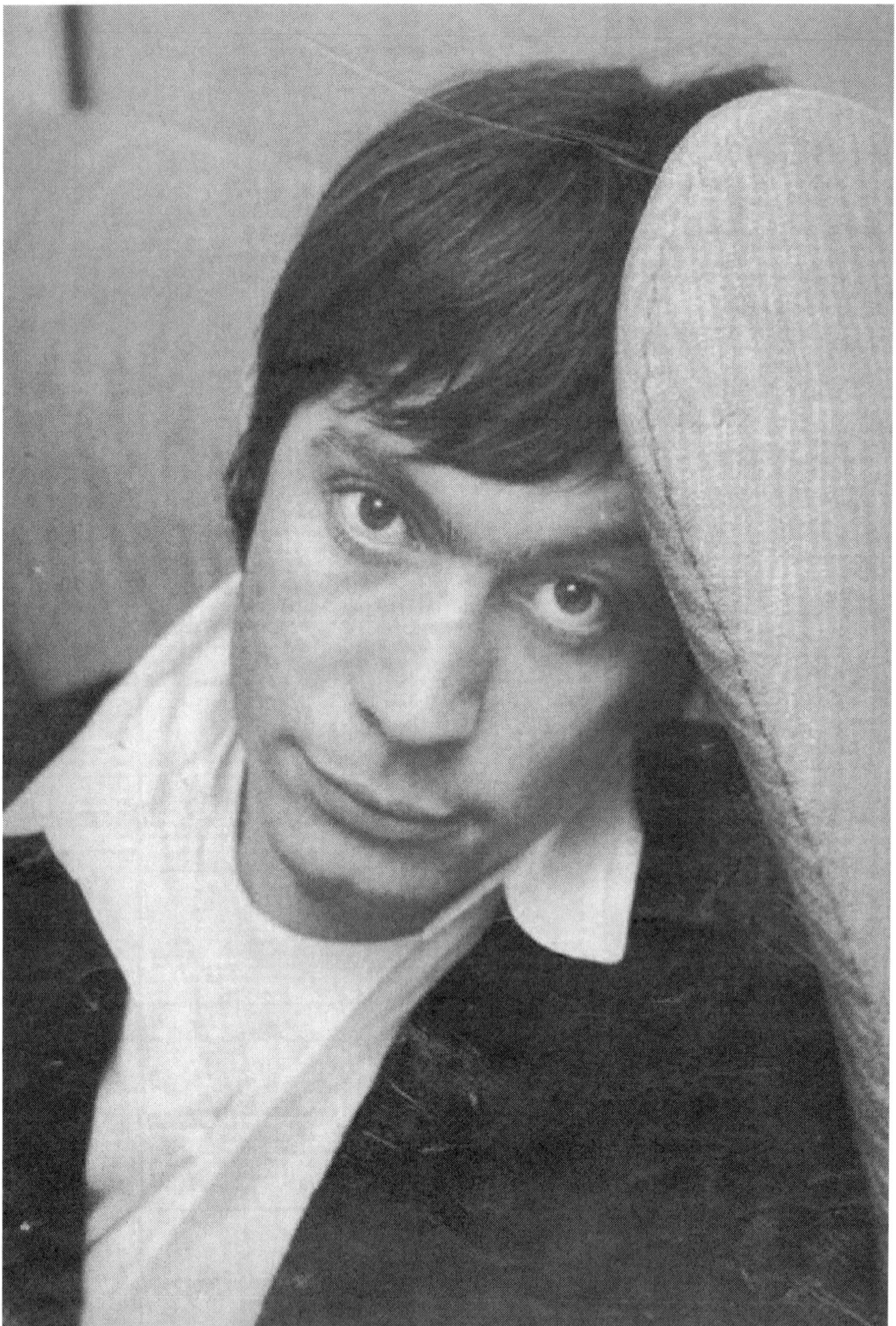

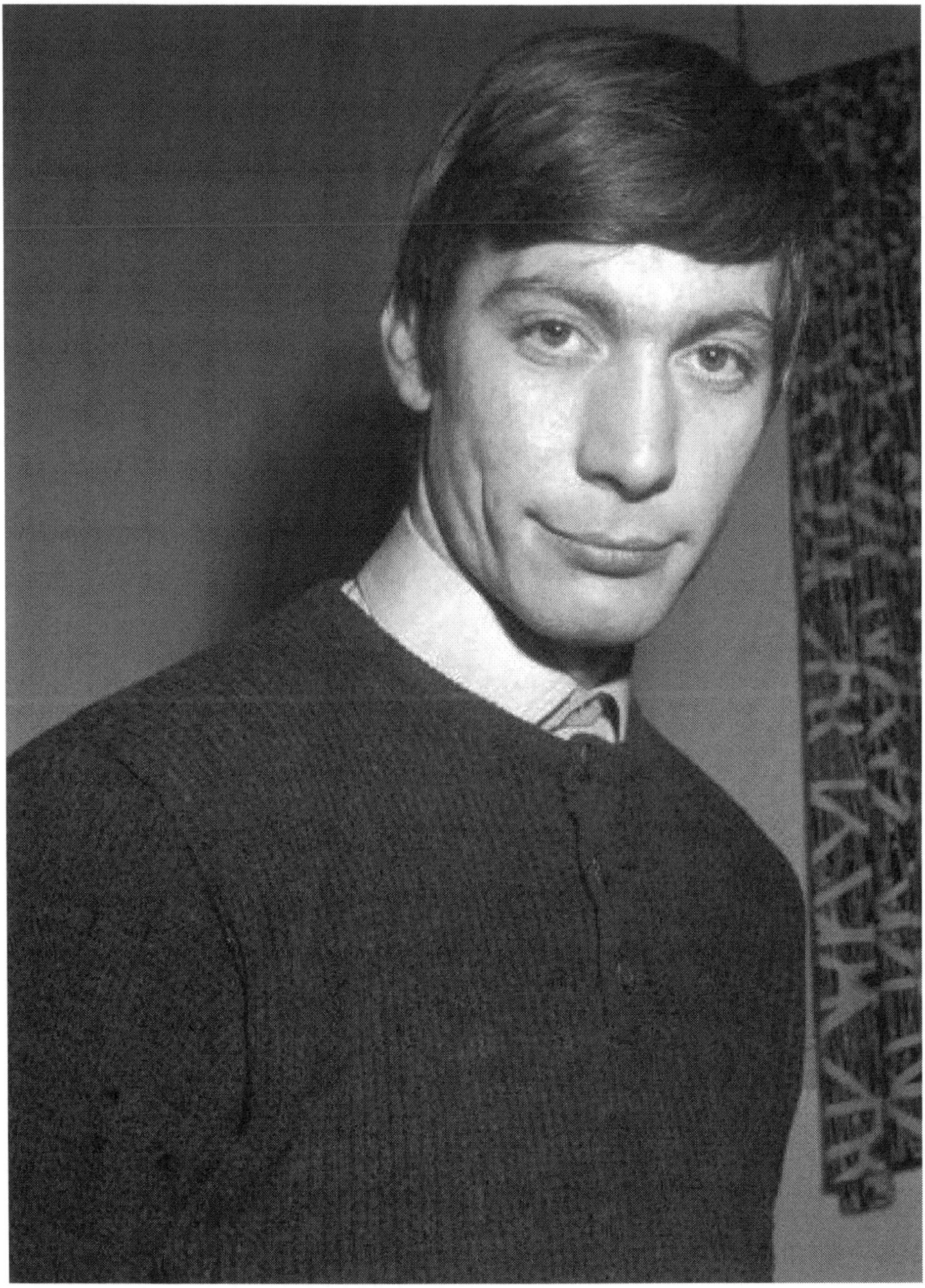

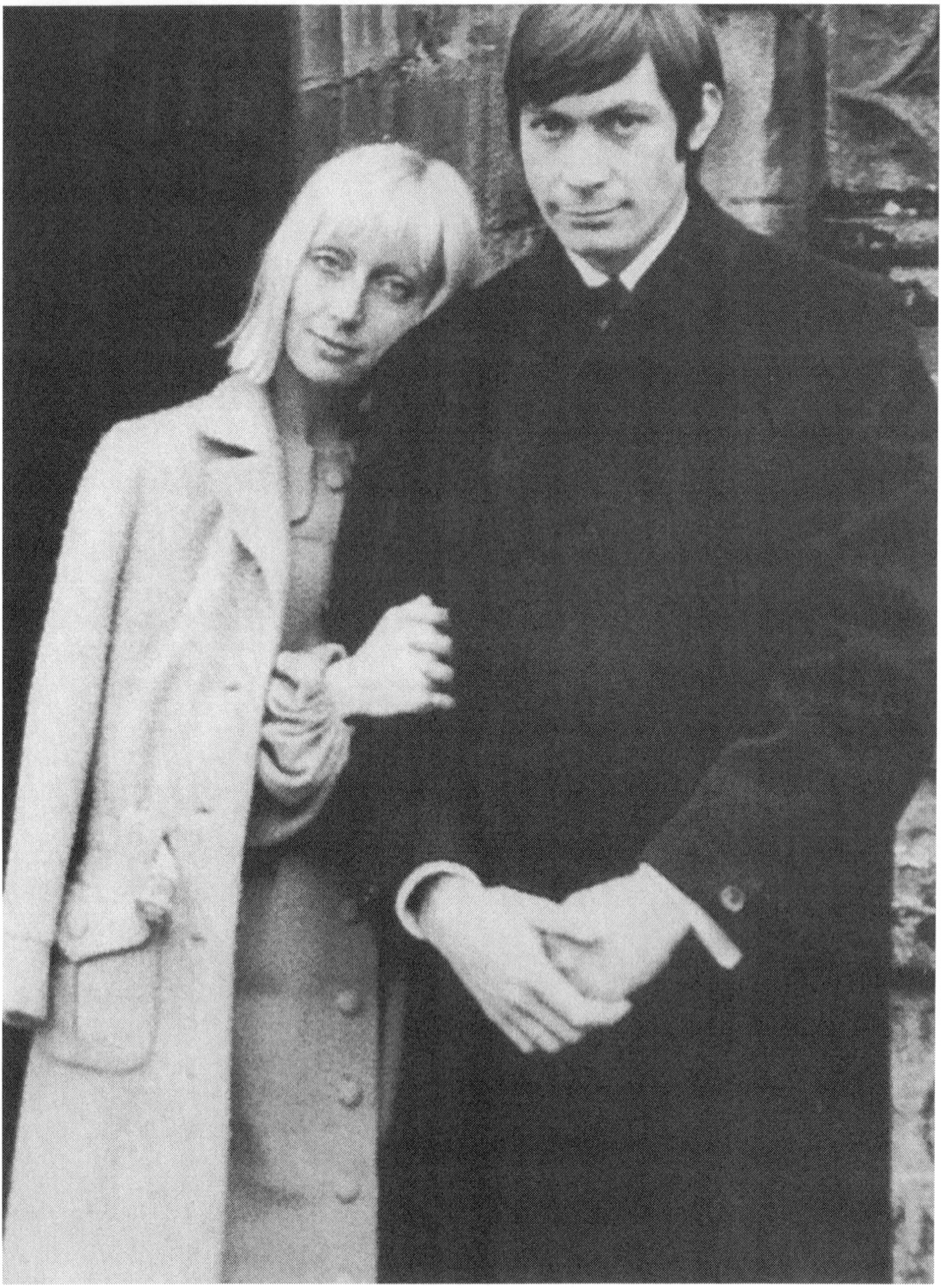

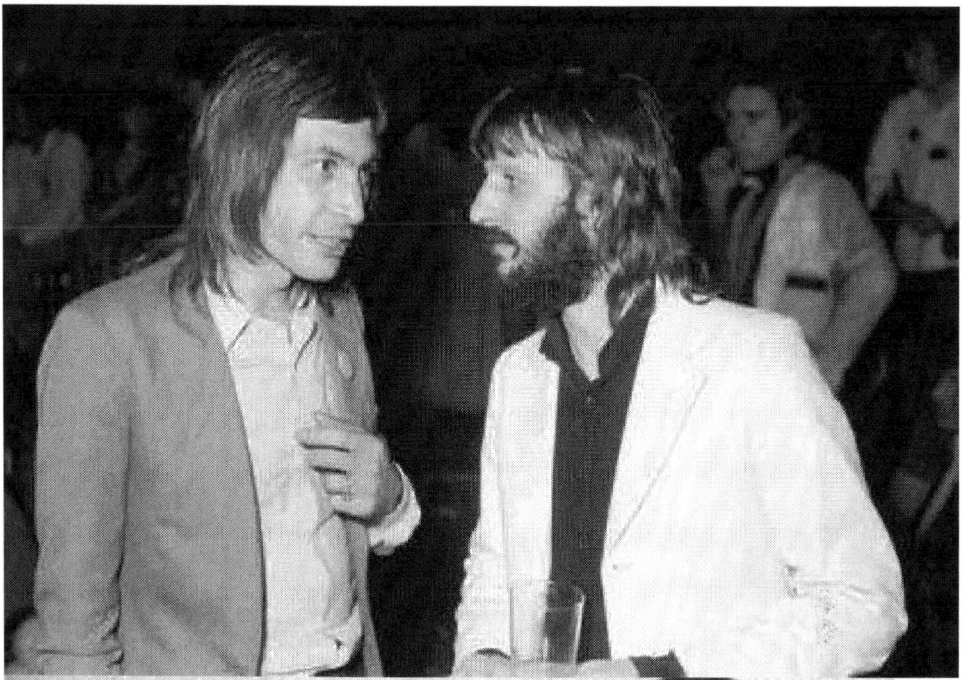

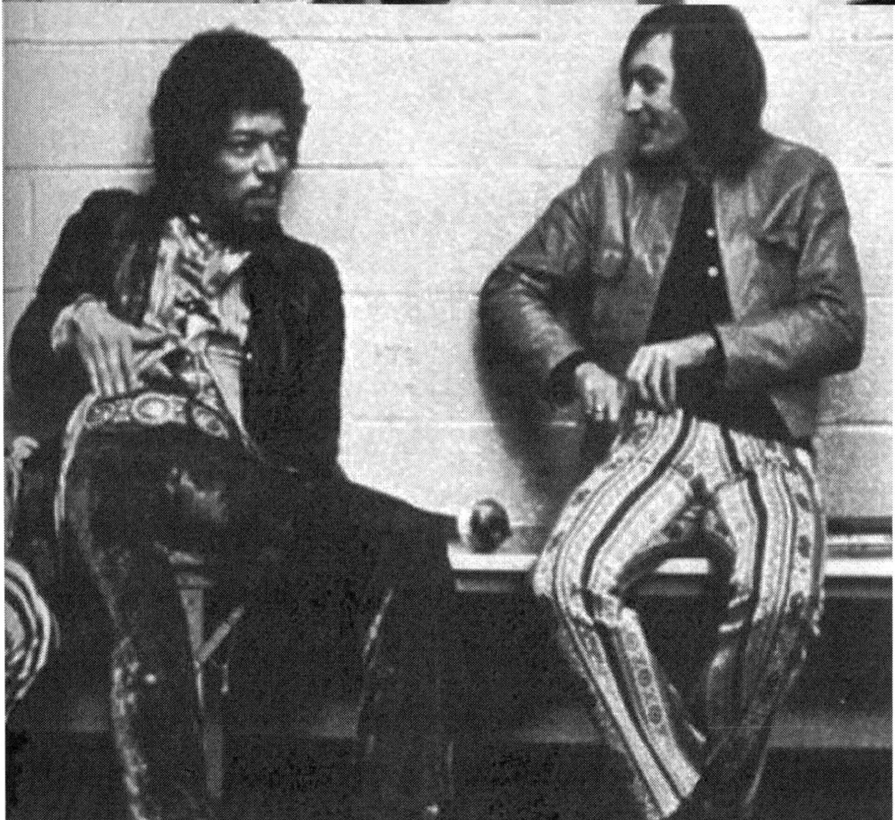

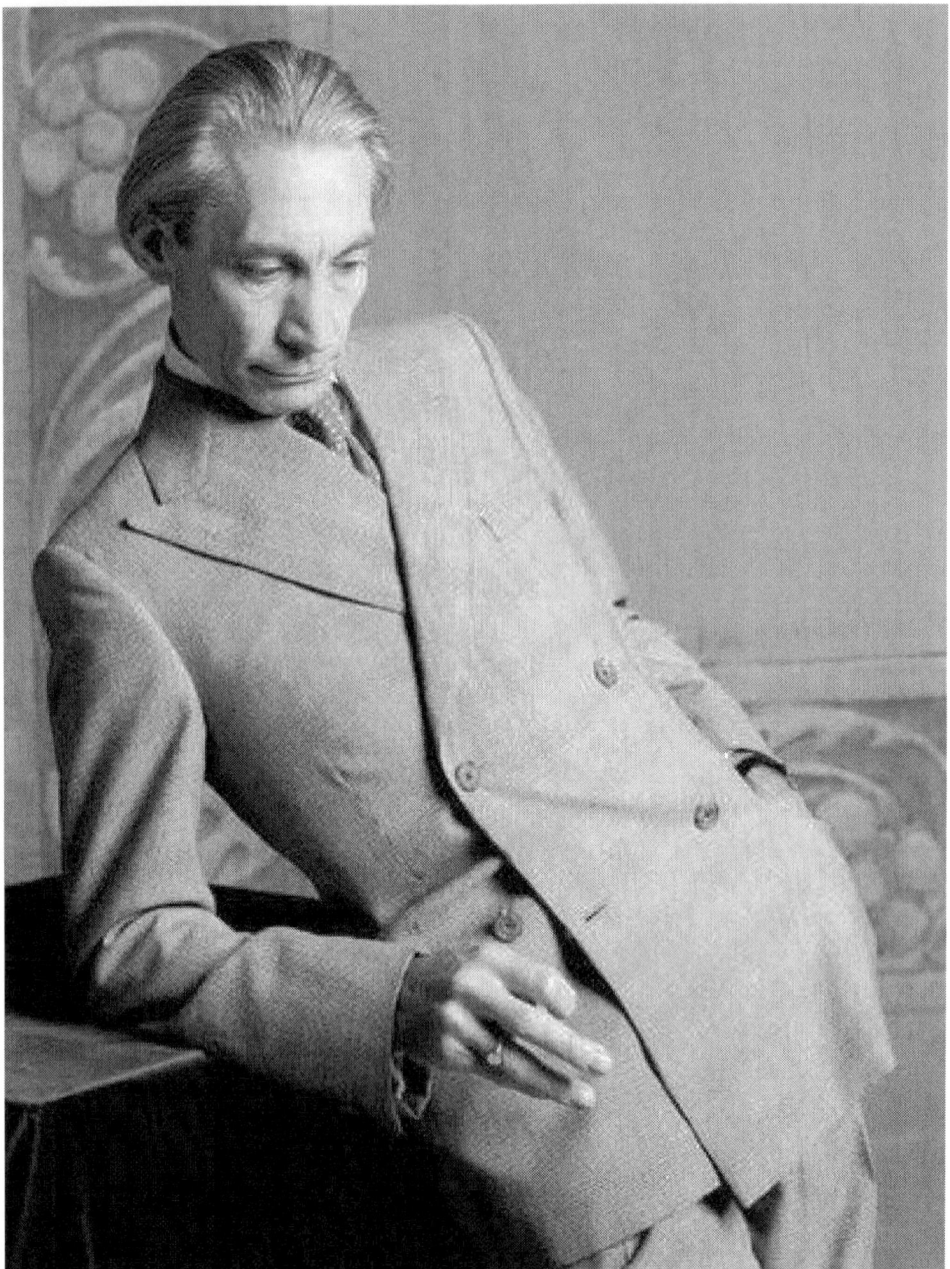

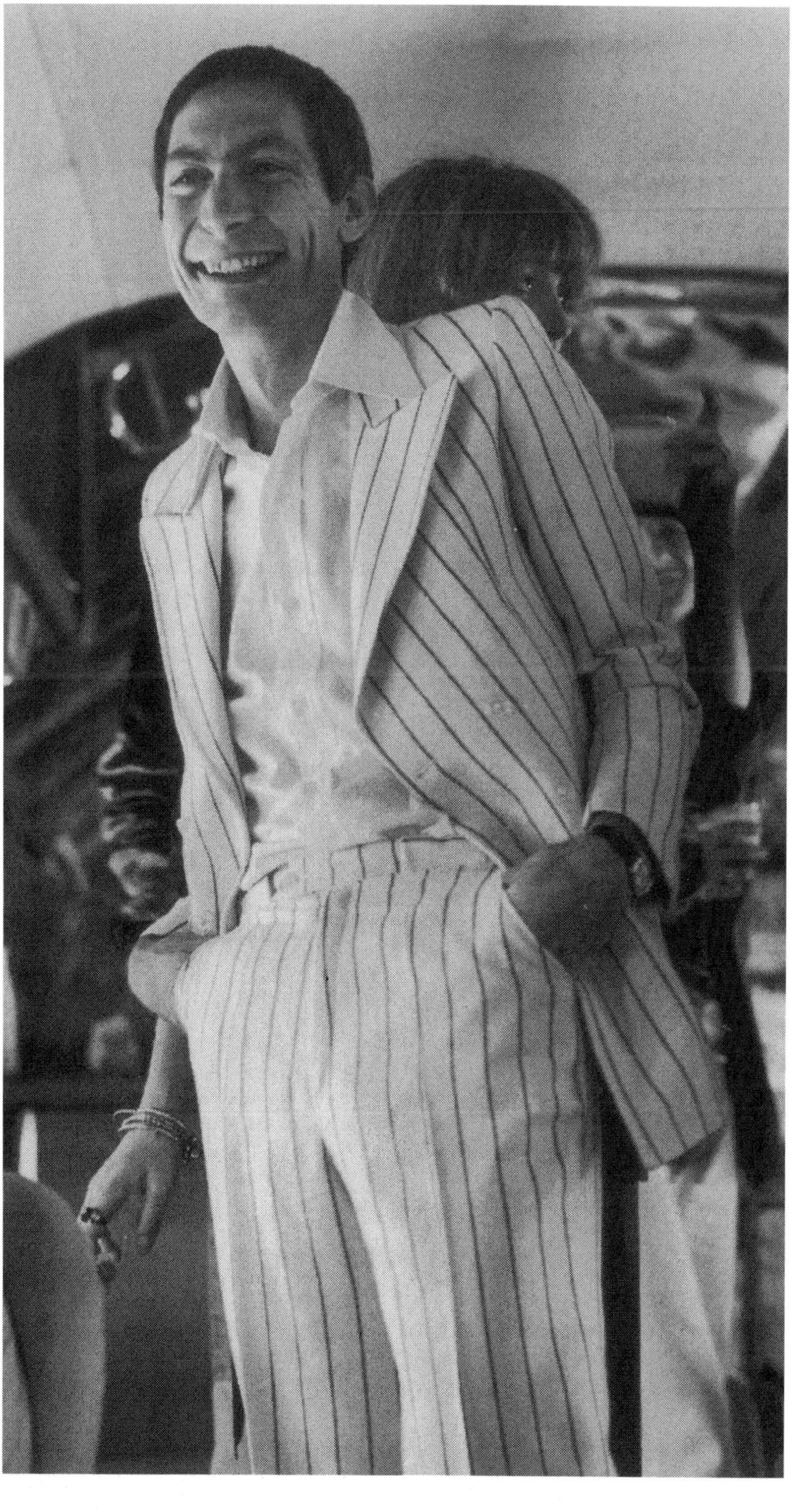

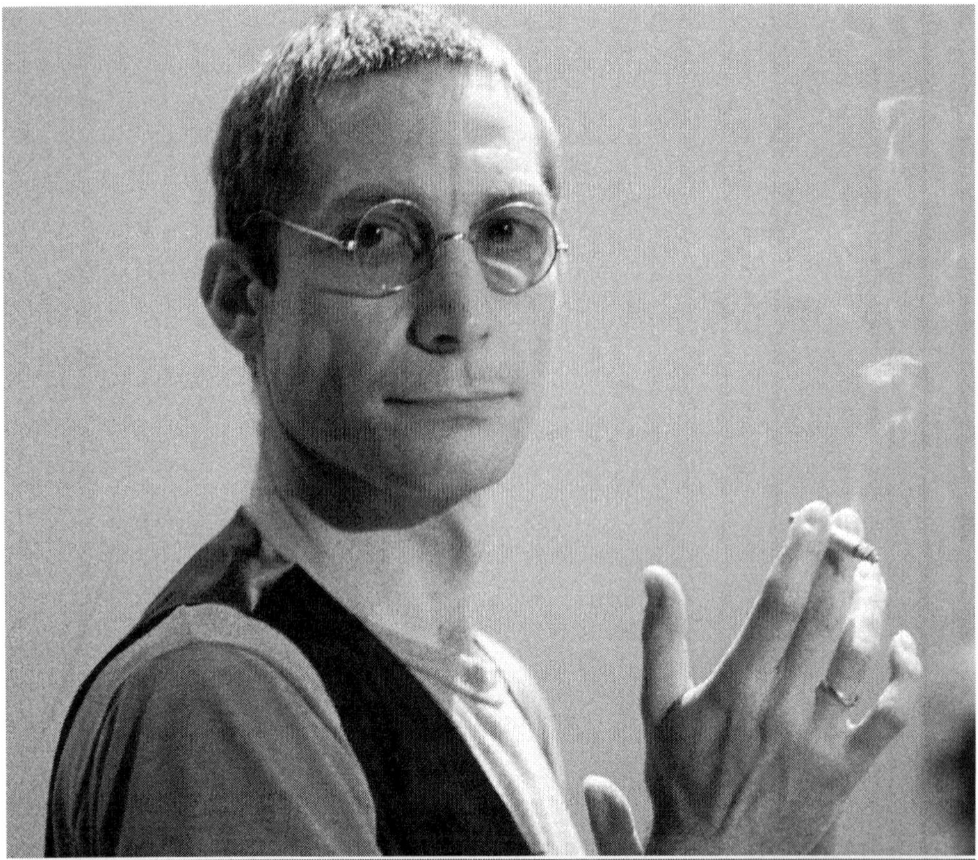

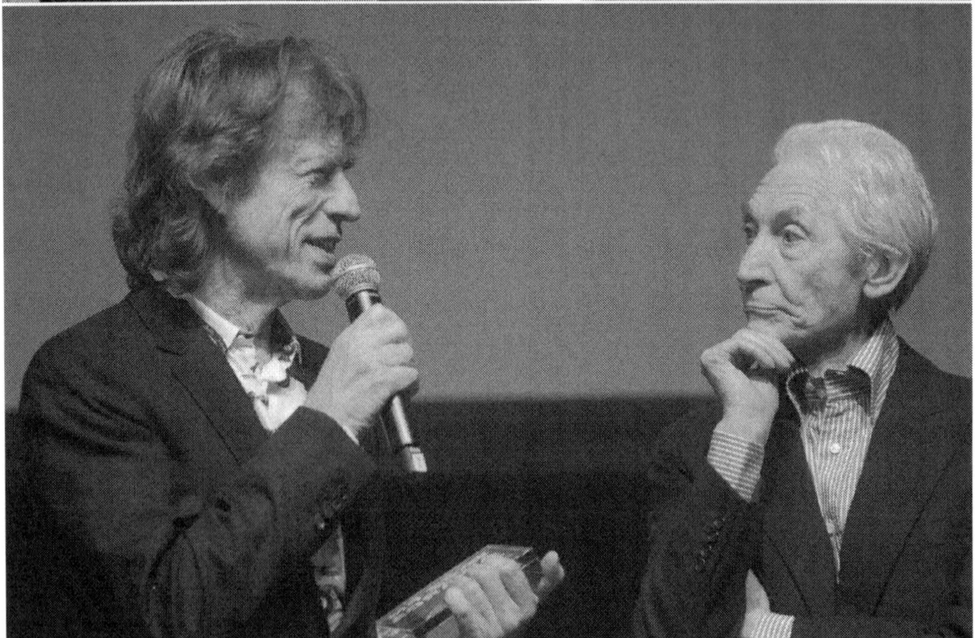

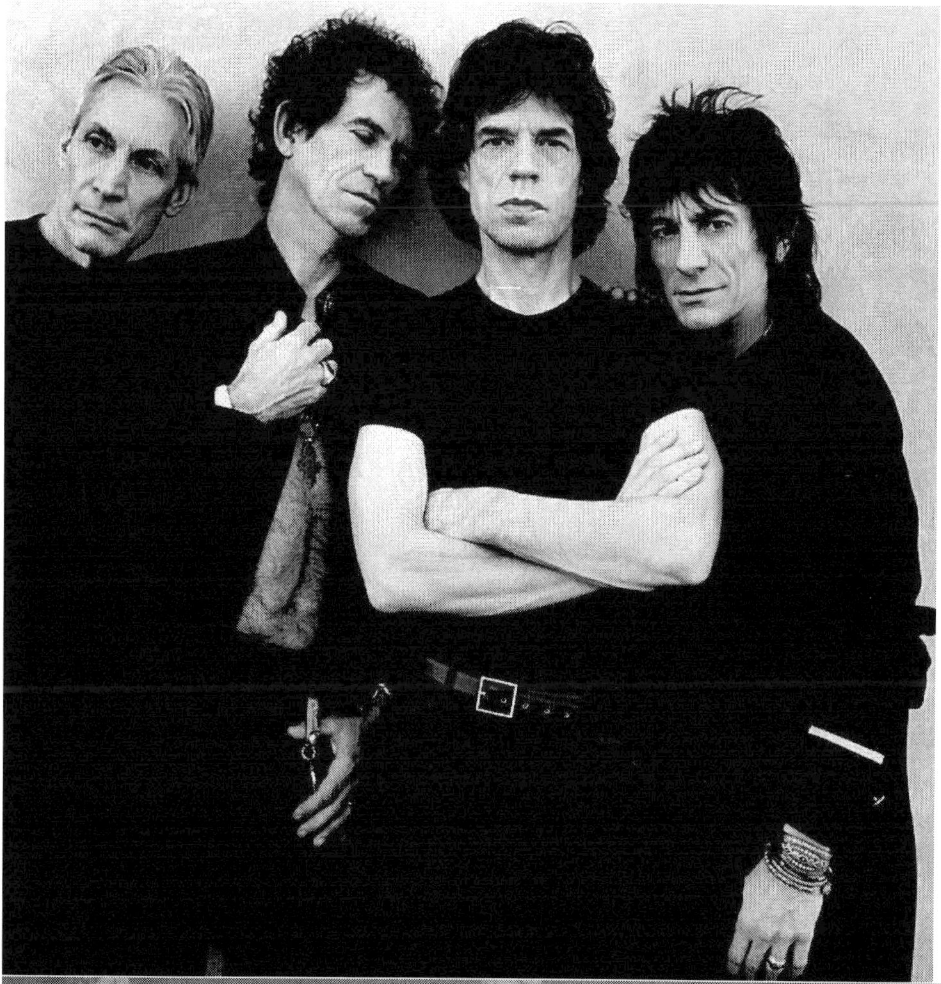

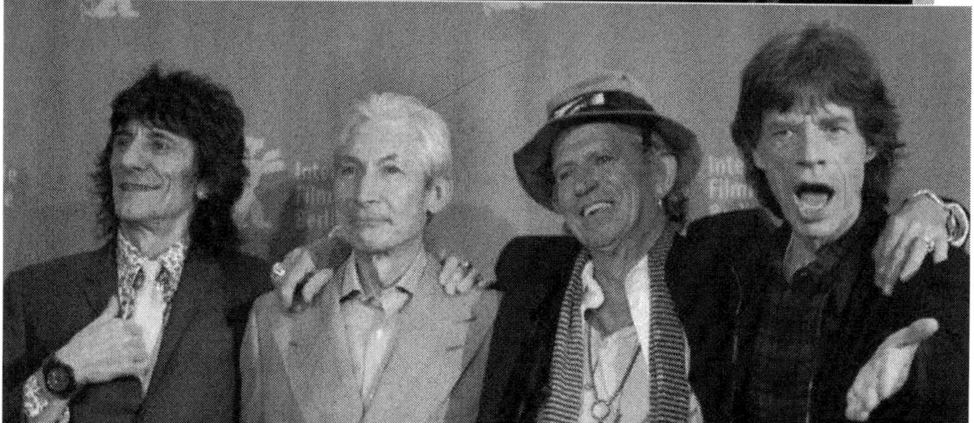

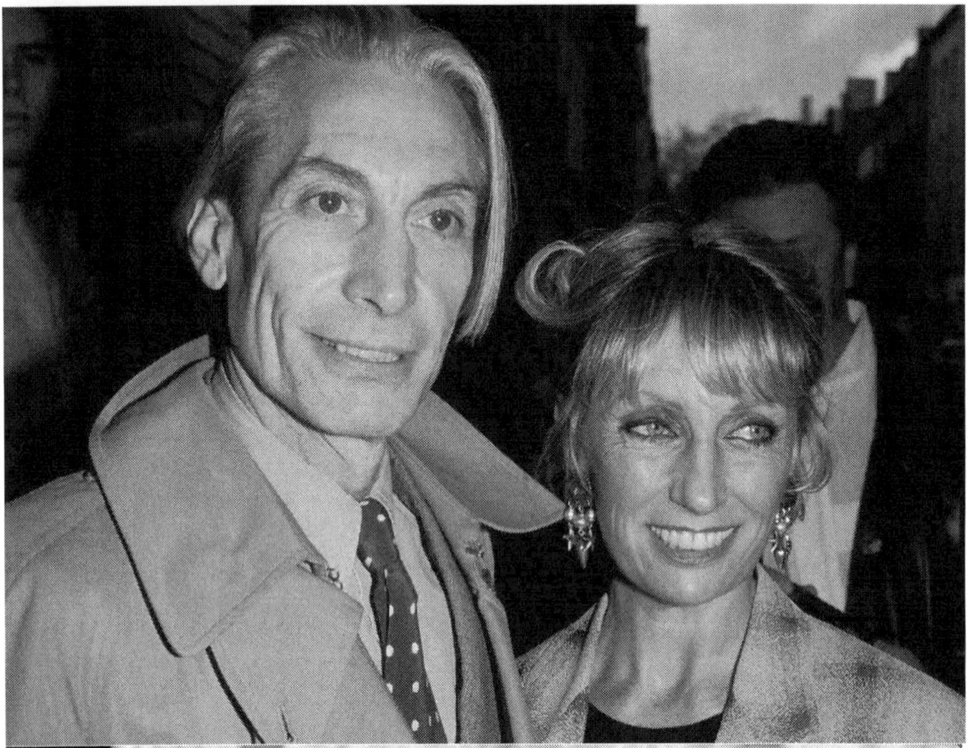

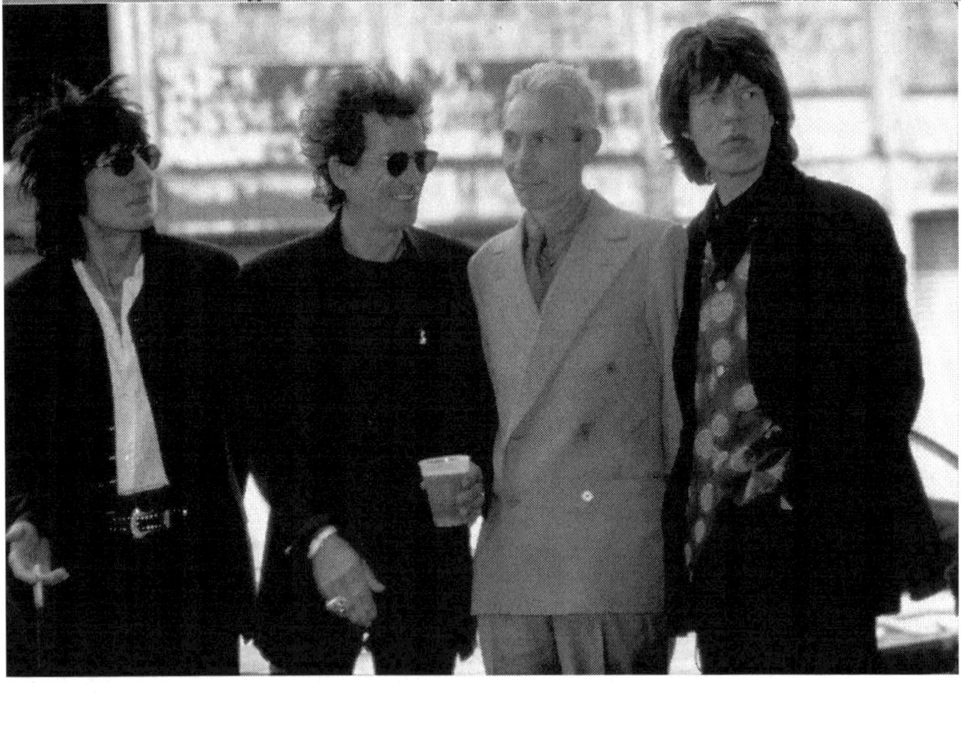

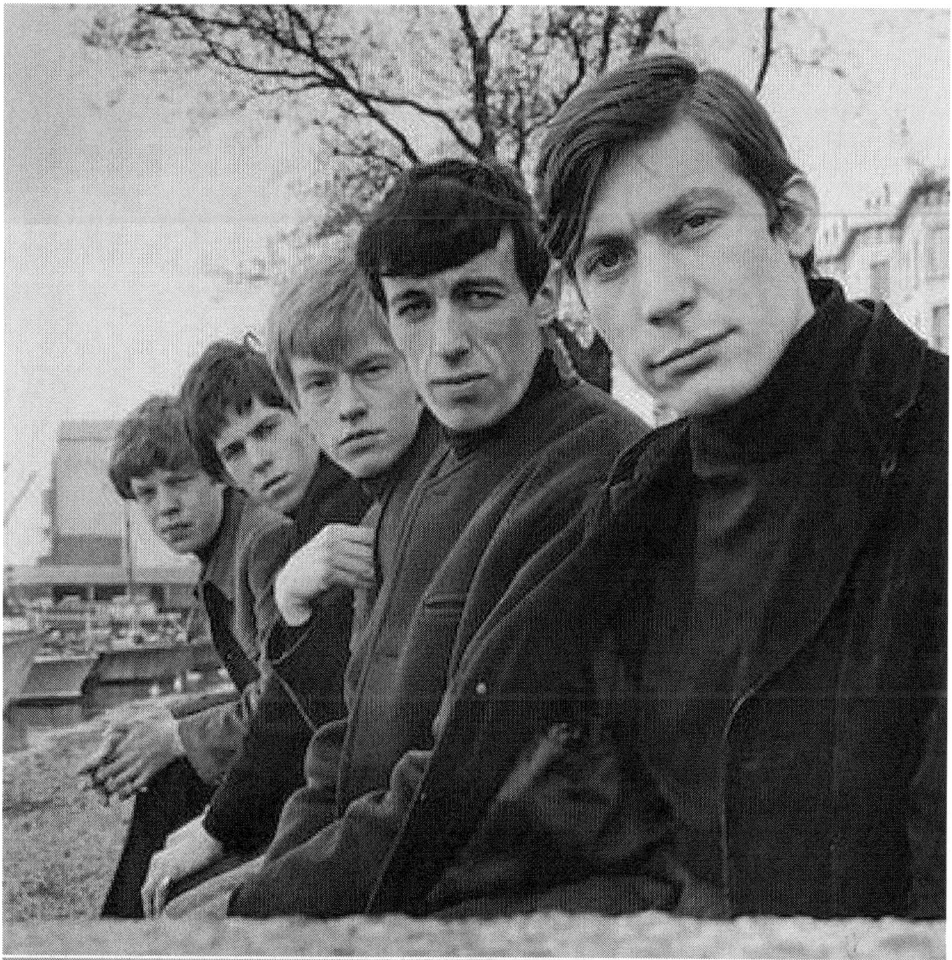

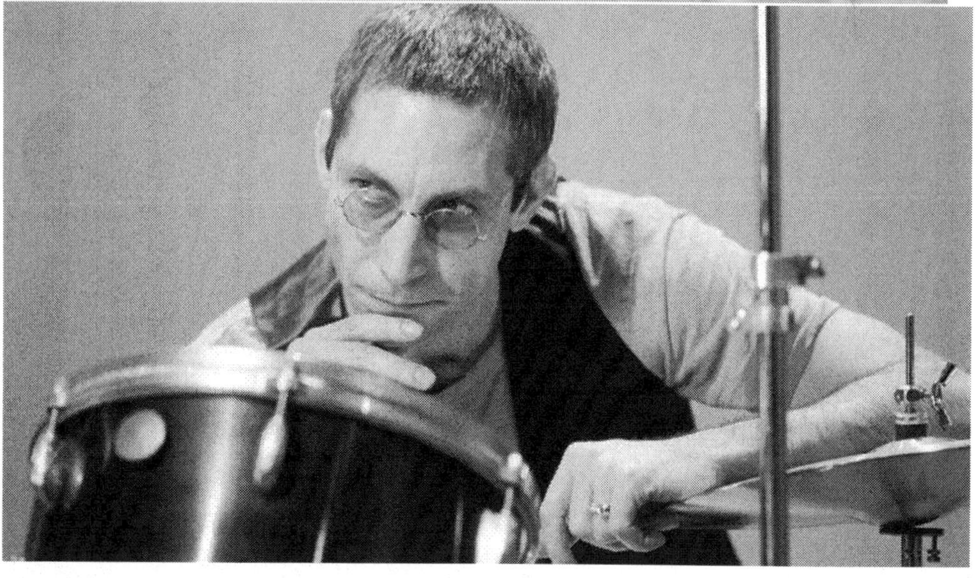

82

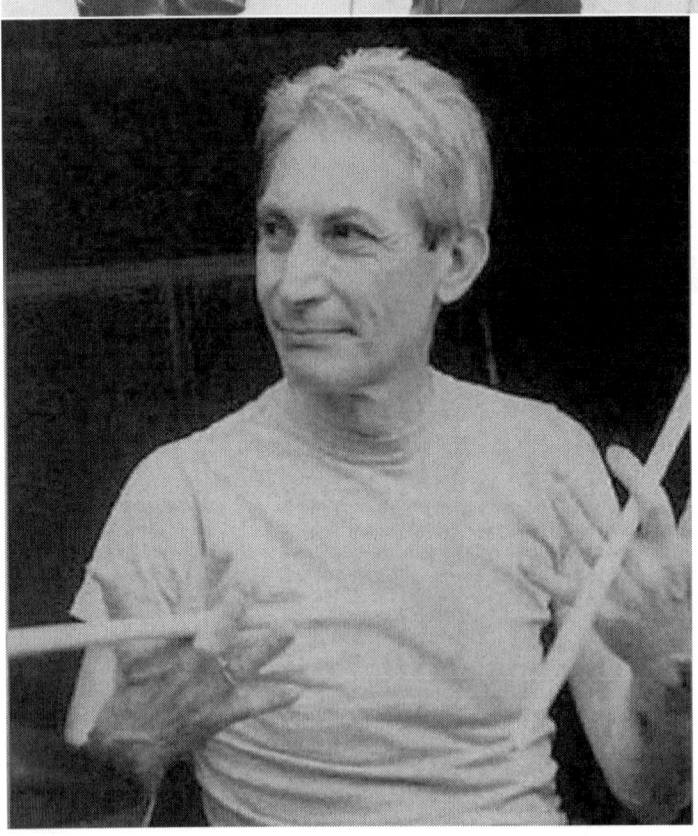

83

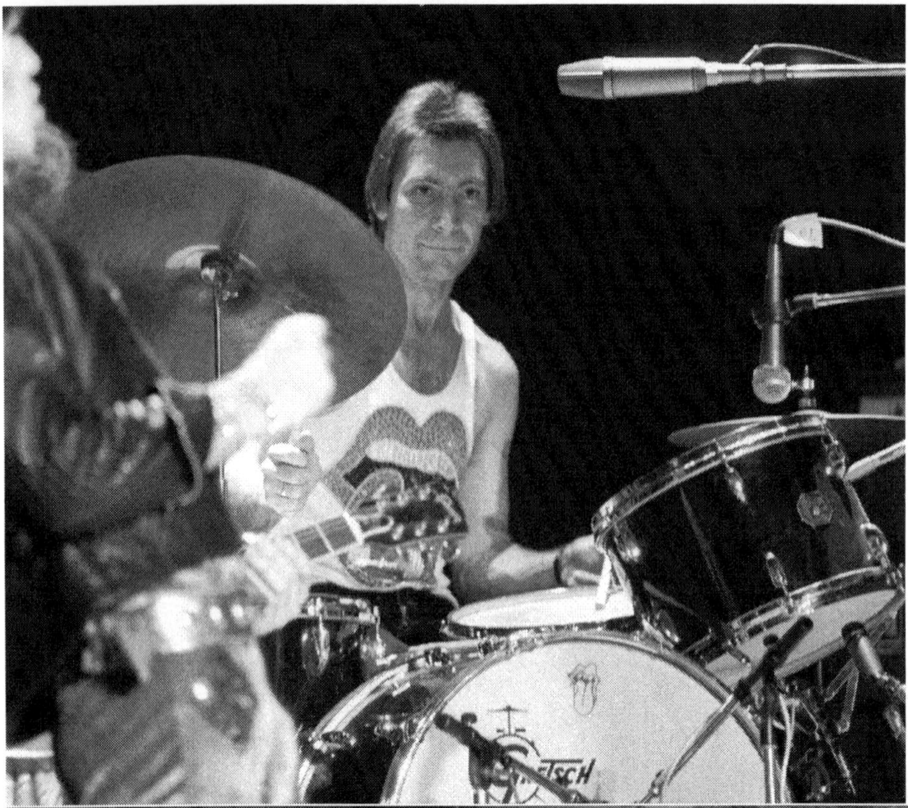

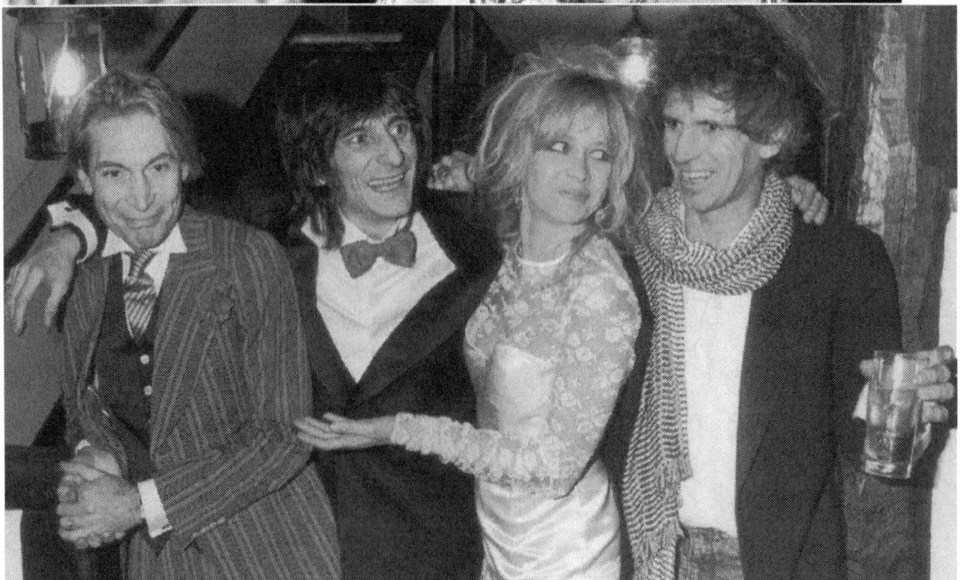

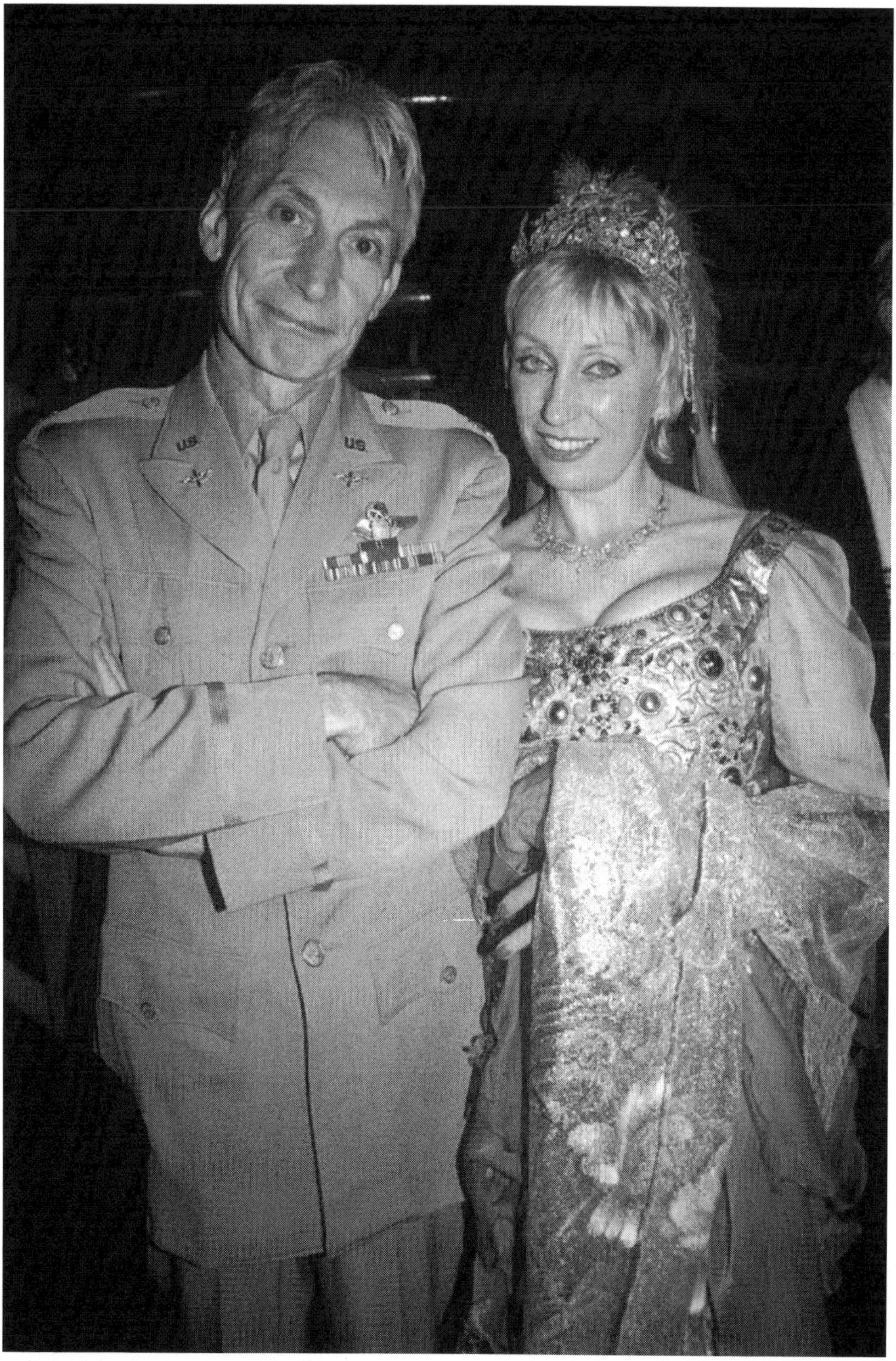
US
US

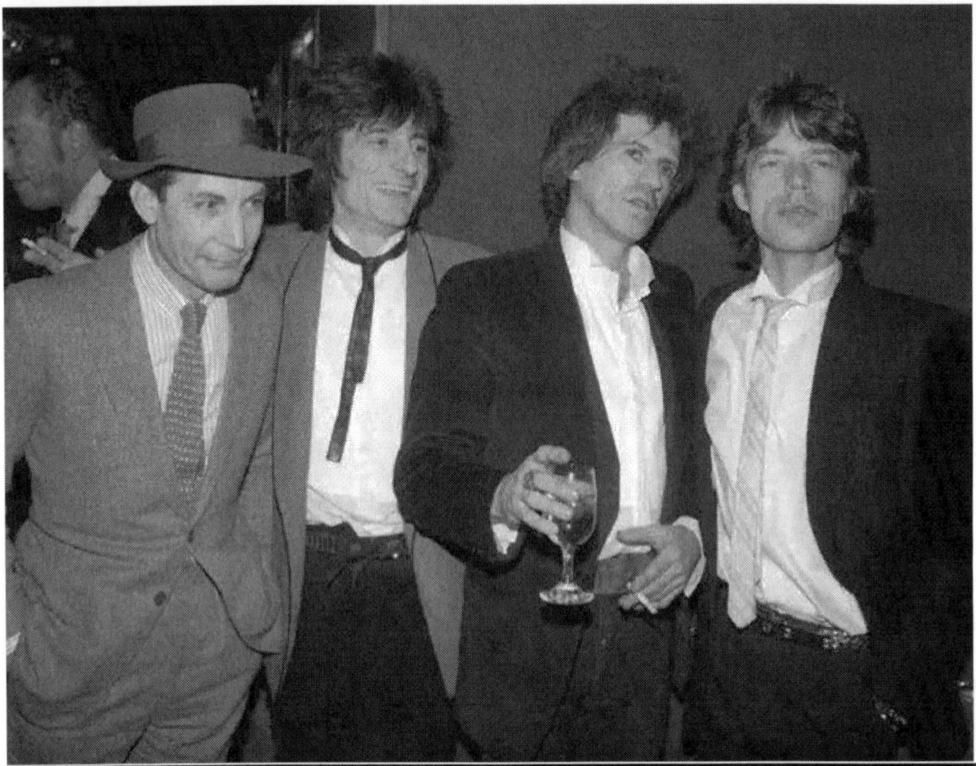

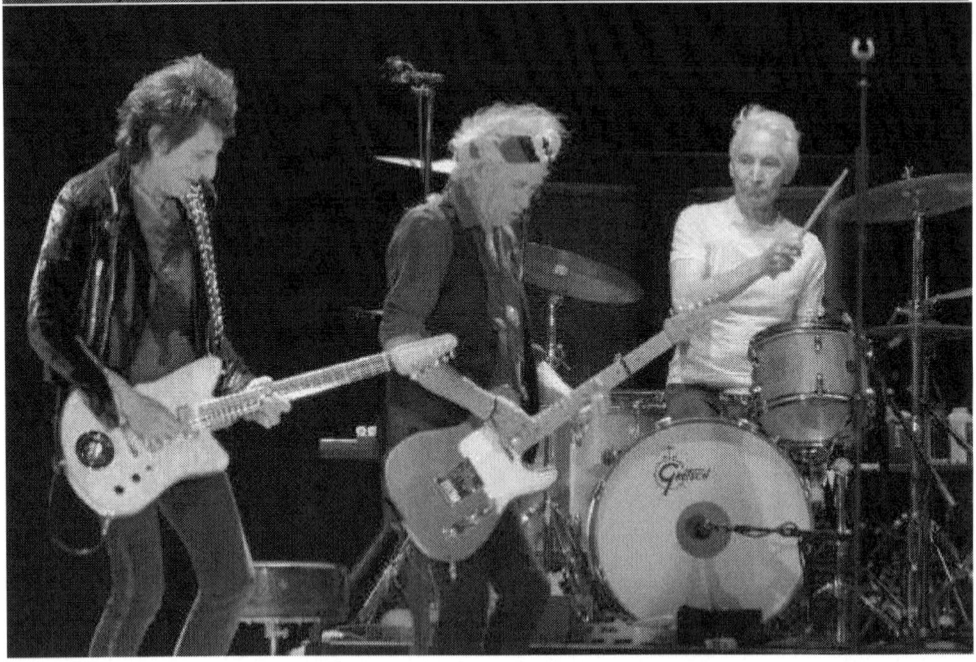
Gretsch

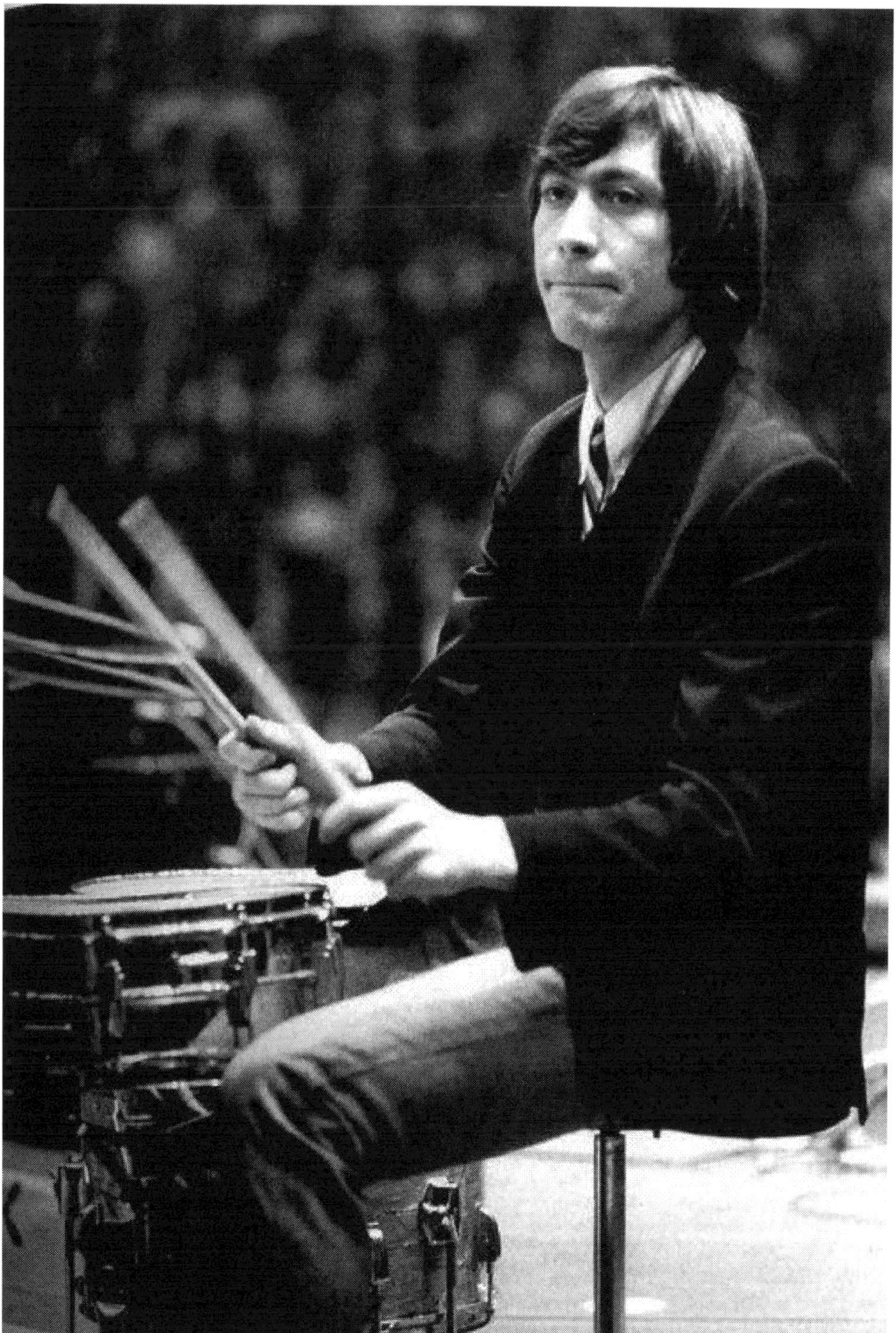

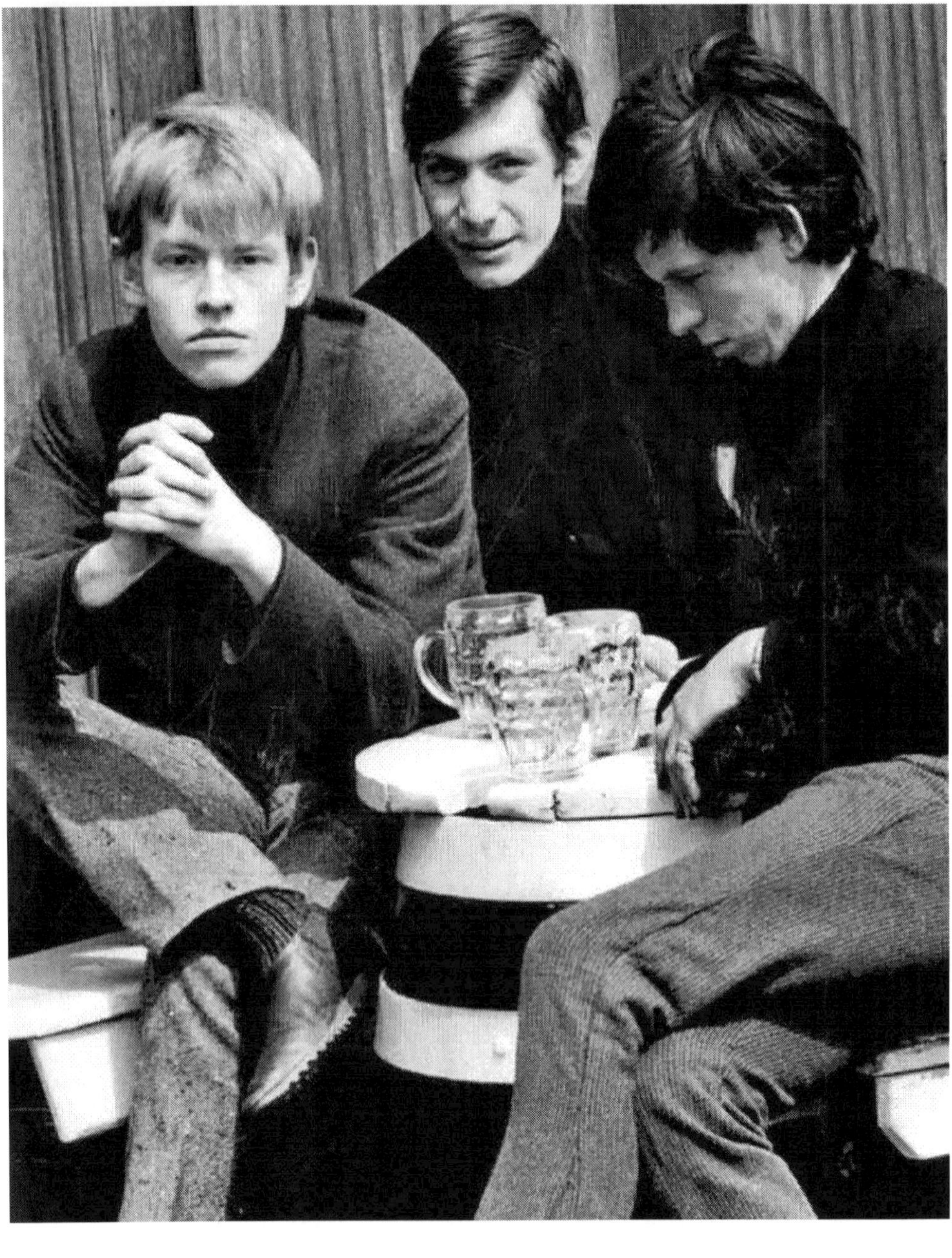

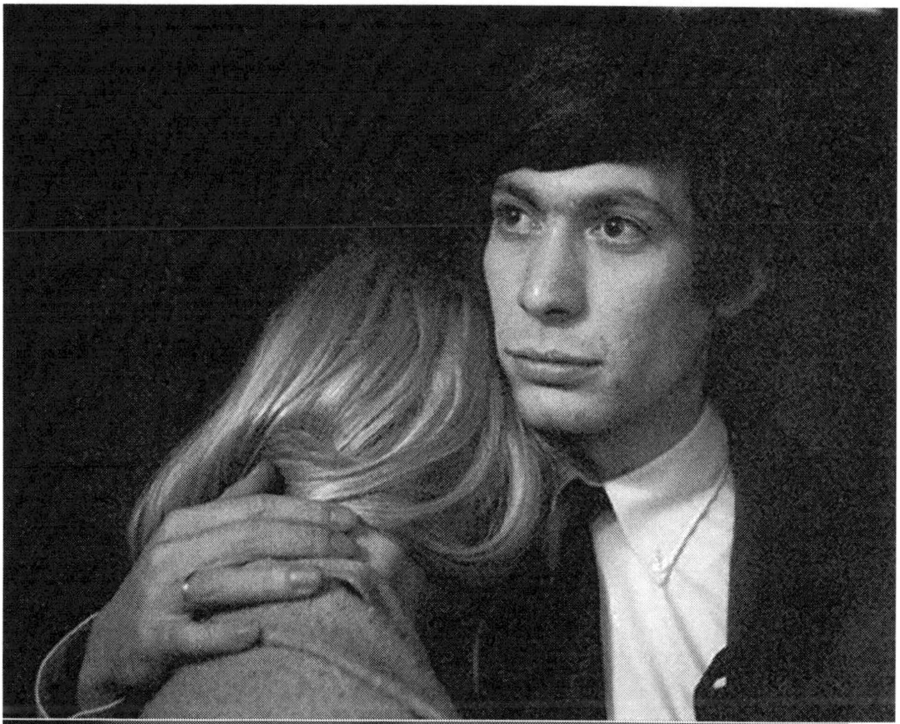

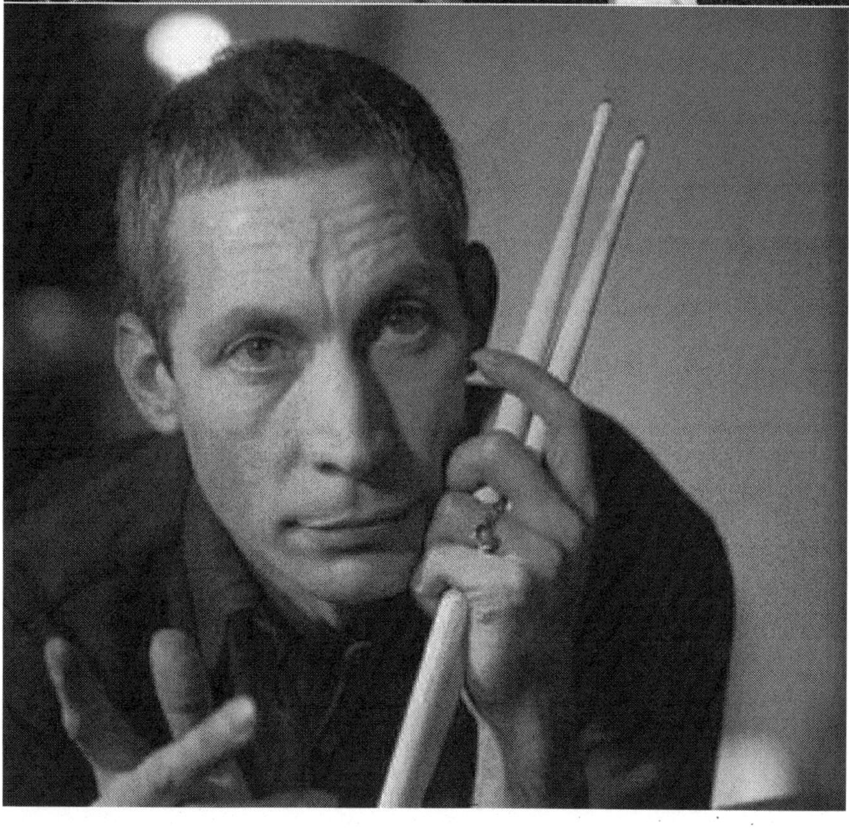

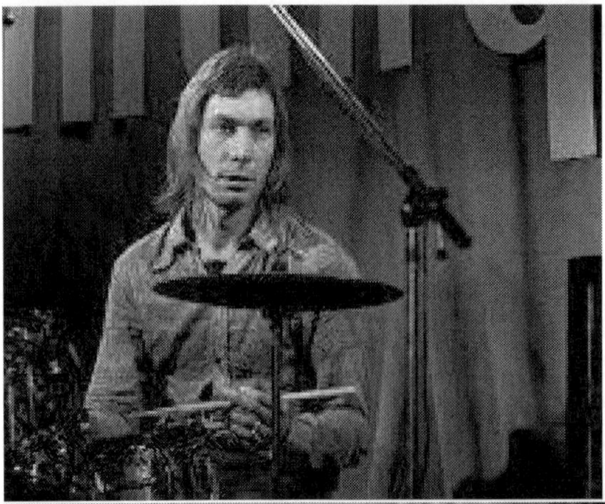

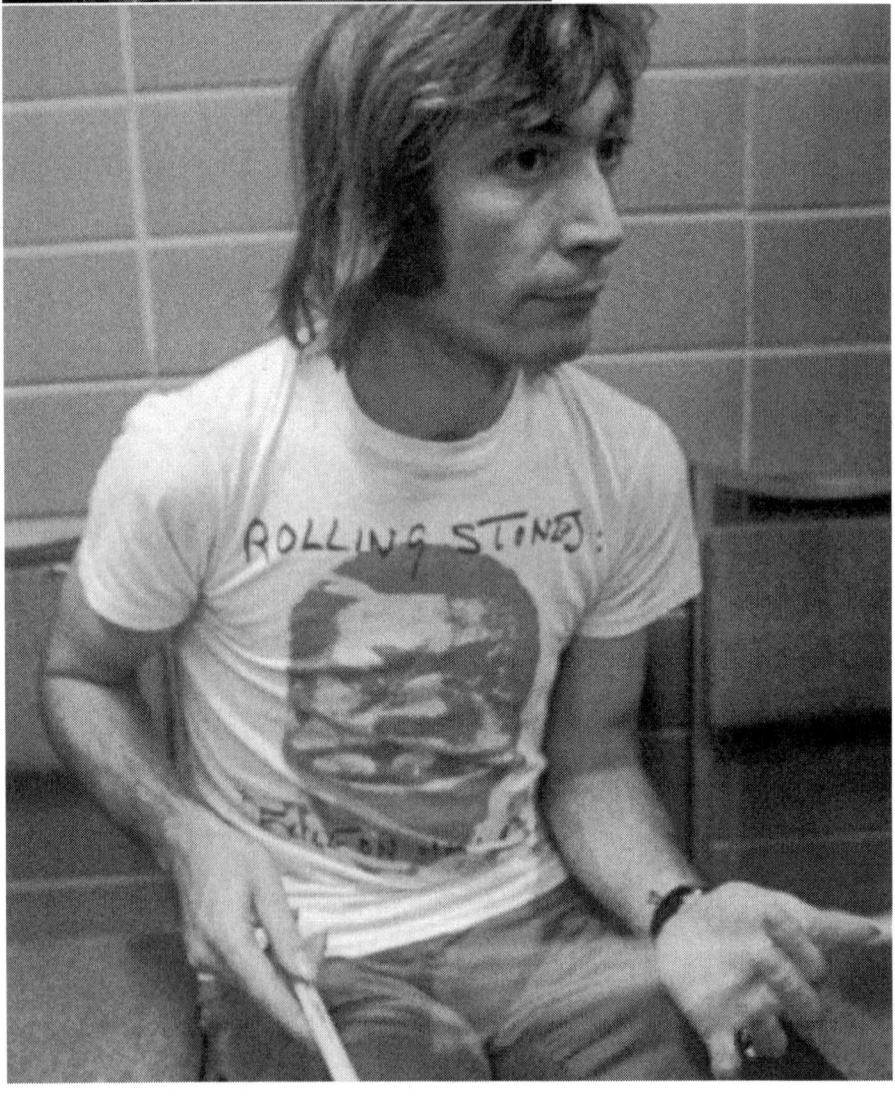
ROLLING STONES

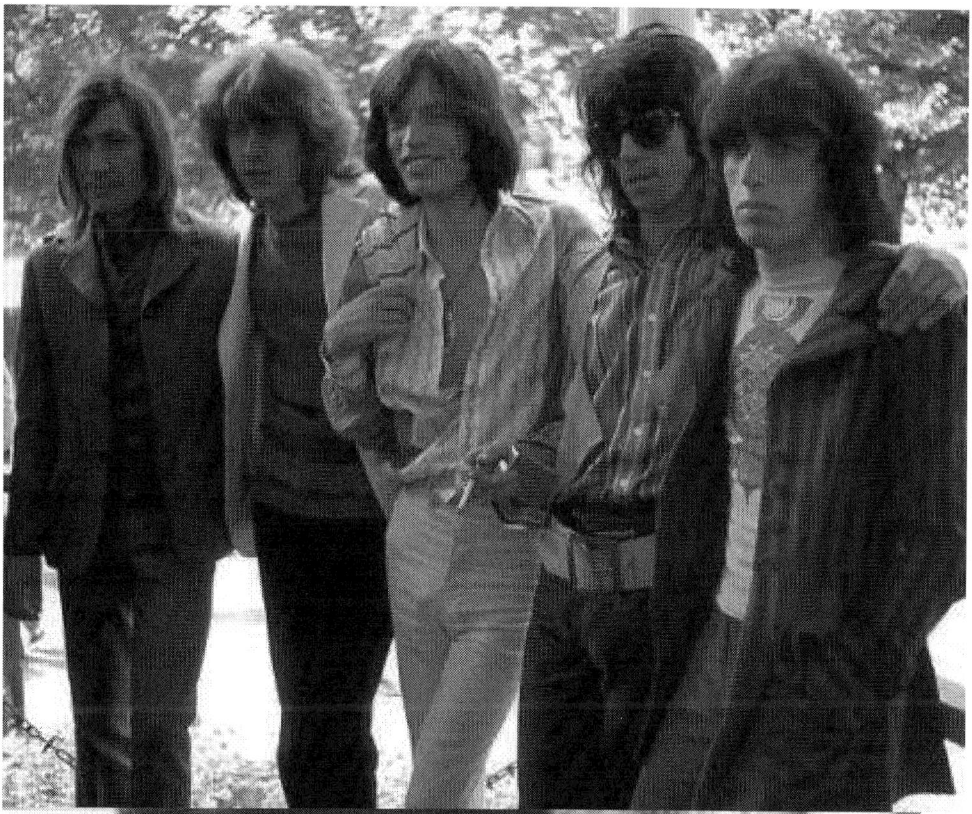

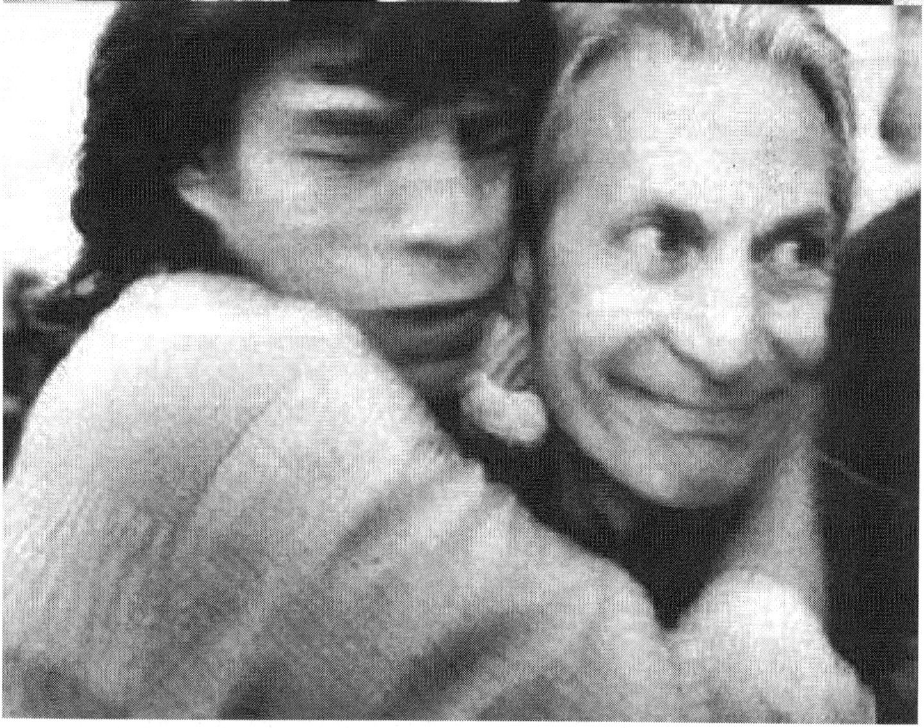

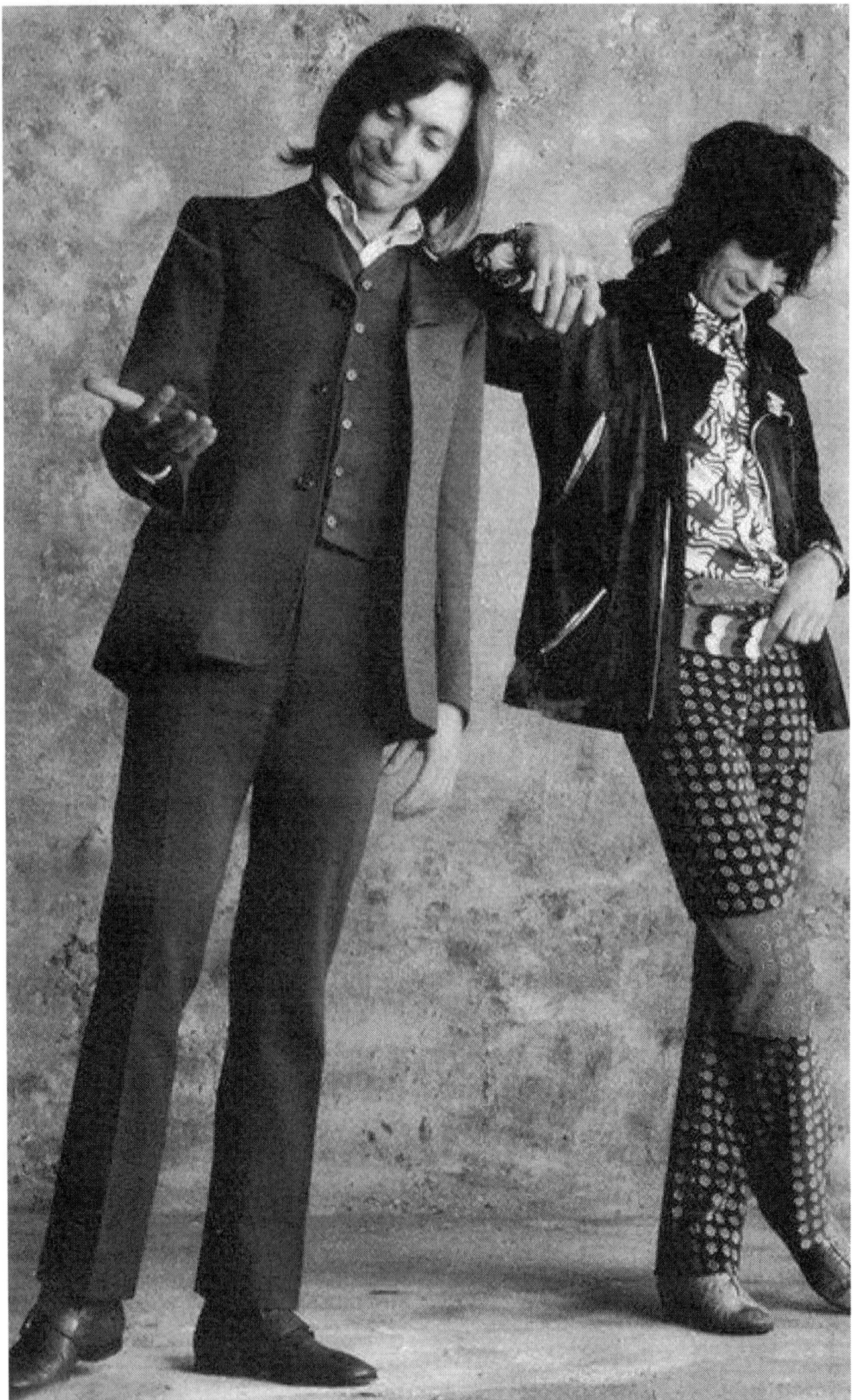

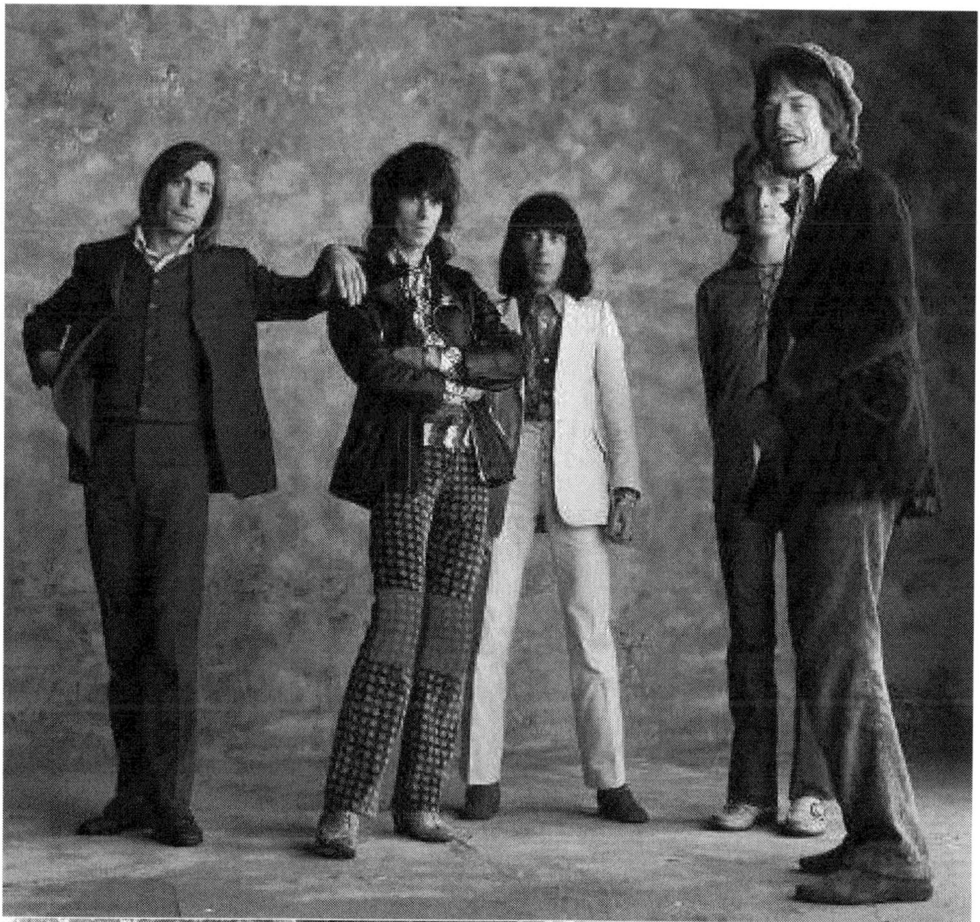

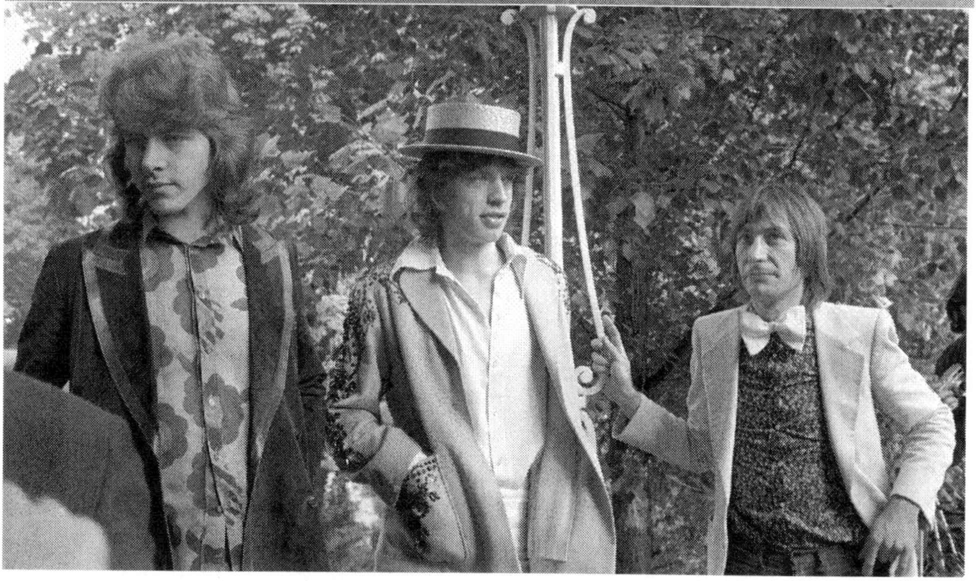

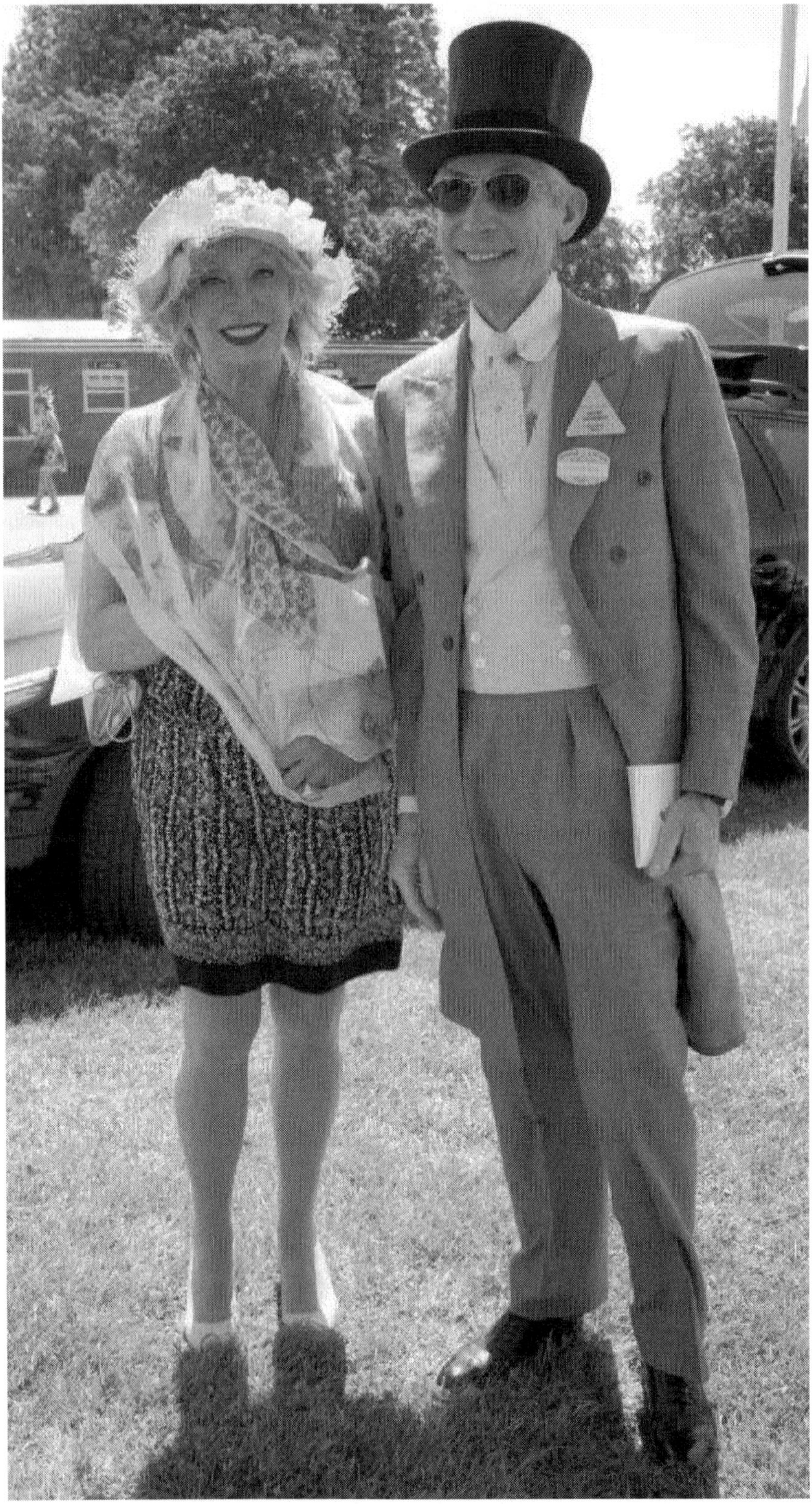

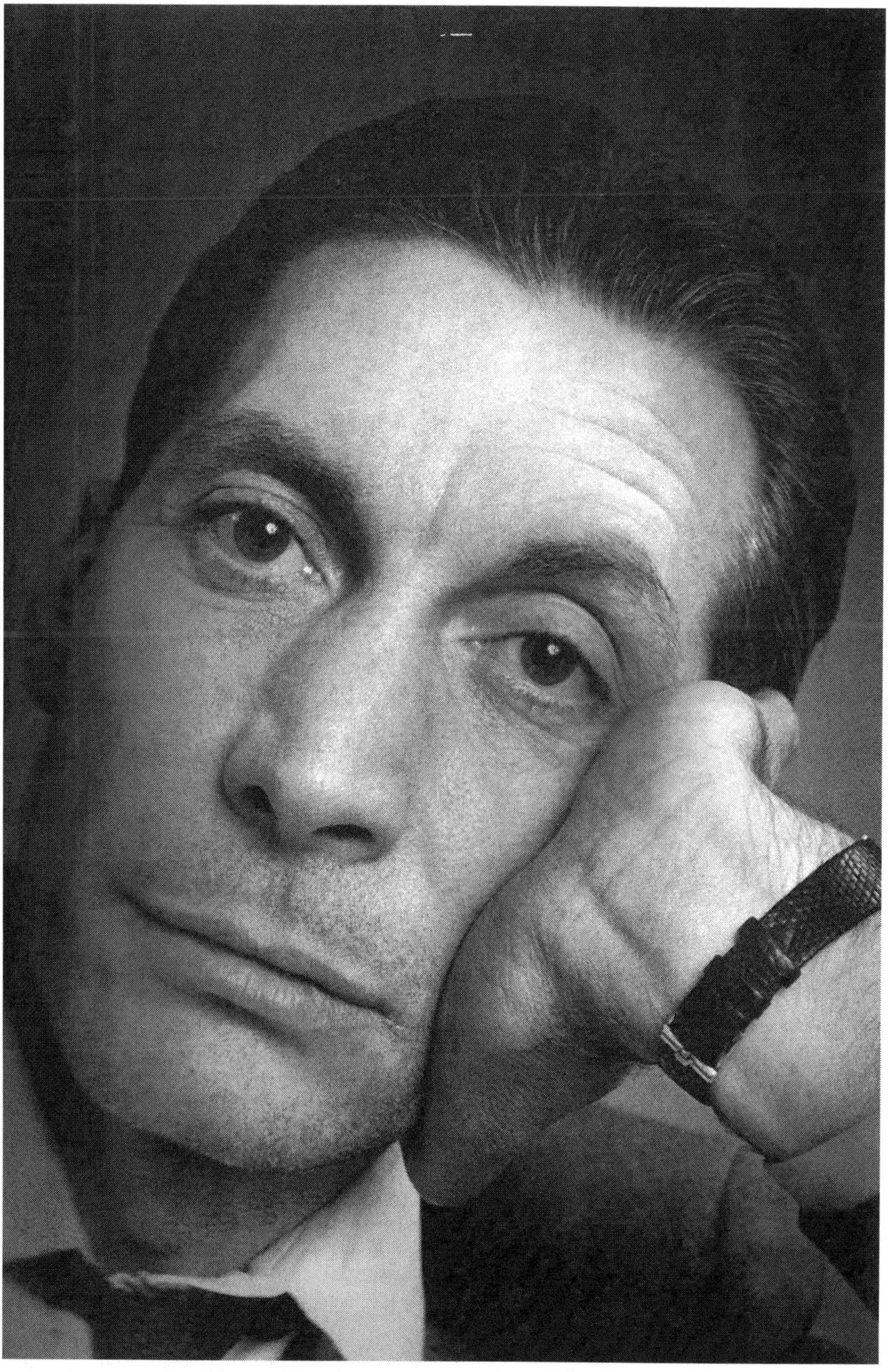

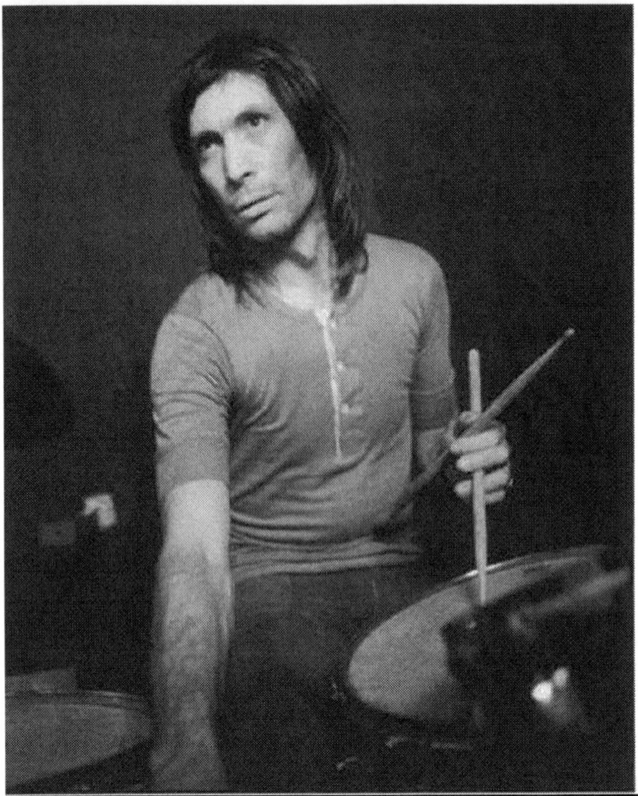

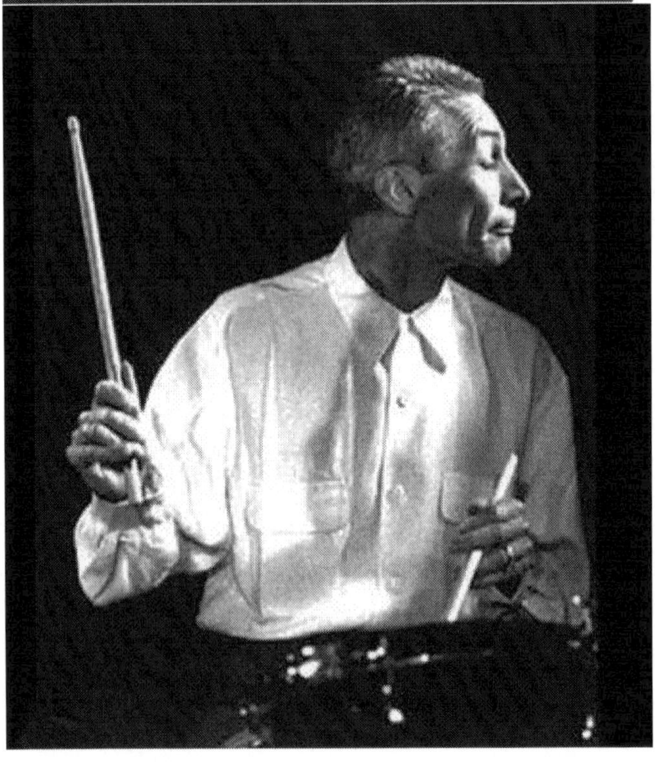

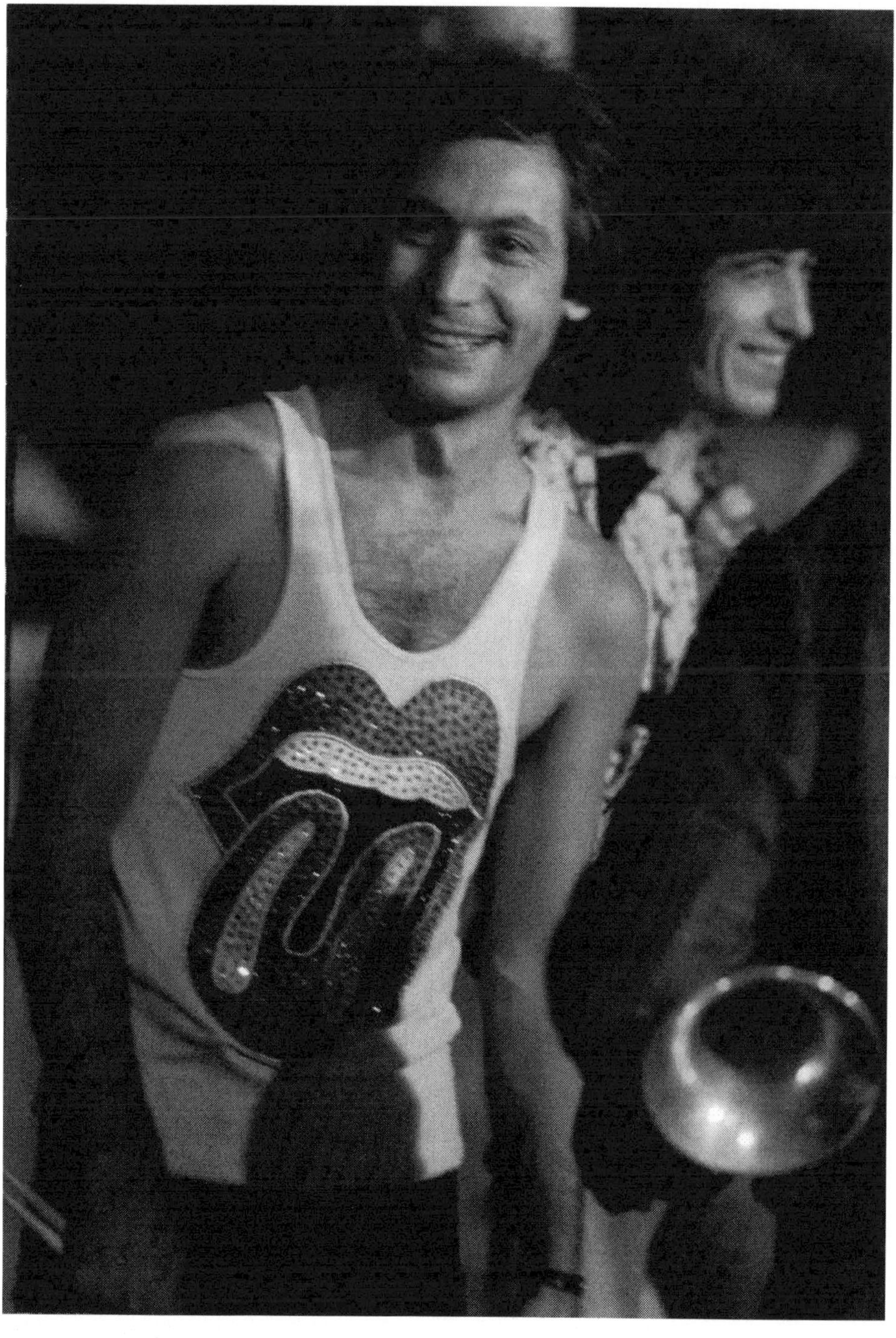

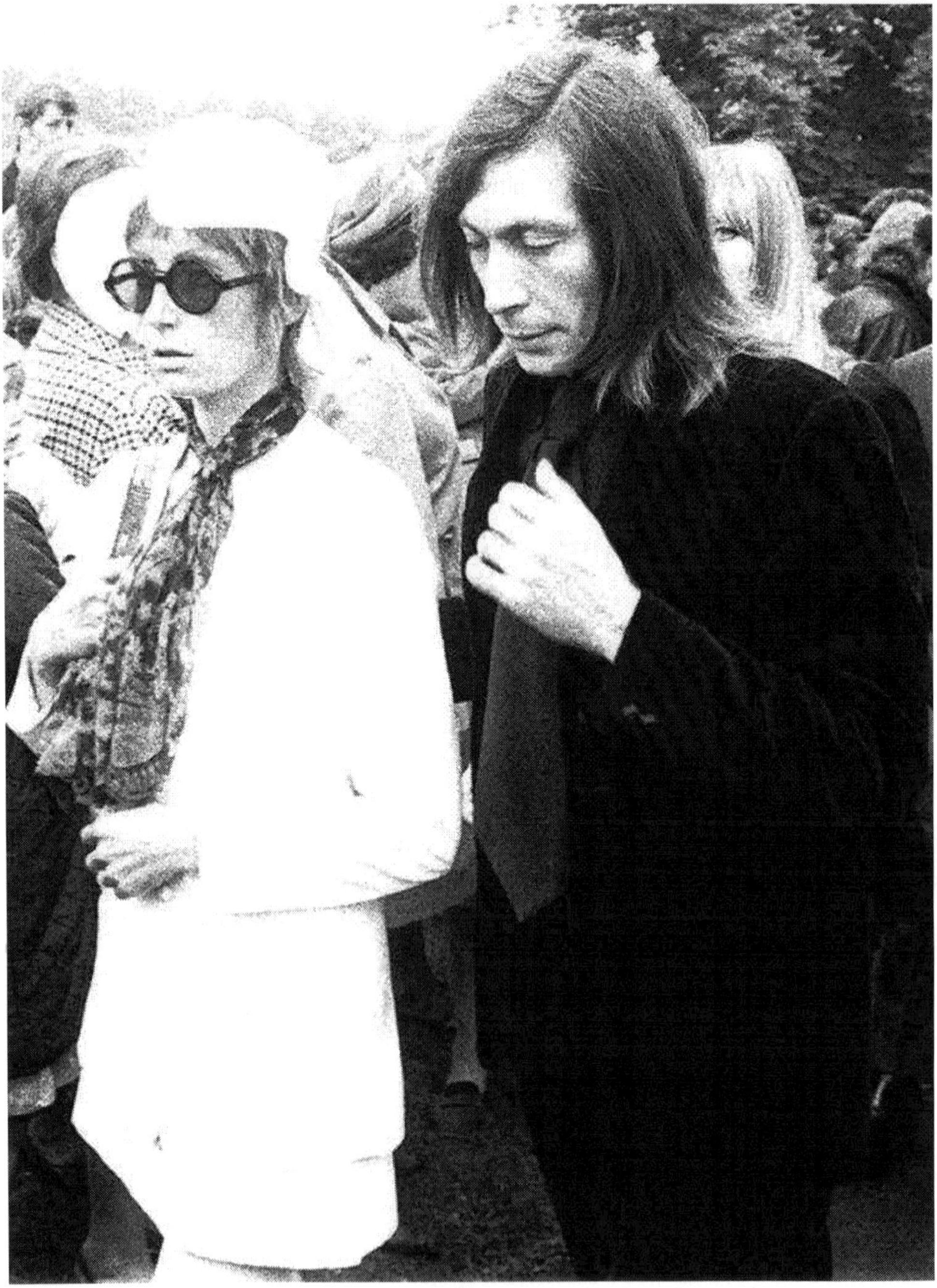

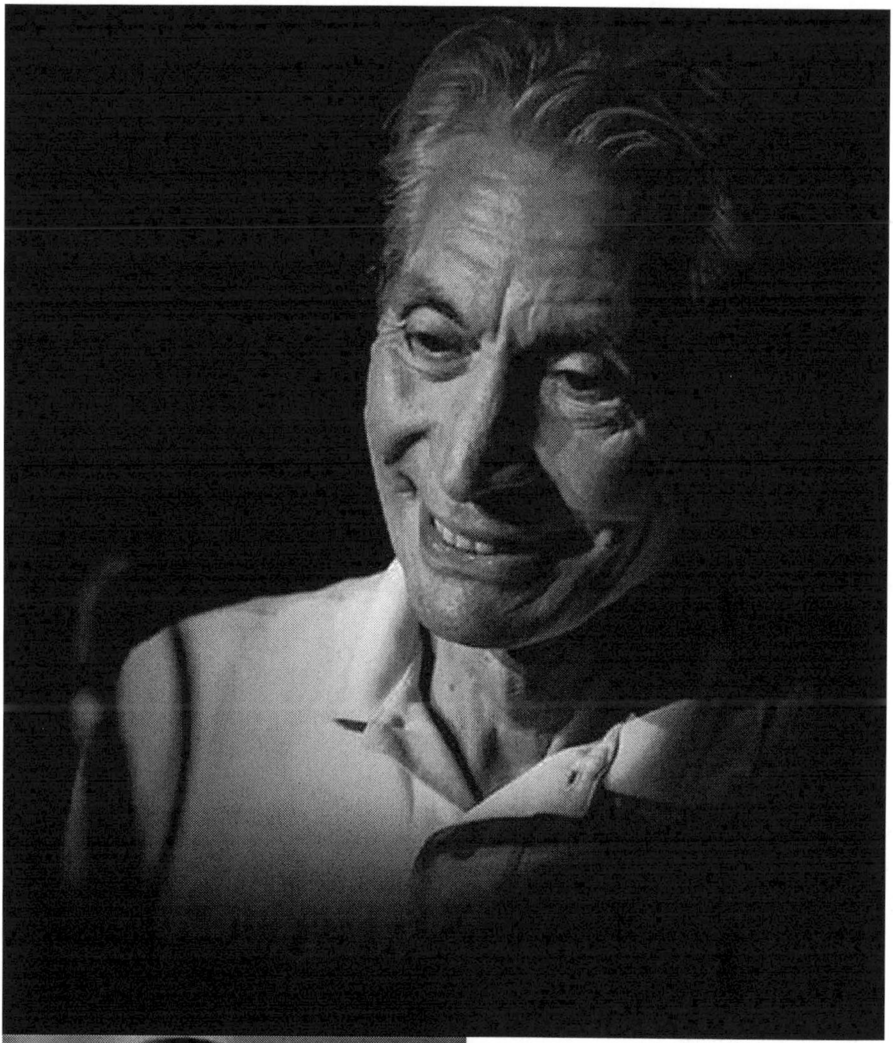

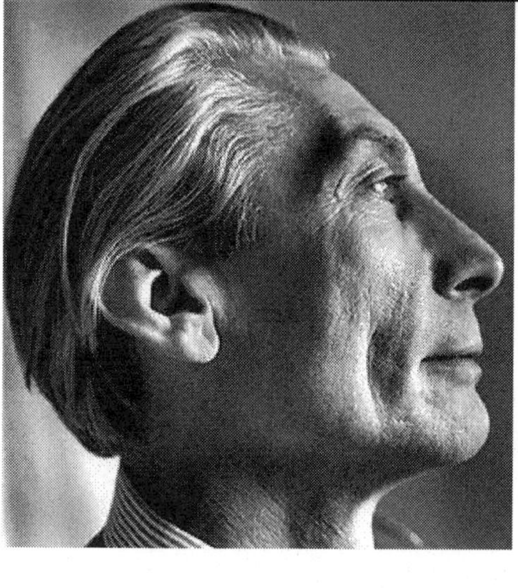

100

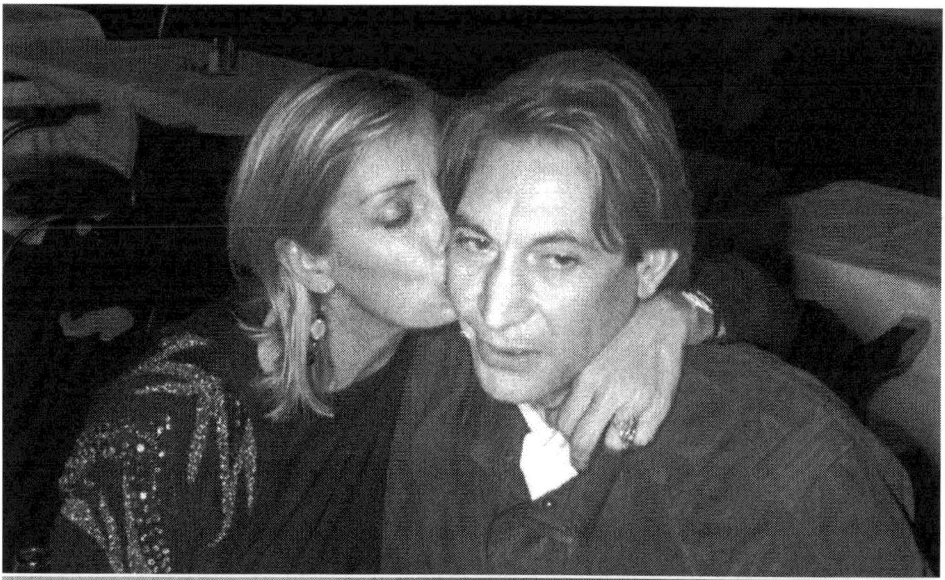

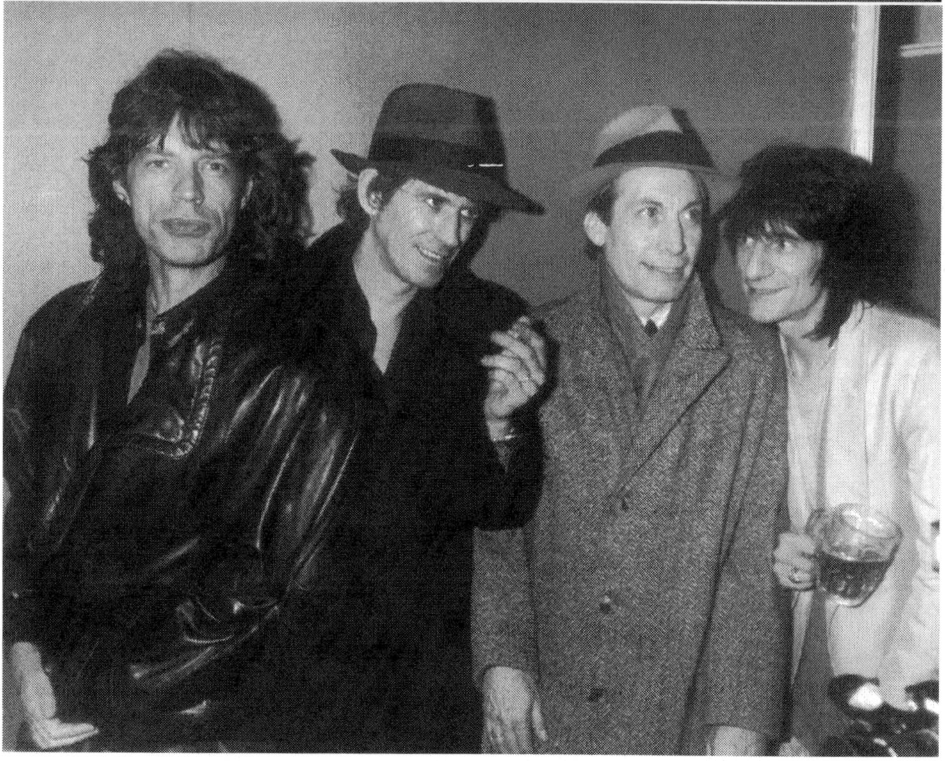

102

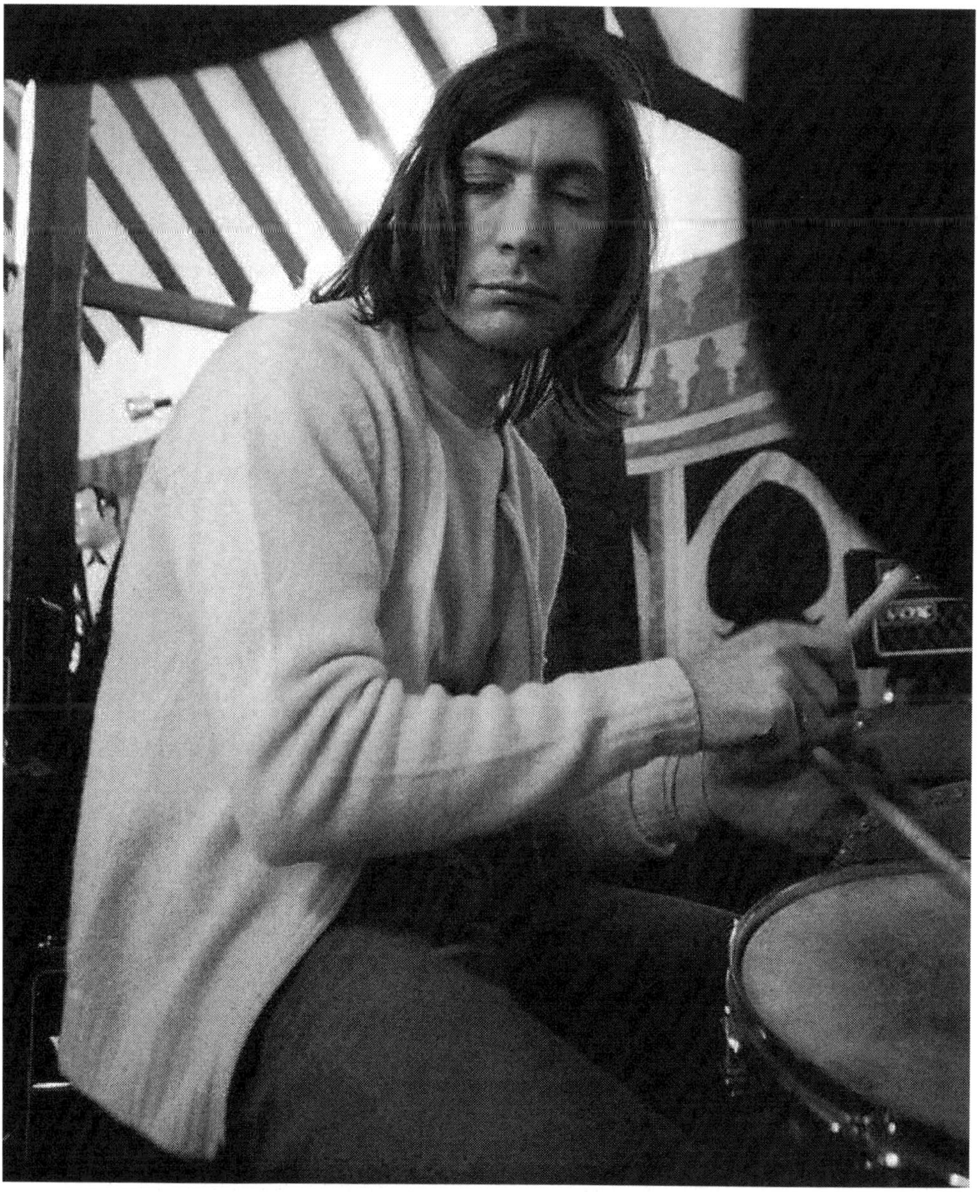

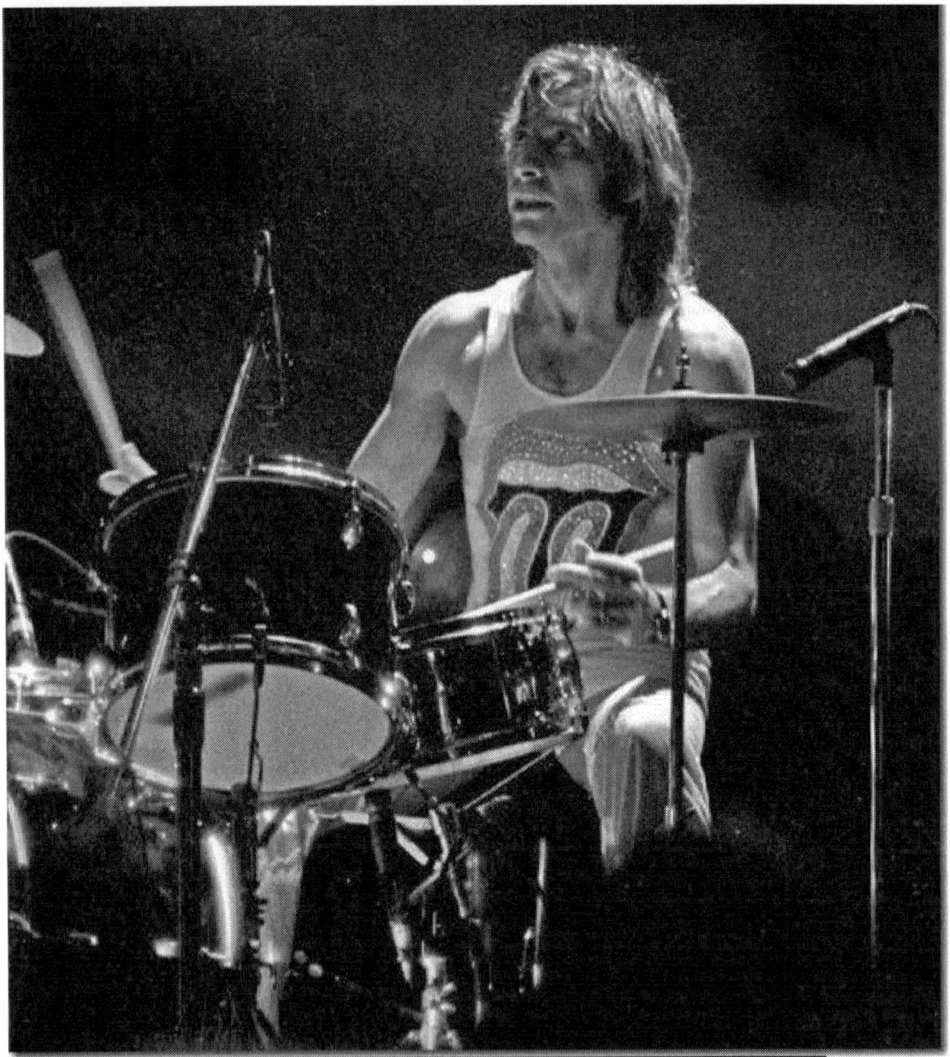

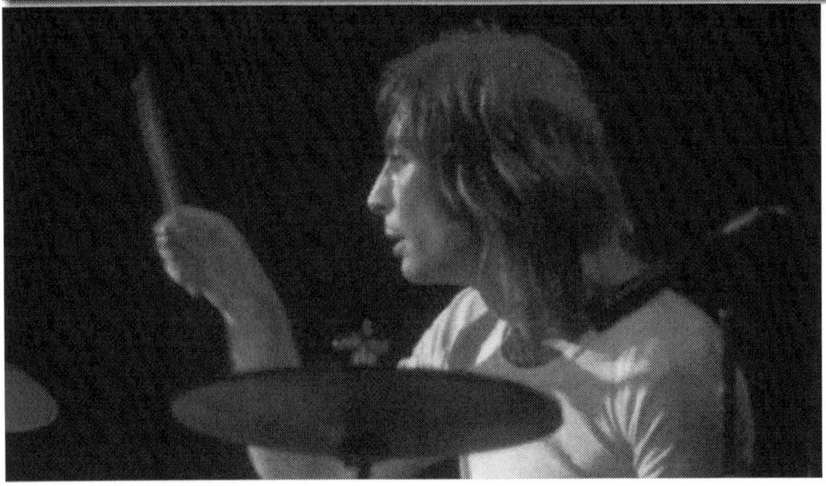

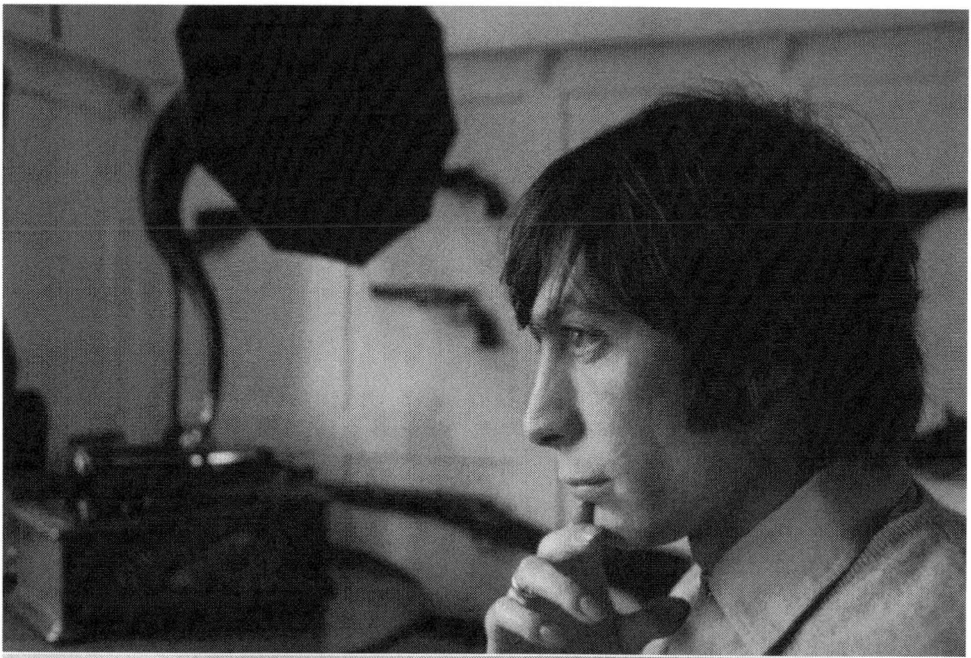

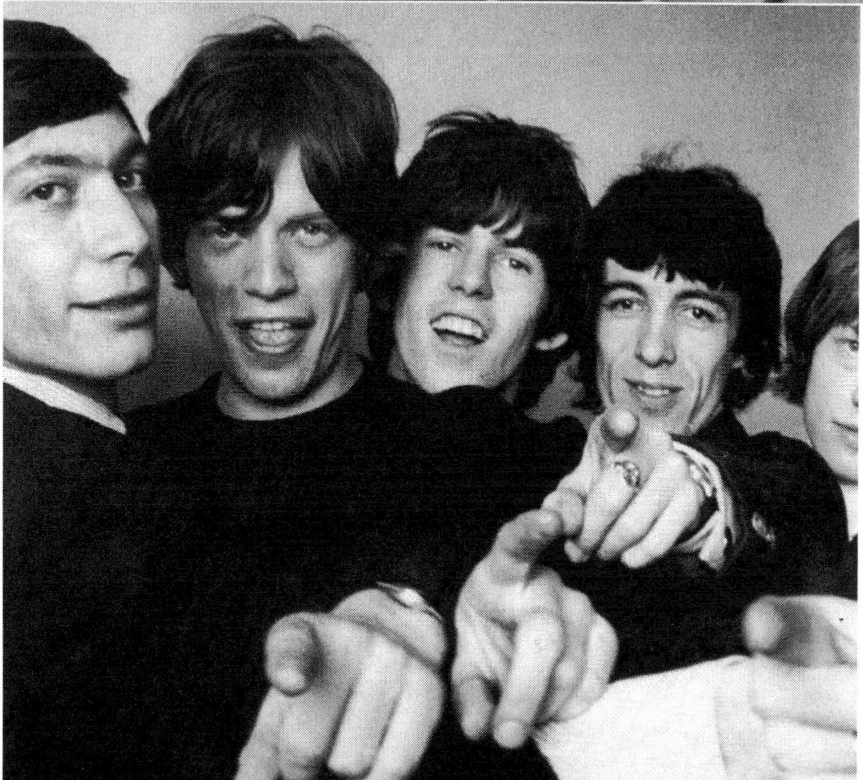

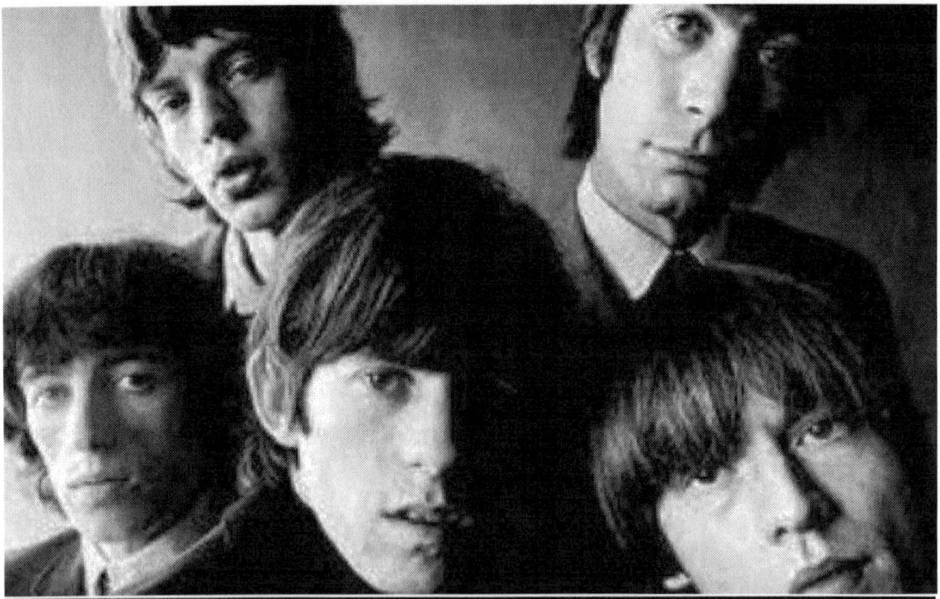

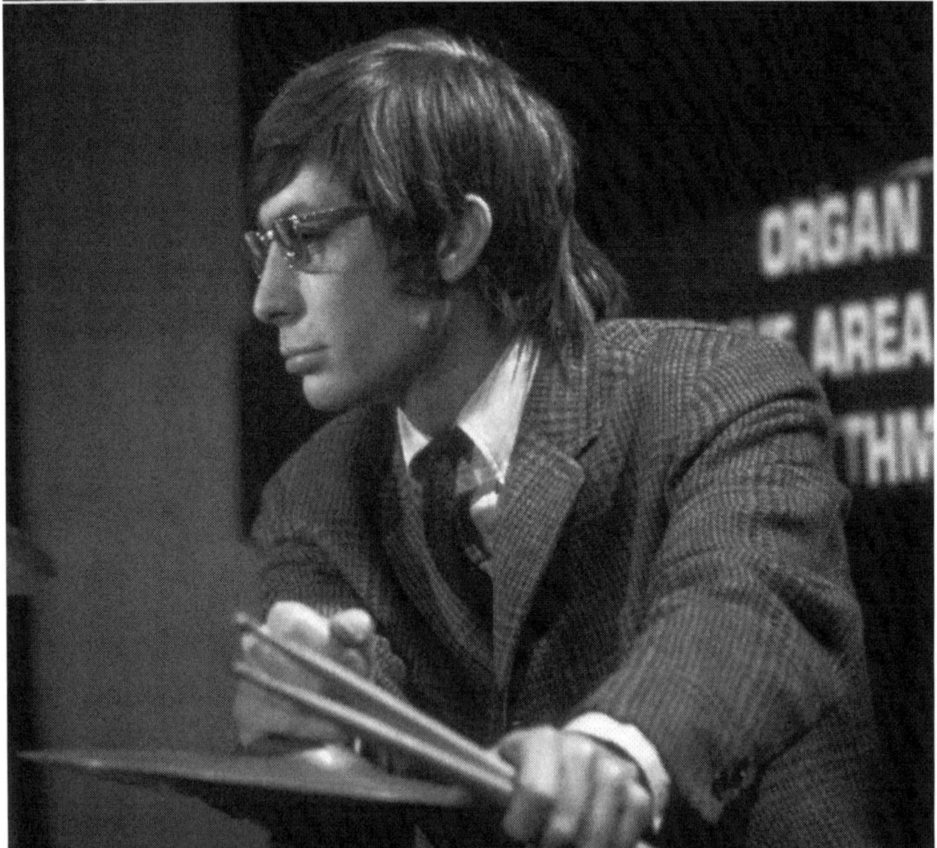
ORGAN
AREA

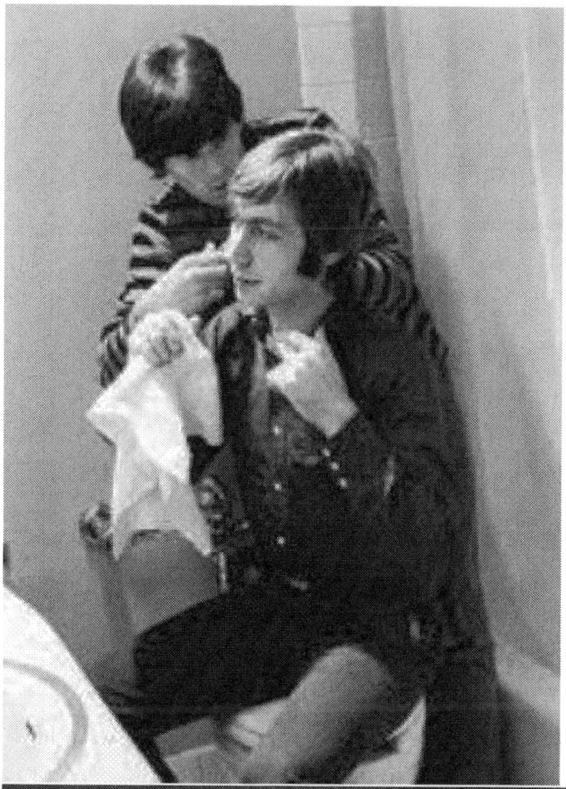

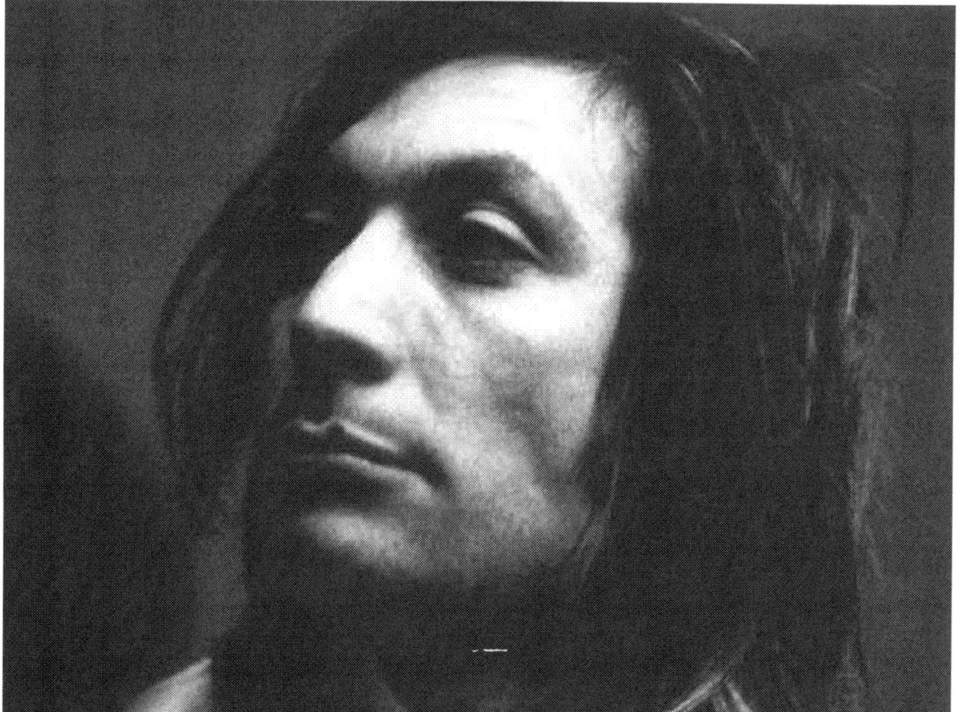

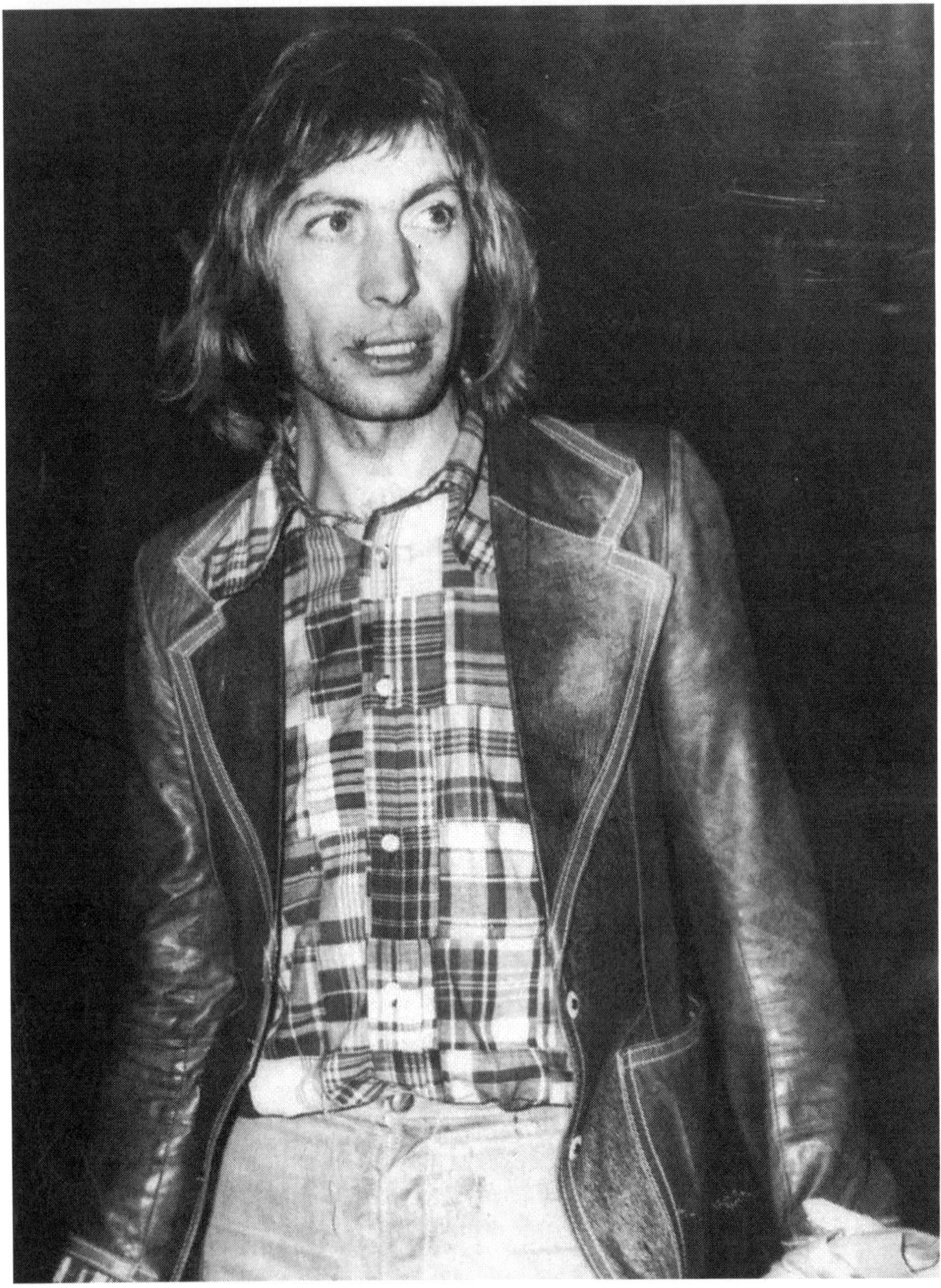

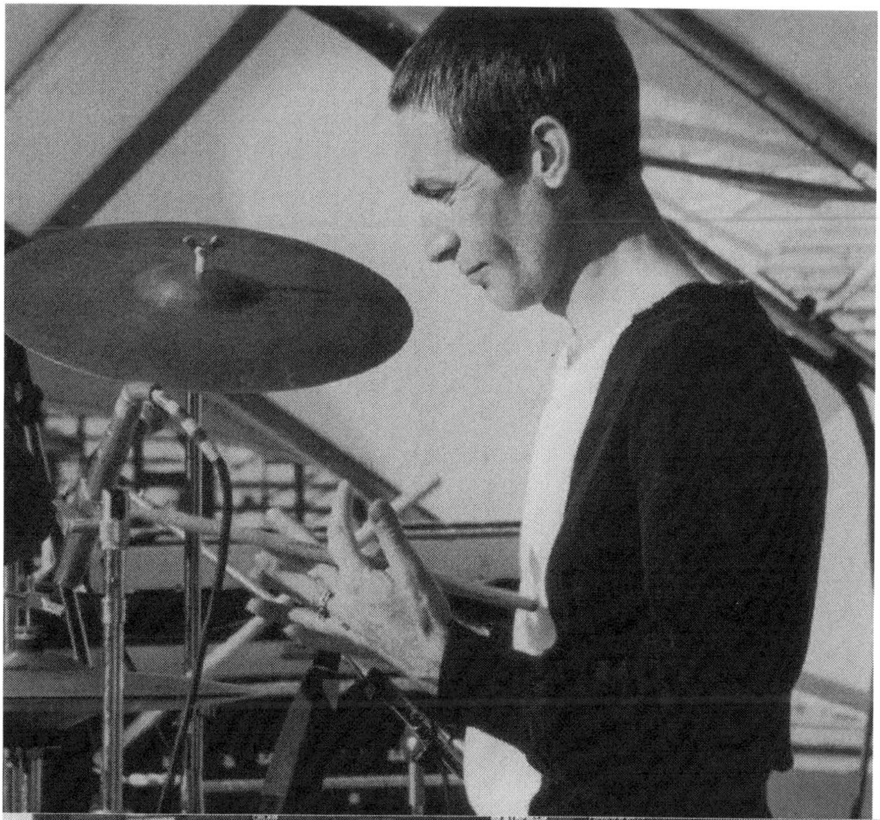

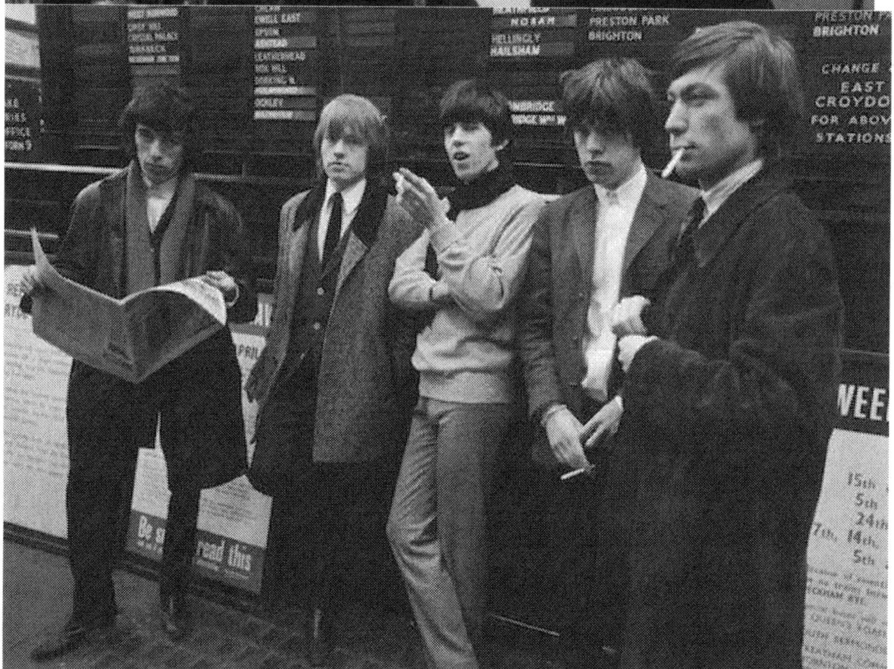
HELLINGLY
HAILSHAM
PRESTON PARK
BRIGHTON
EAST

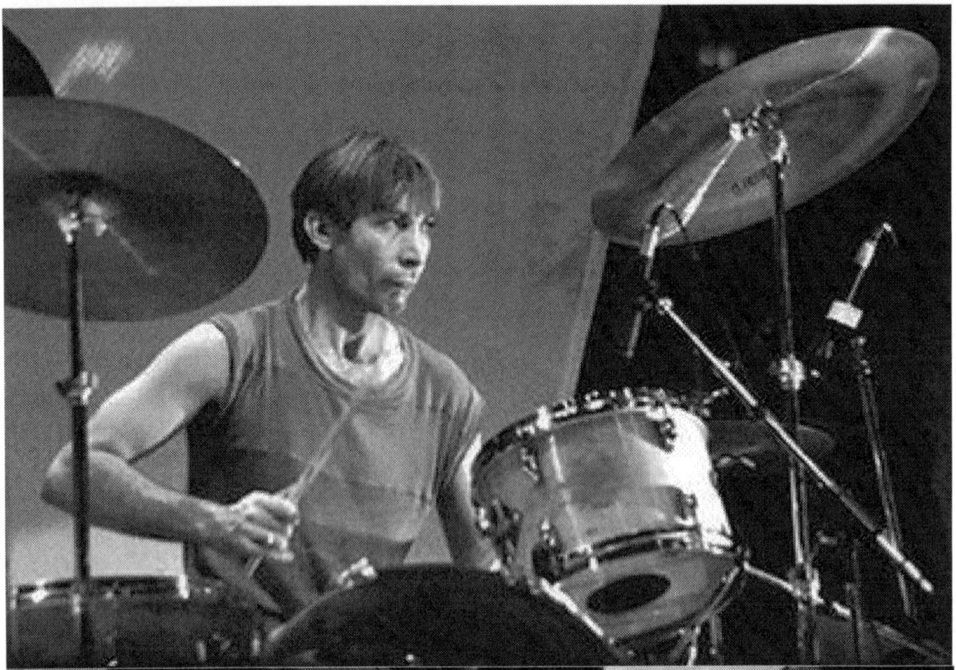

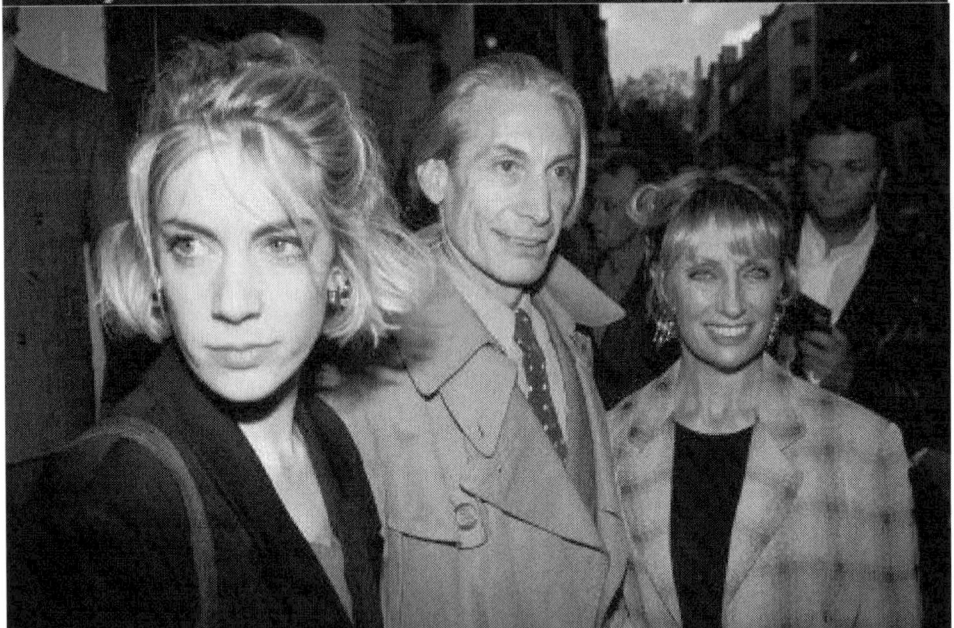

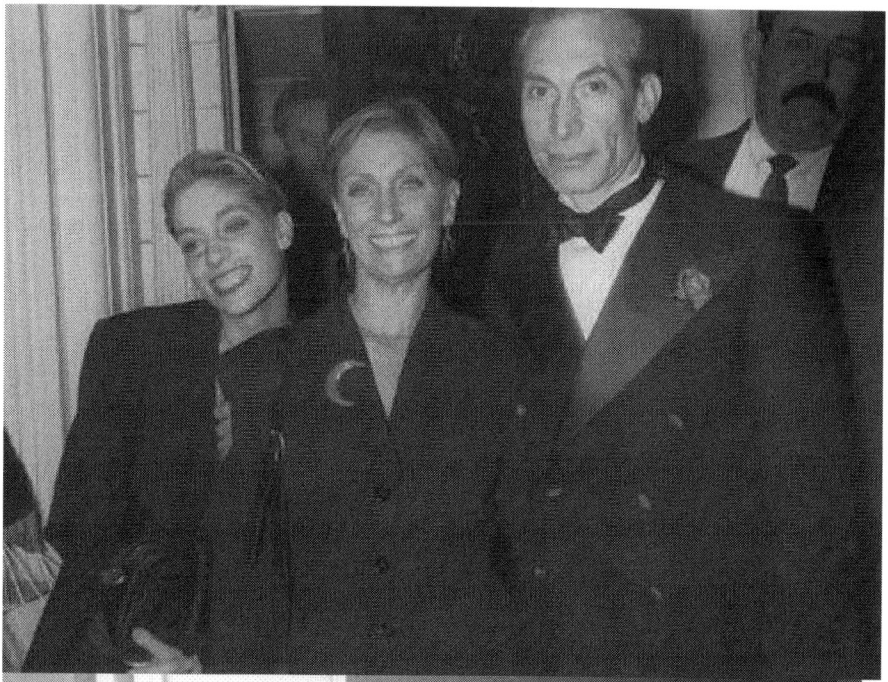

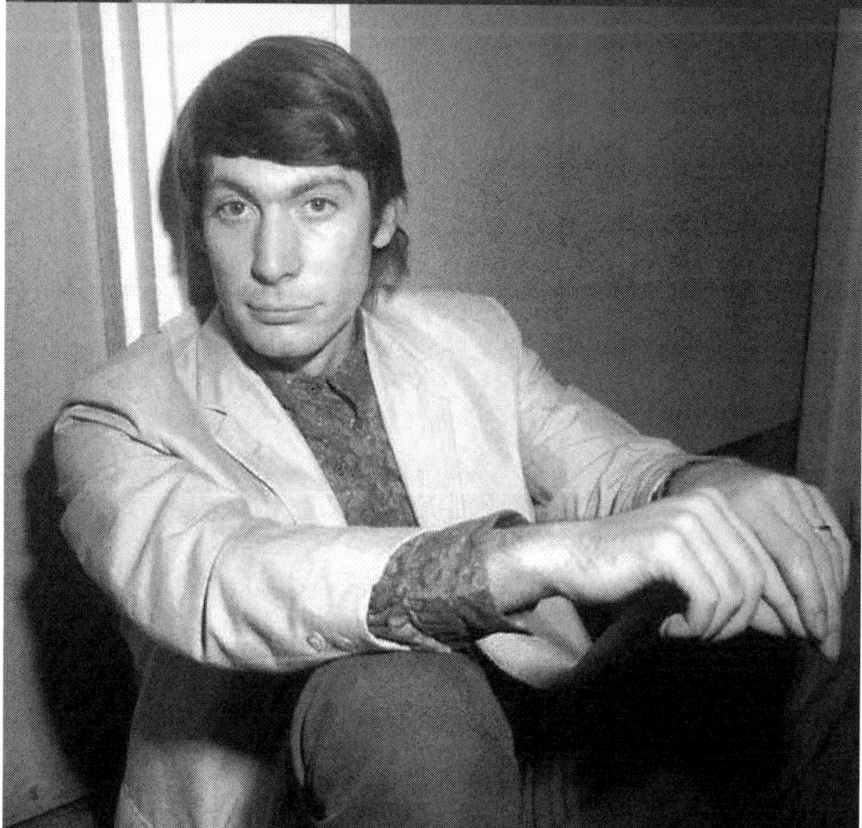

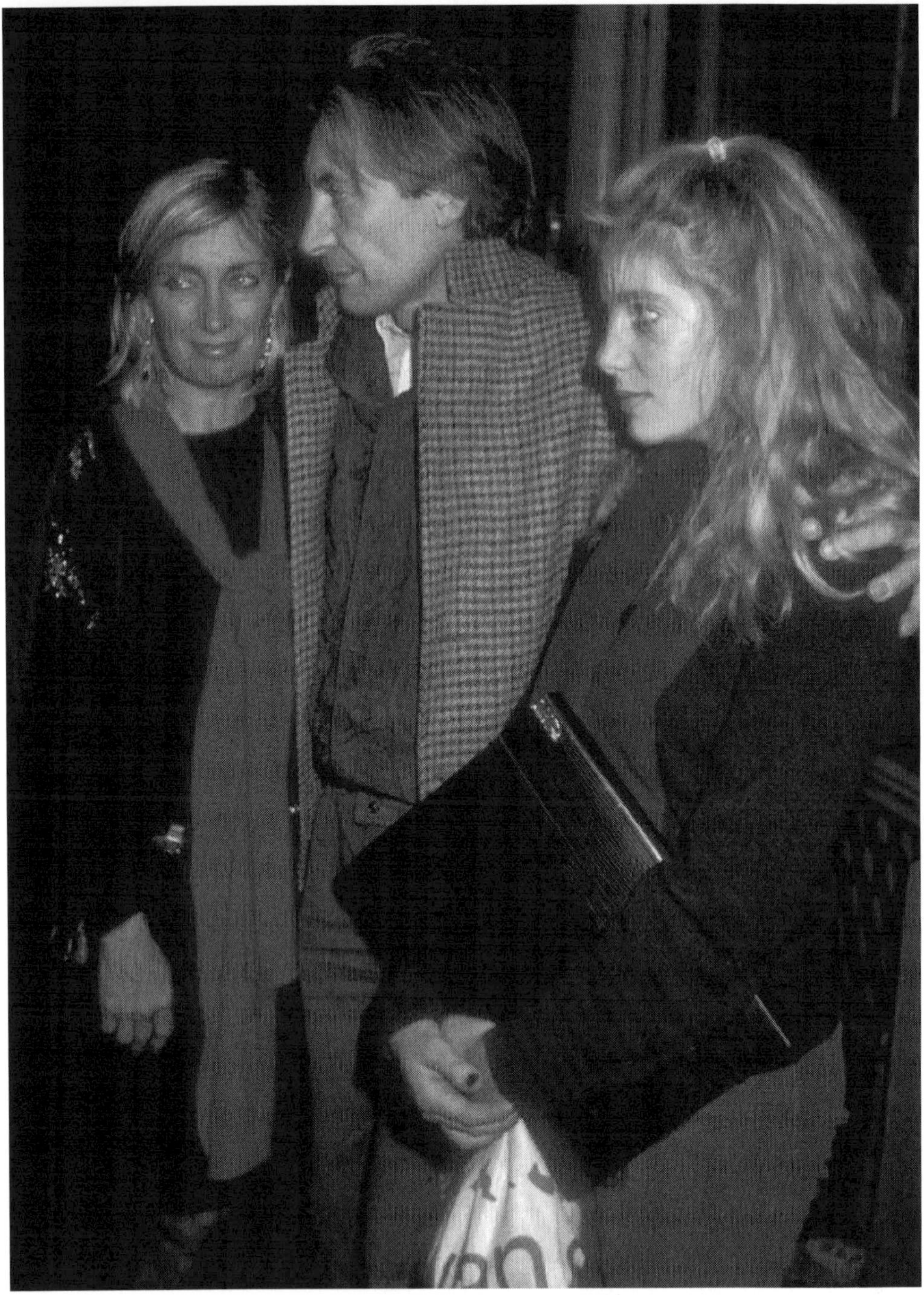

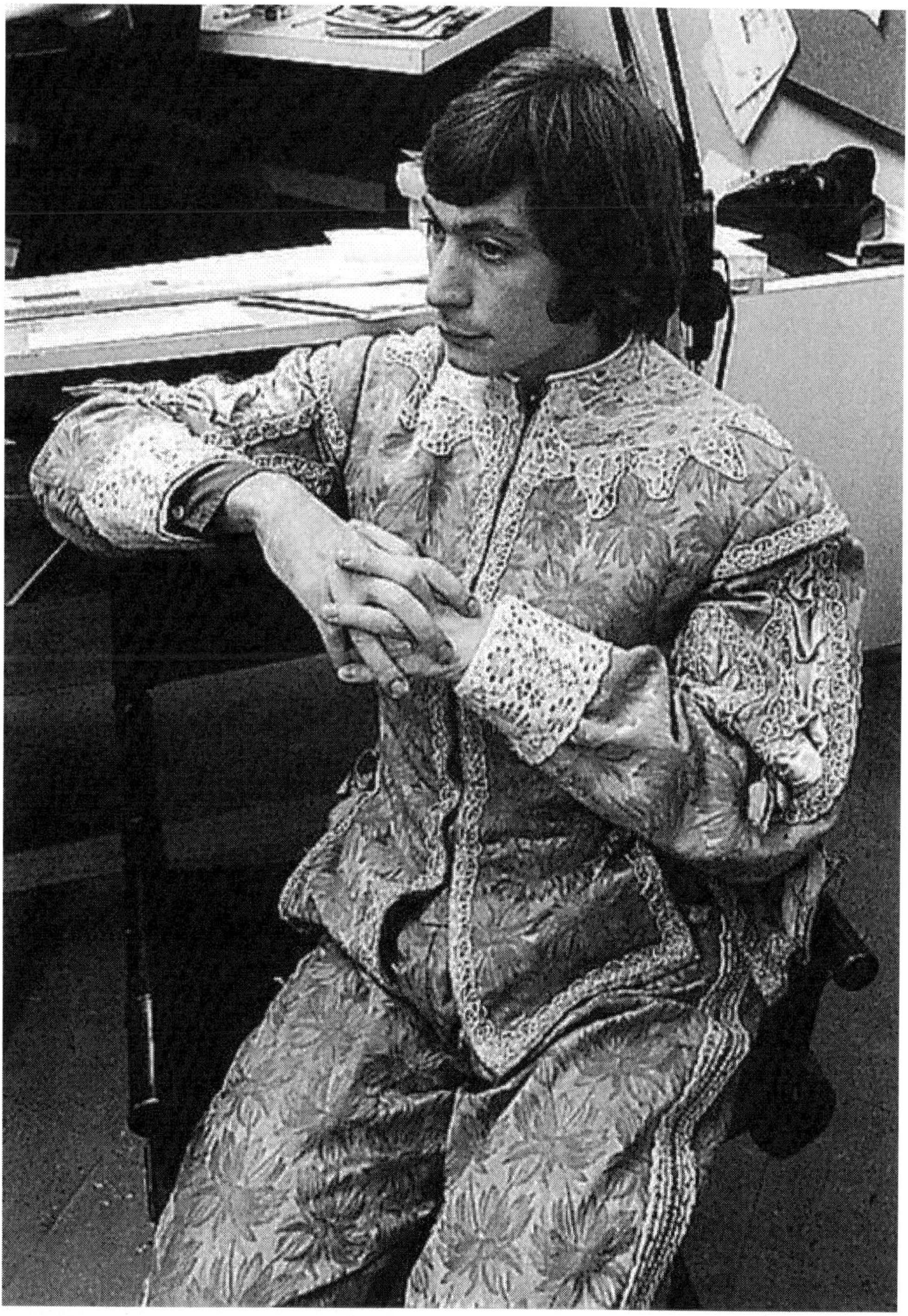

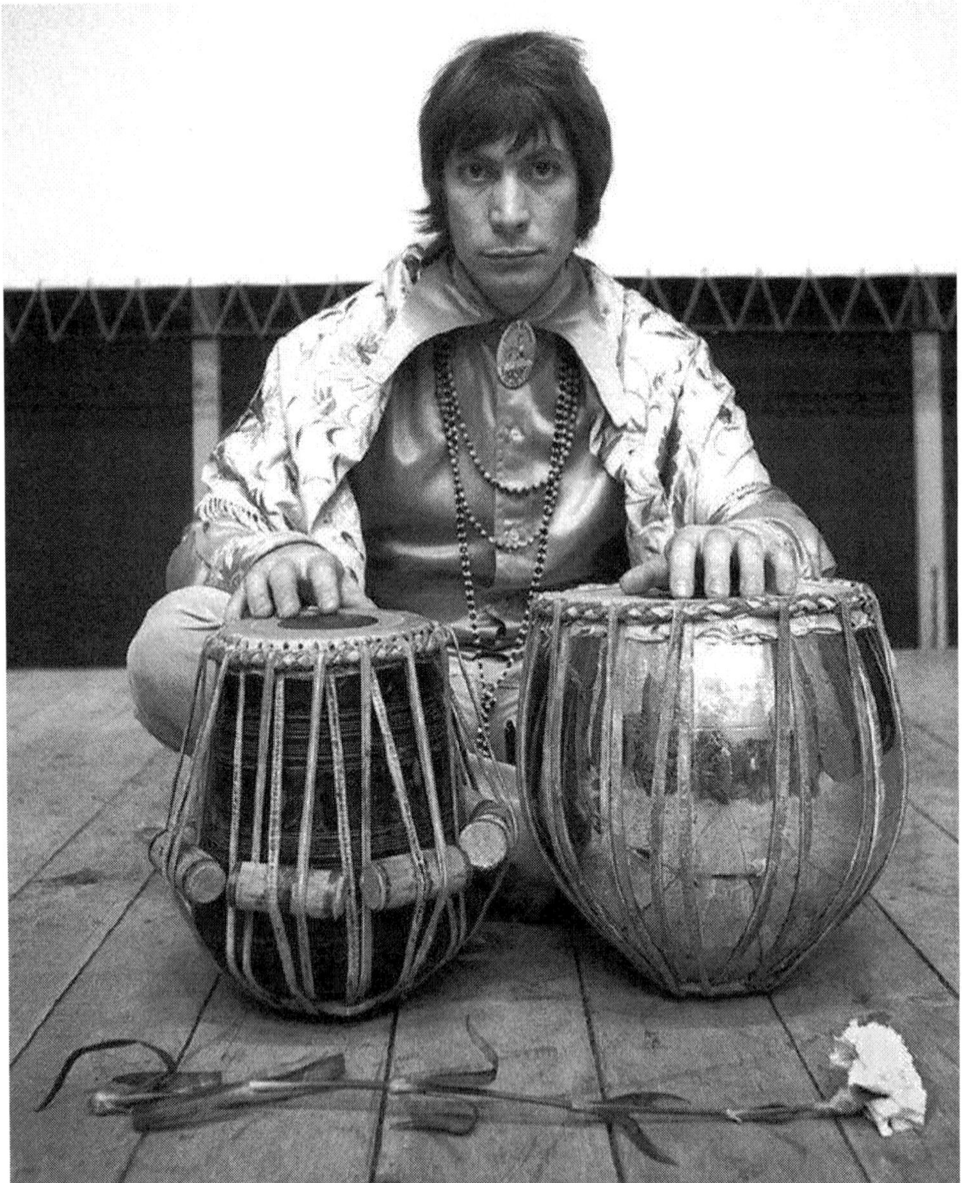

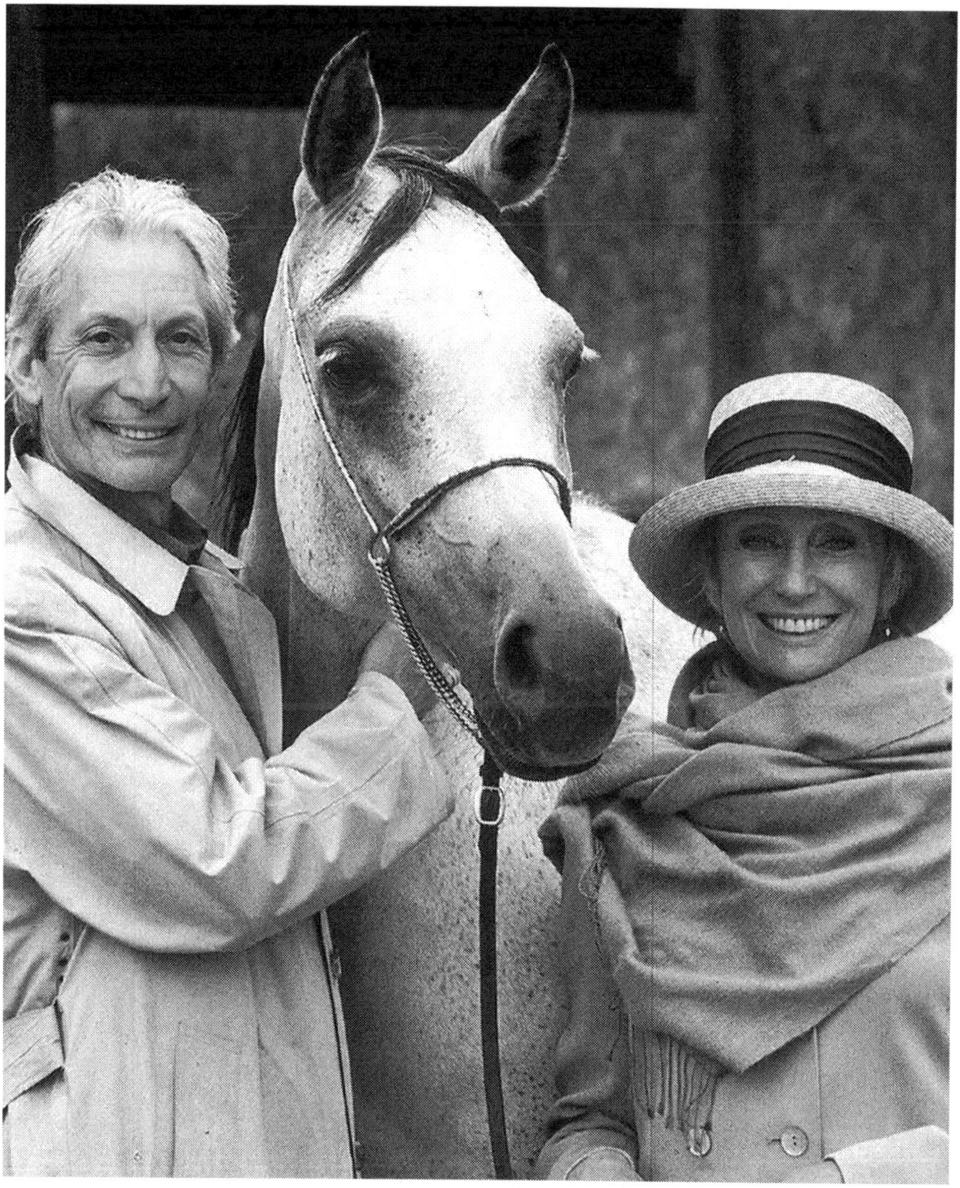

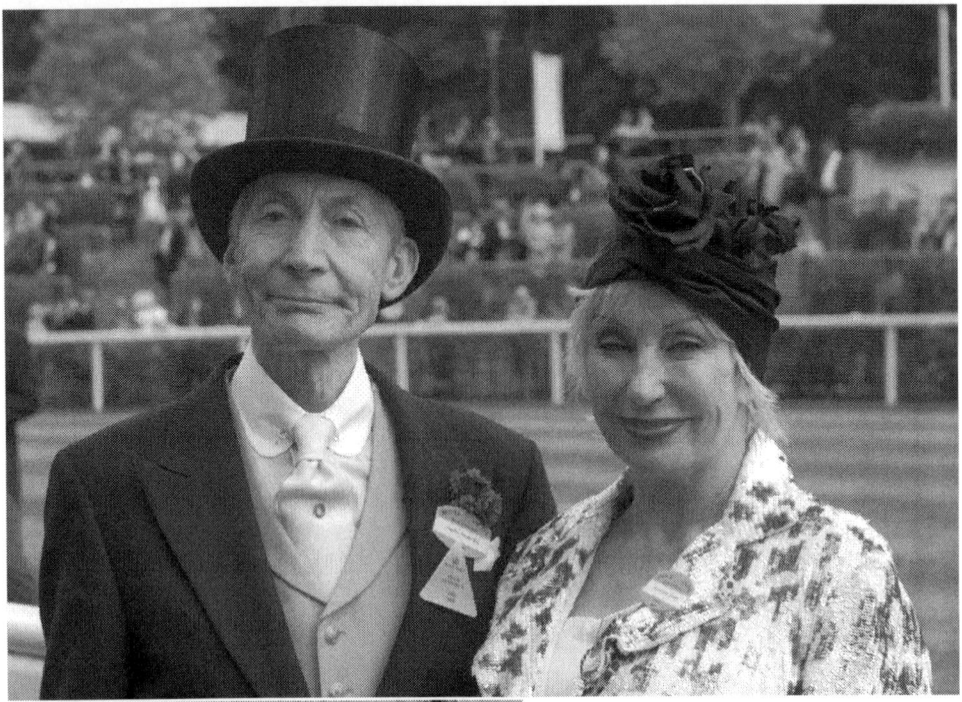

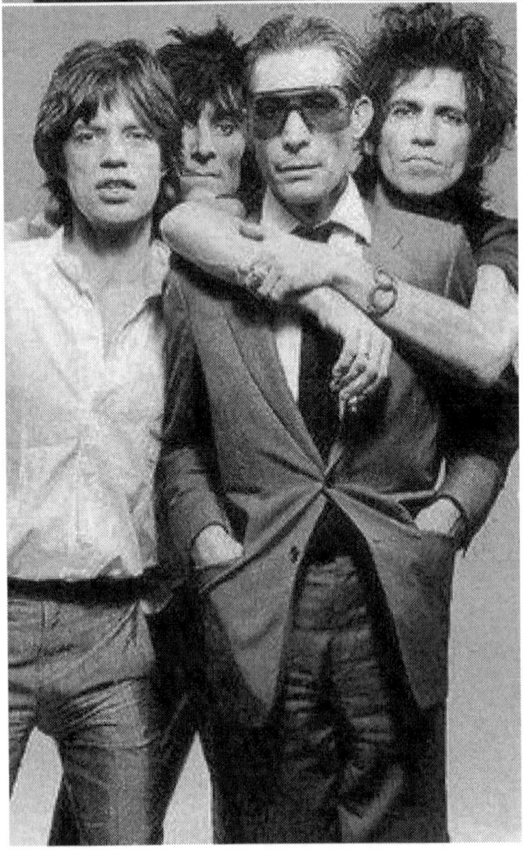

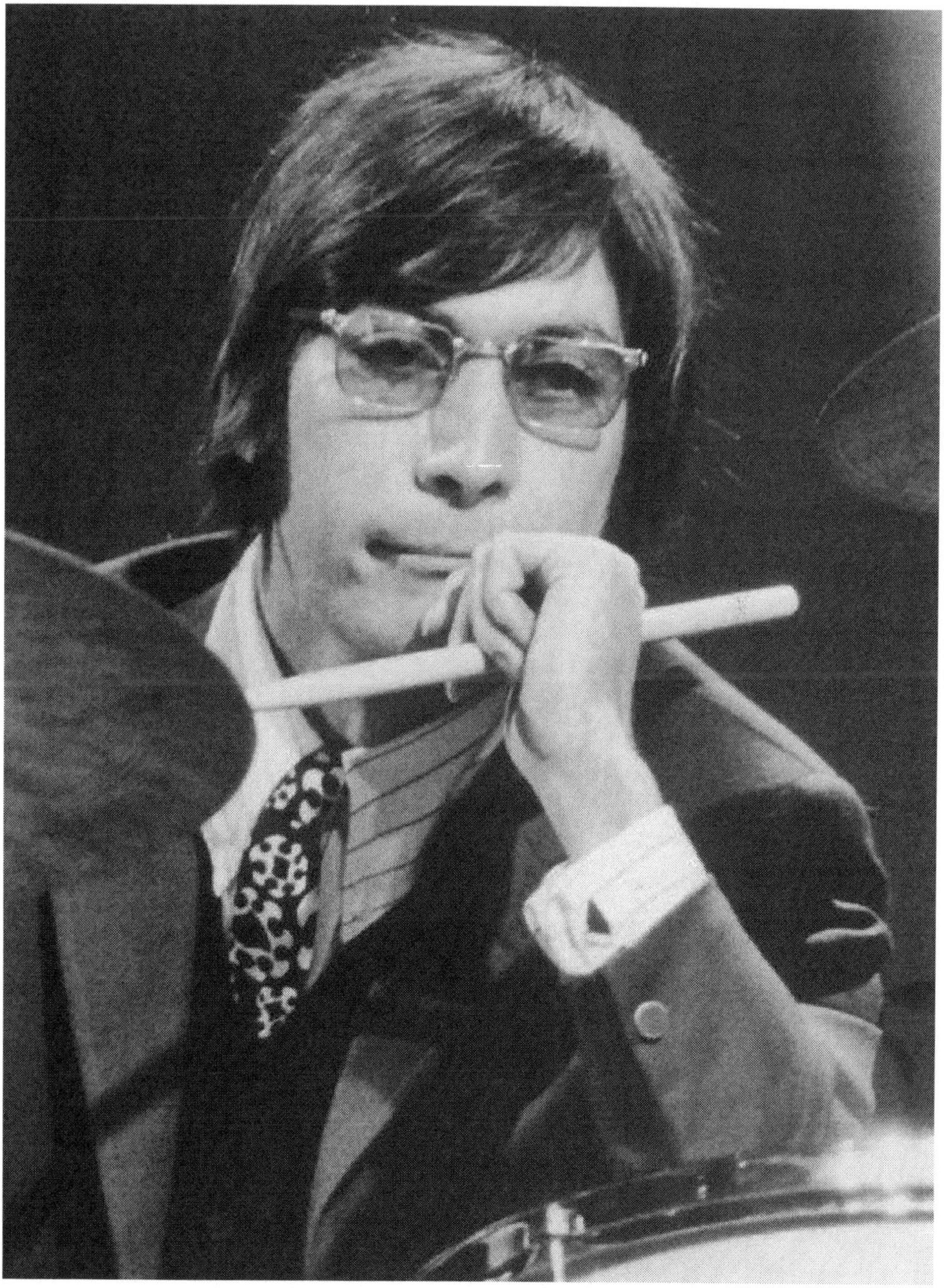

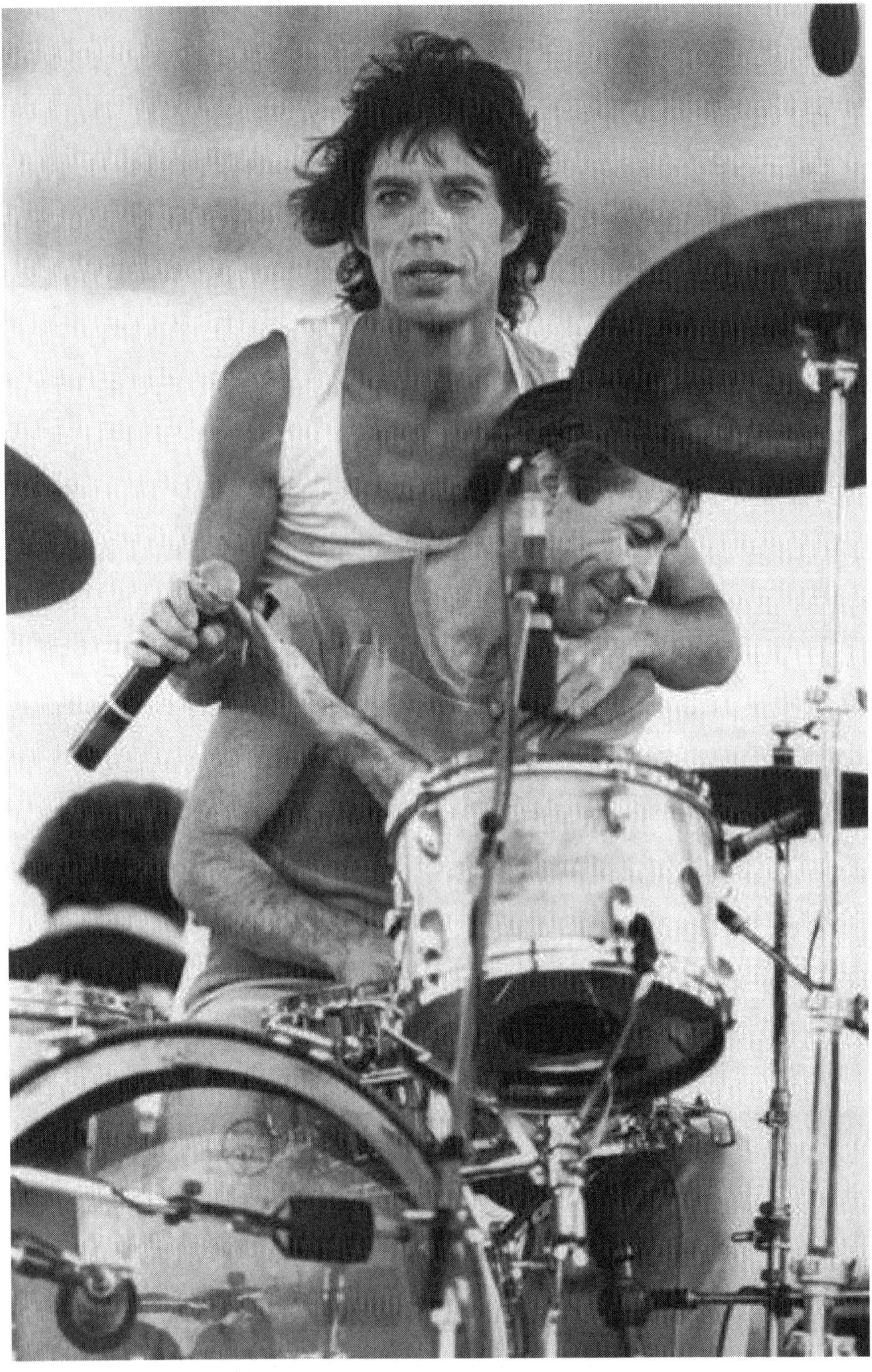

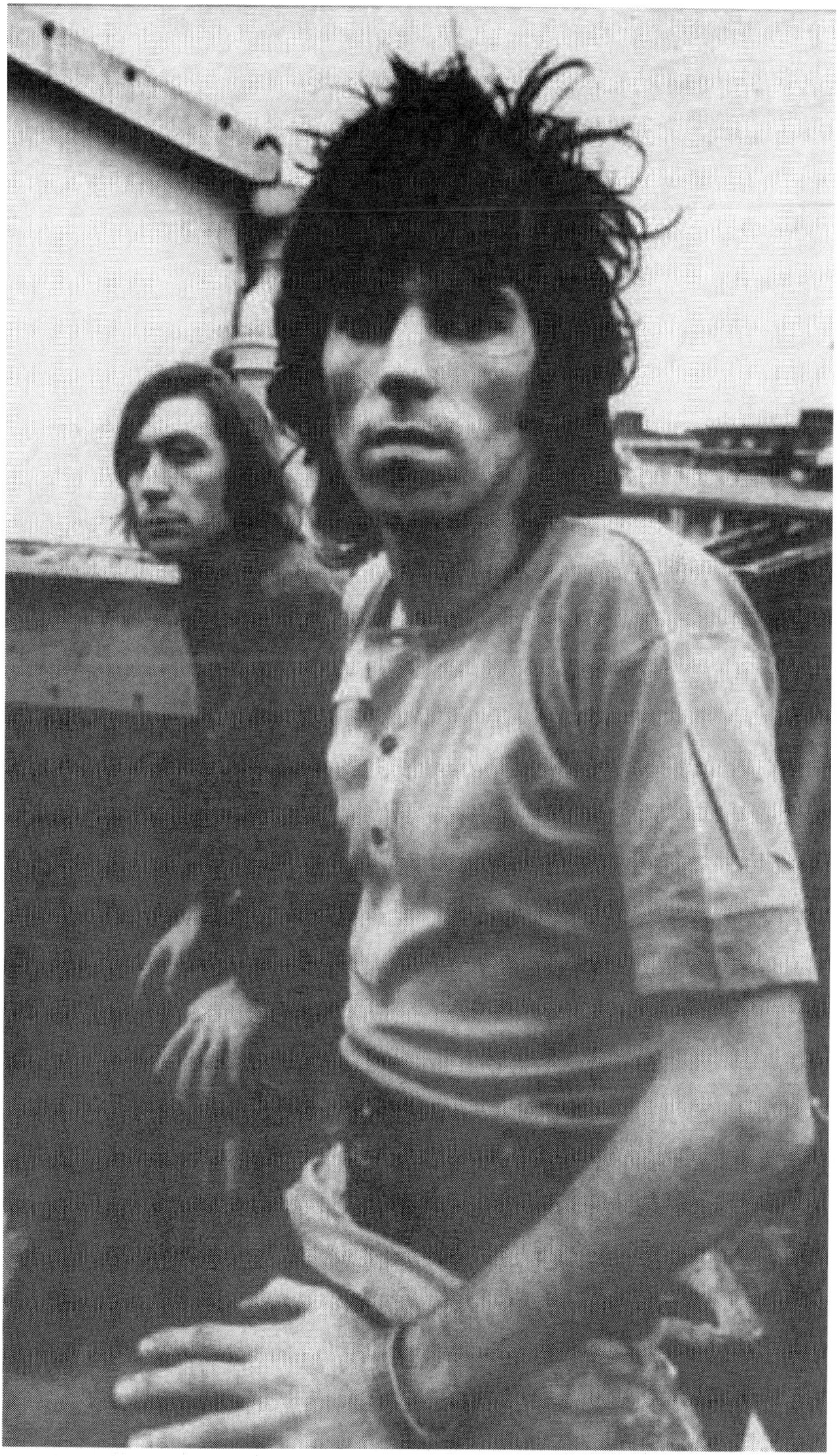

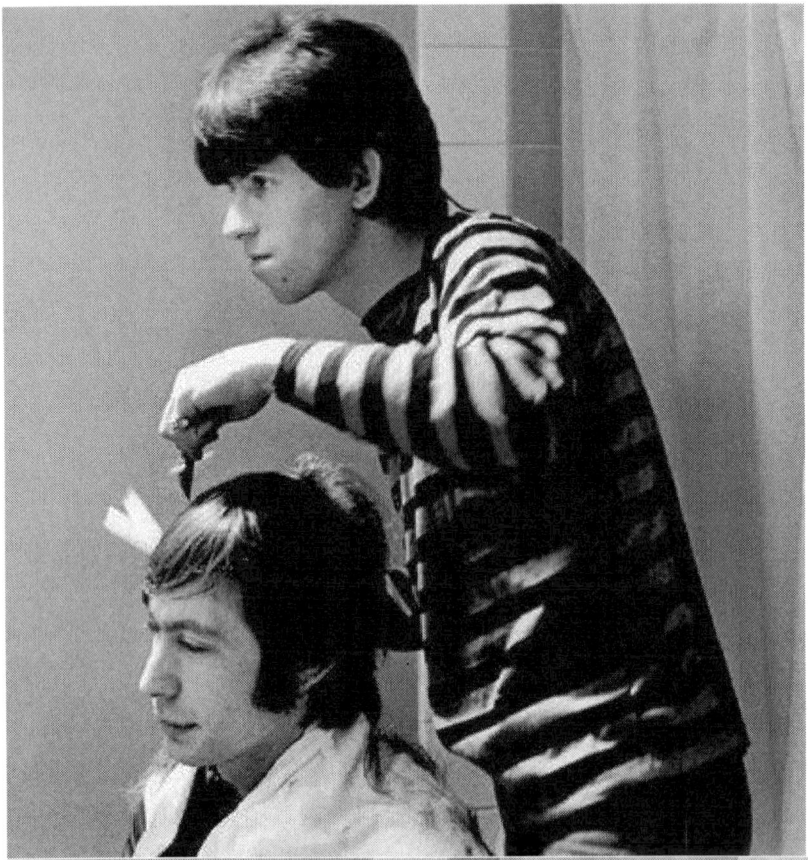

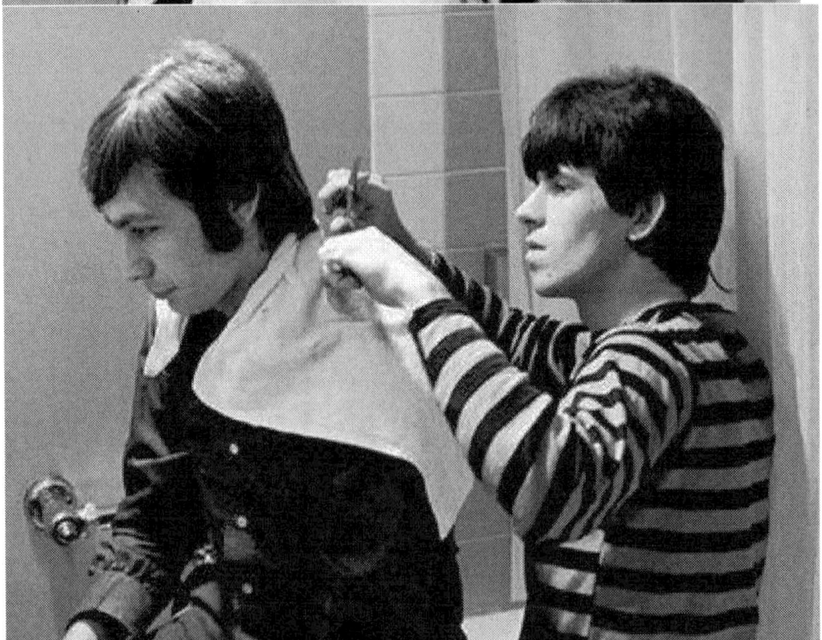

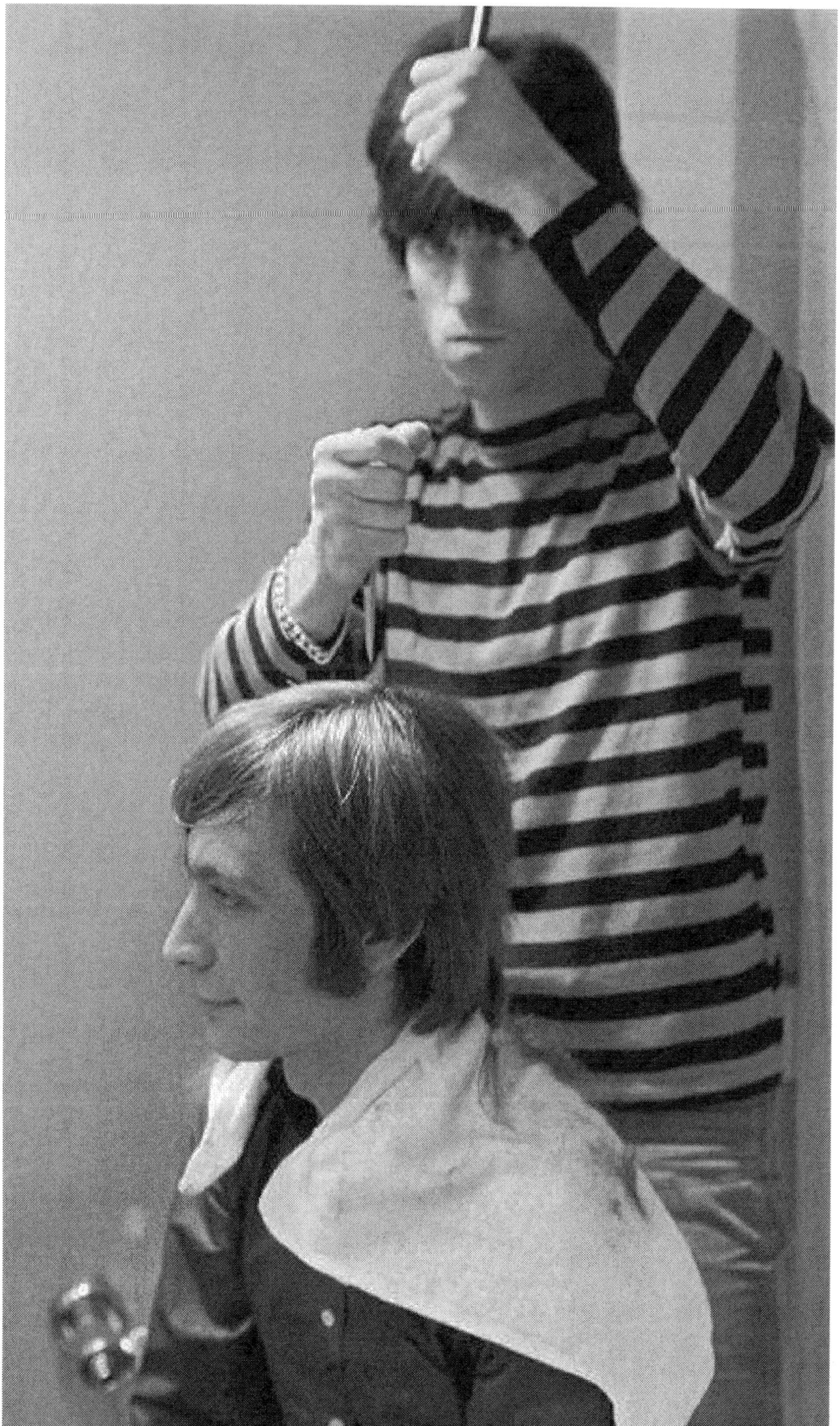

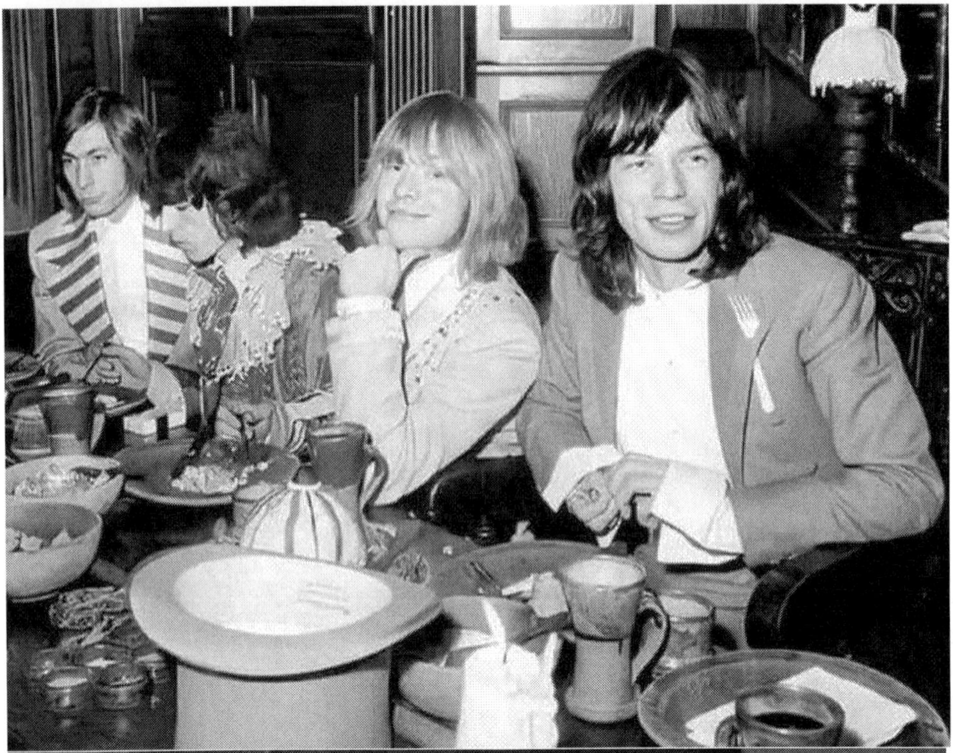

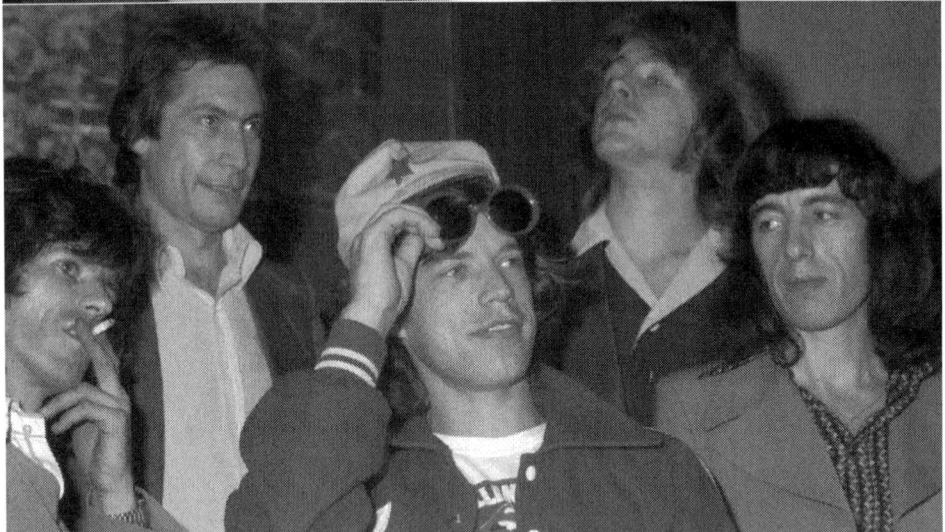

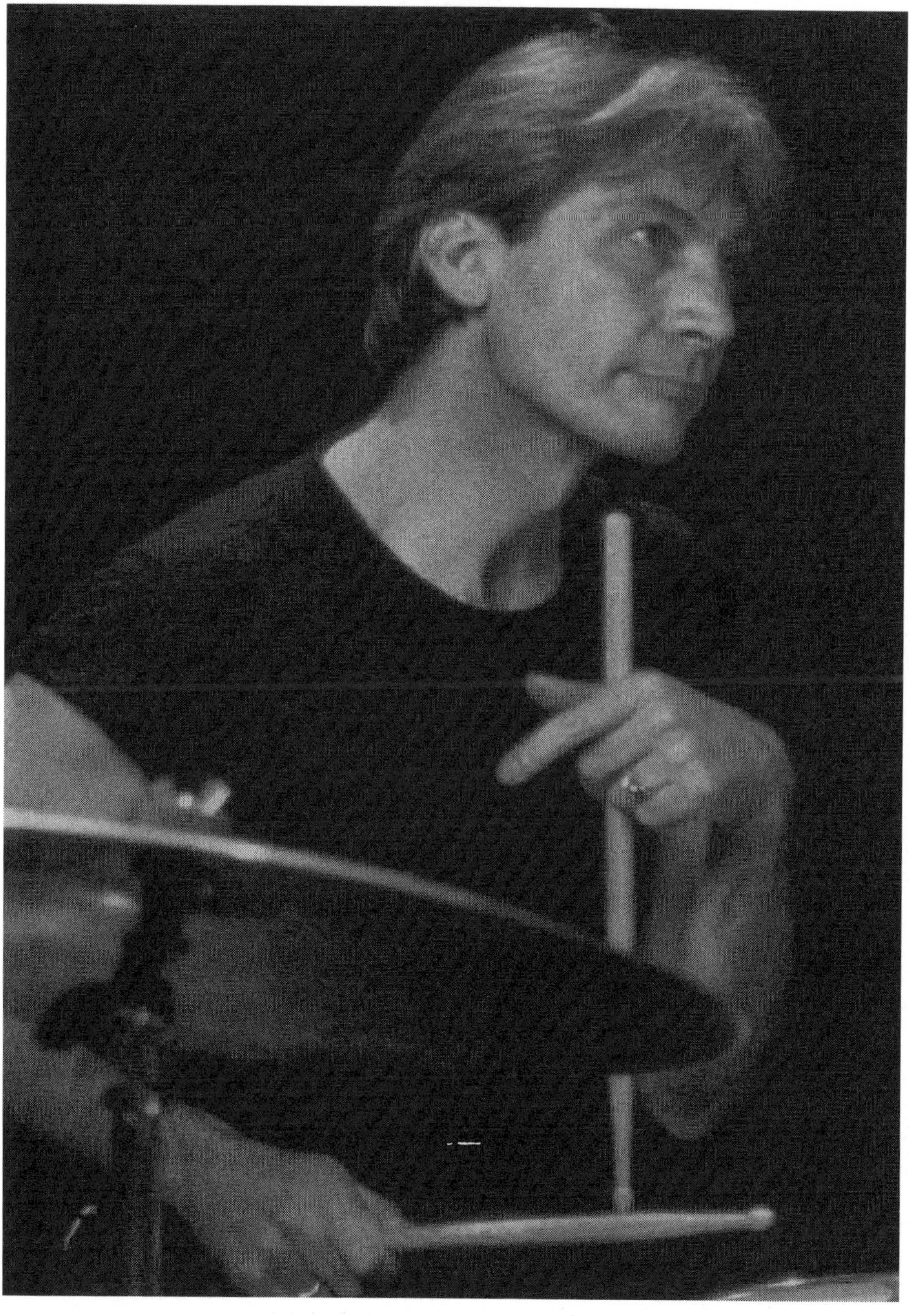

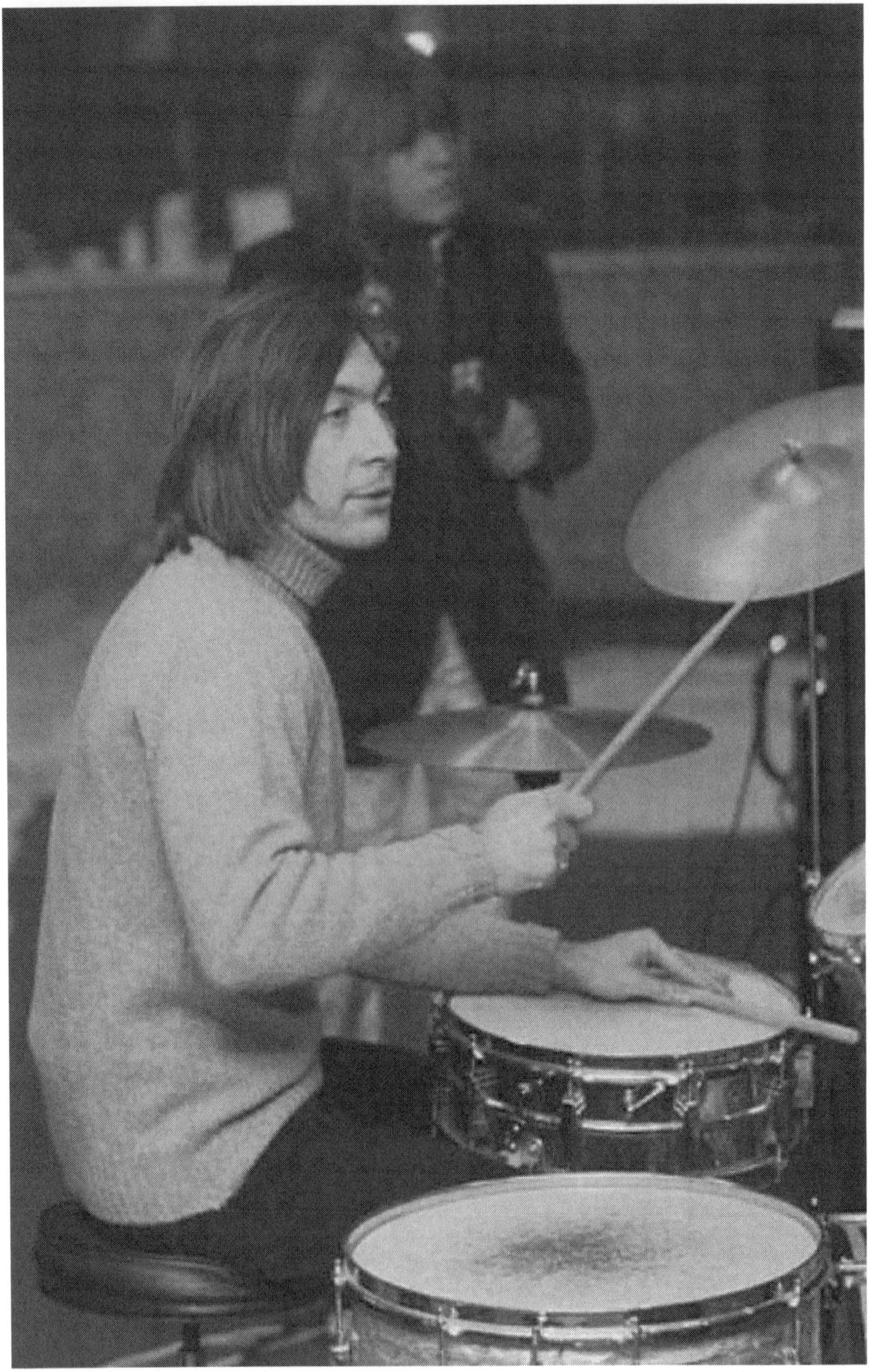

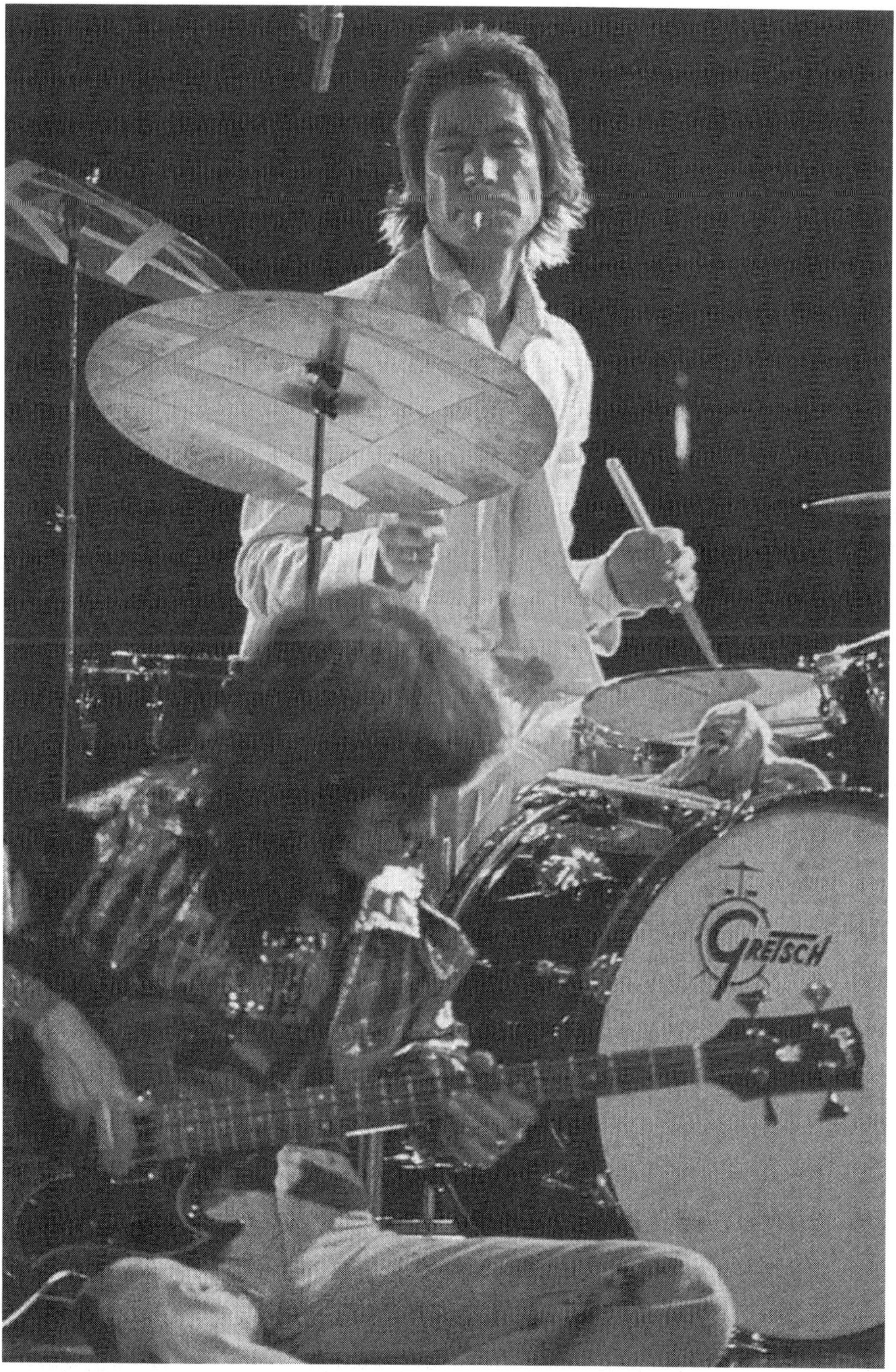
GRETSCH

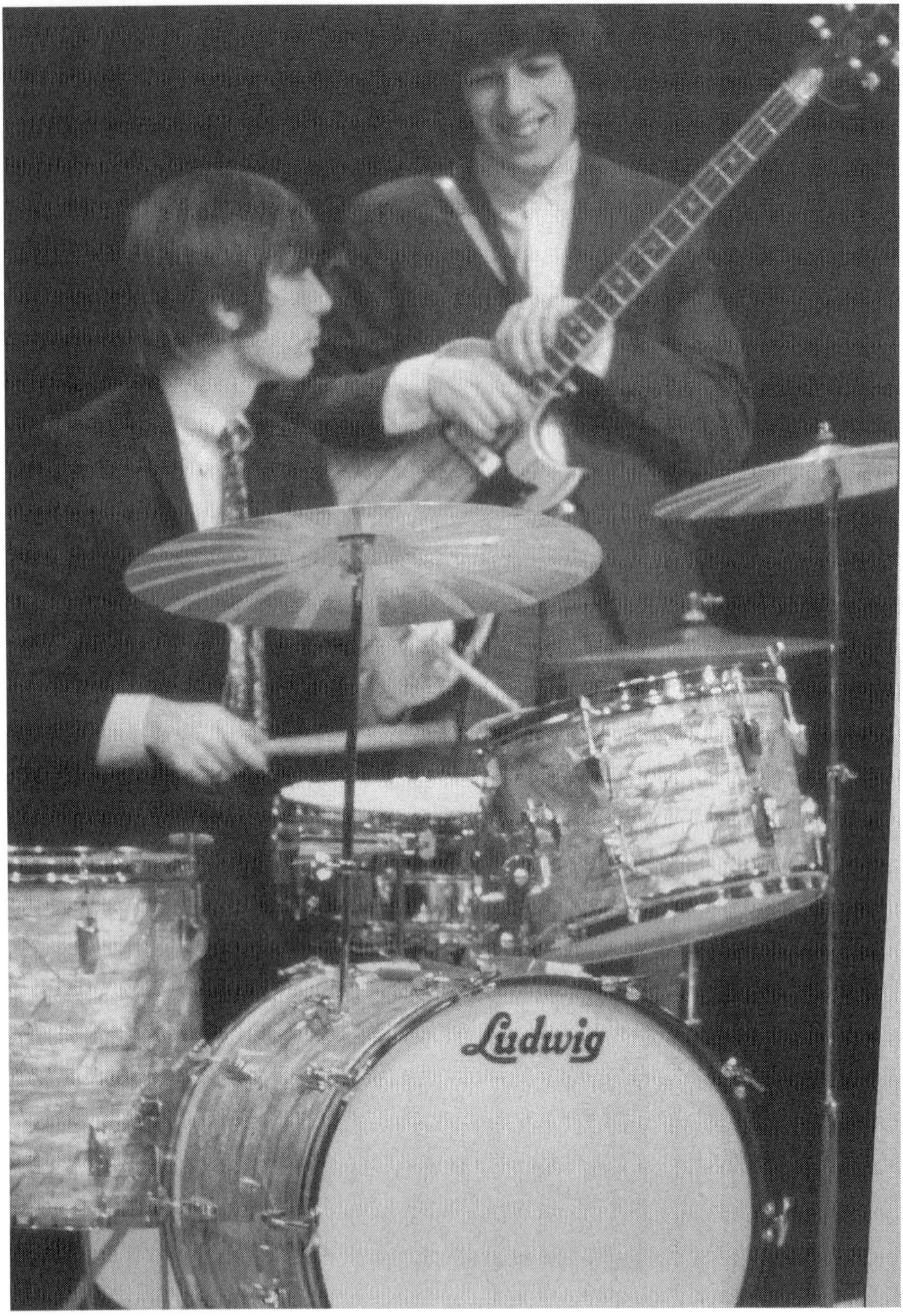
Ludwig

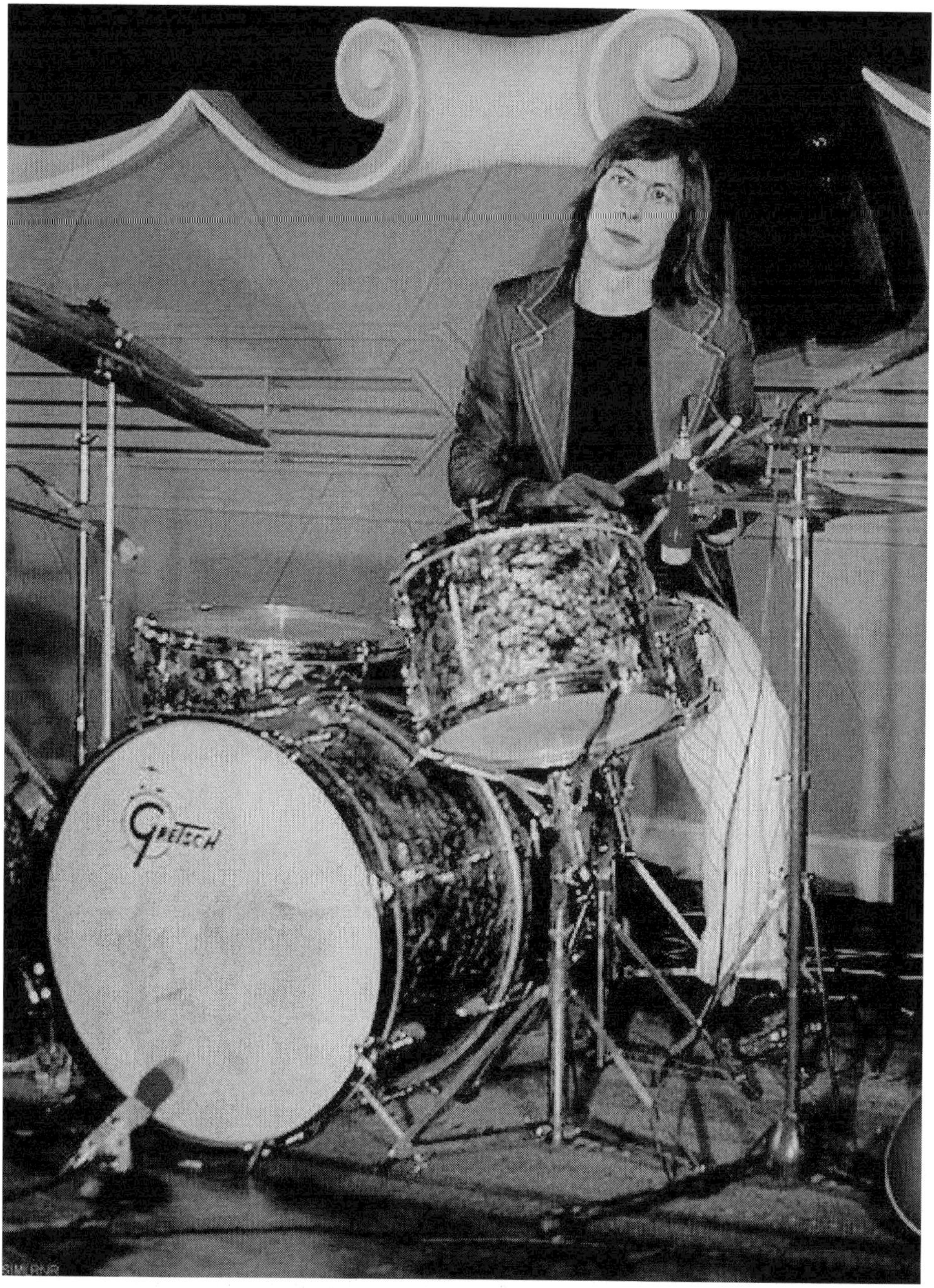
Gretsch

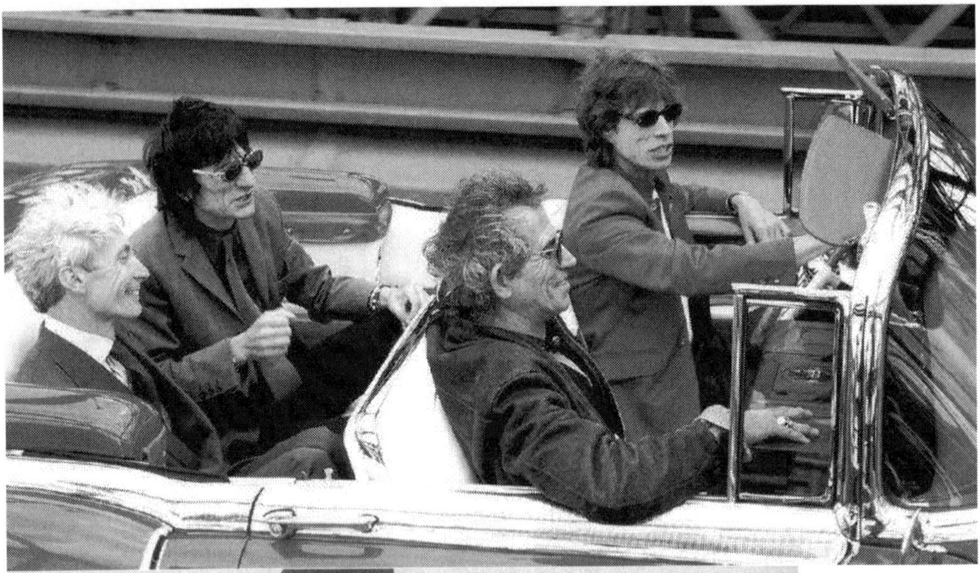

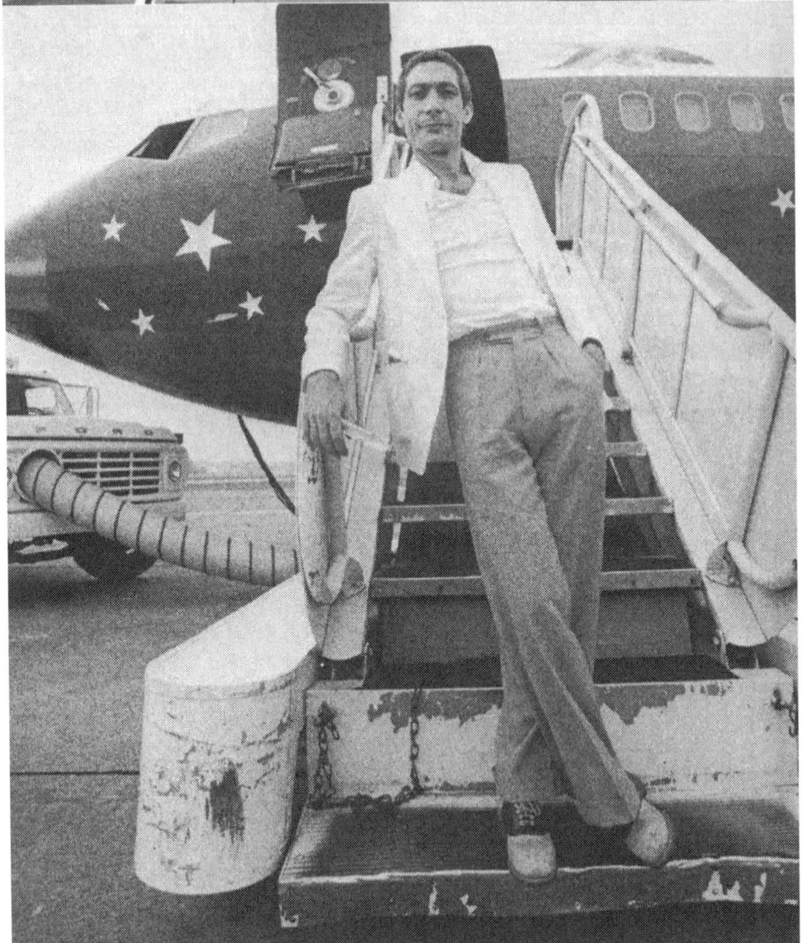

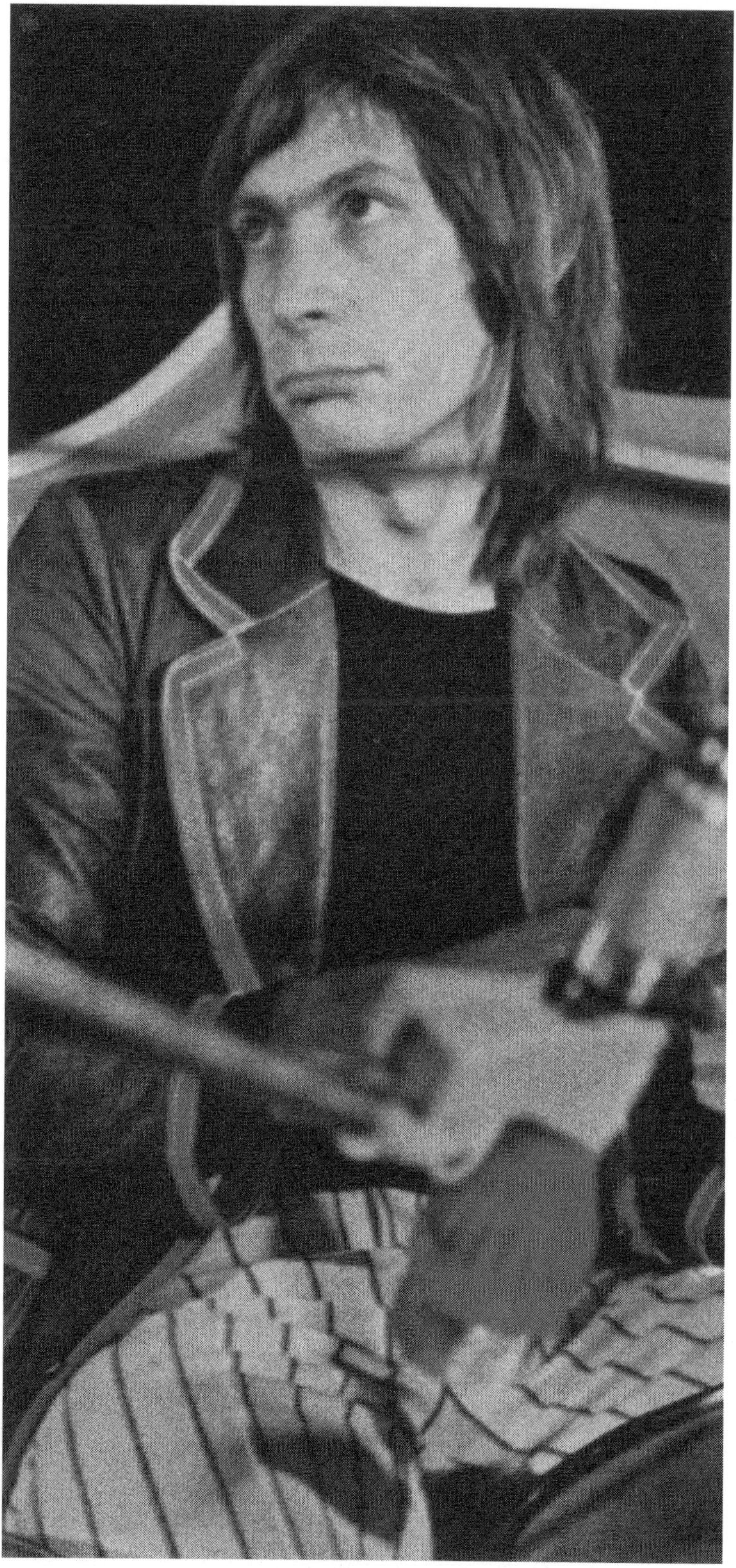

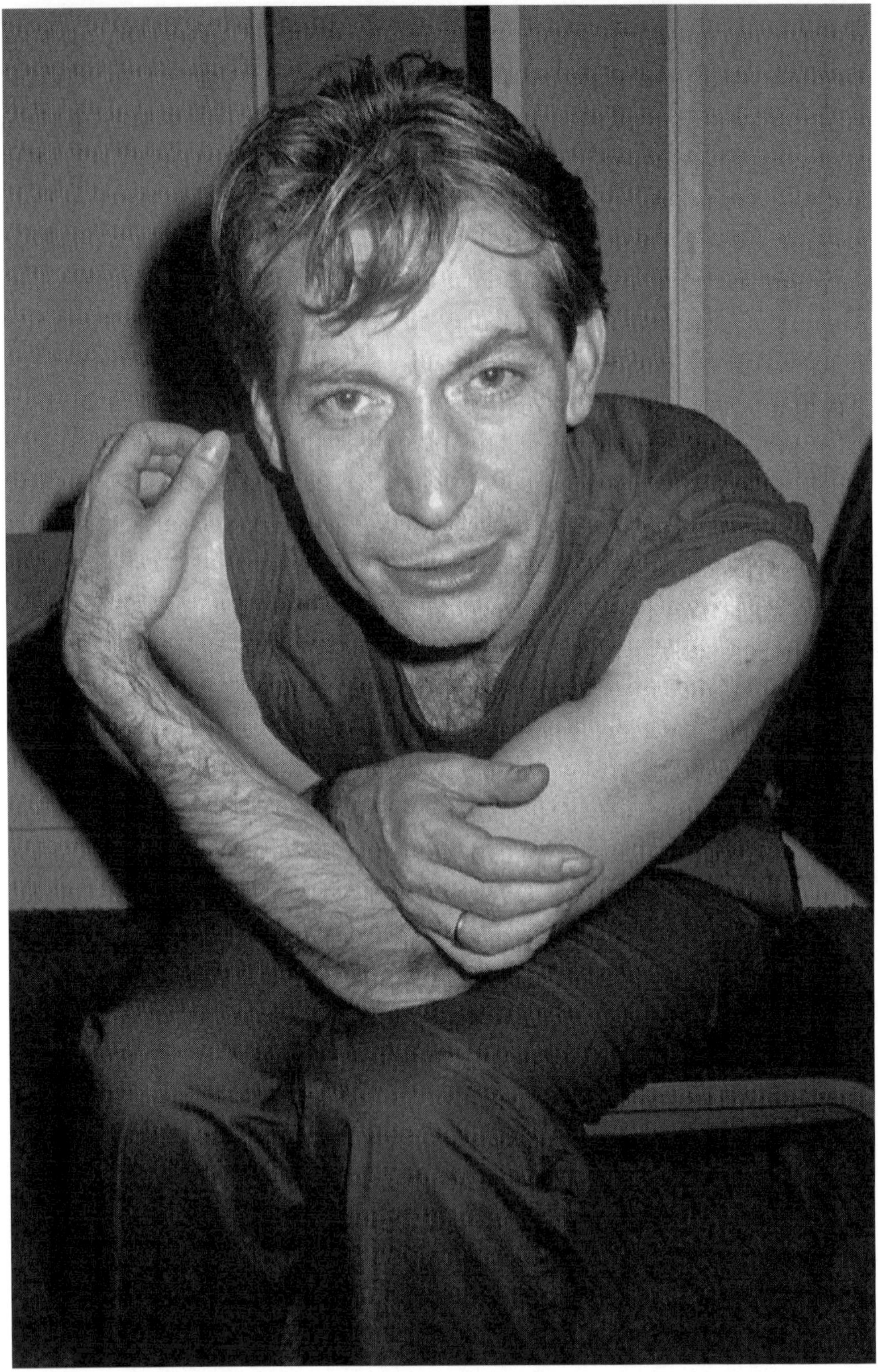

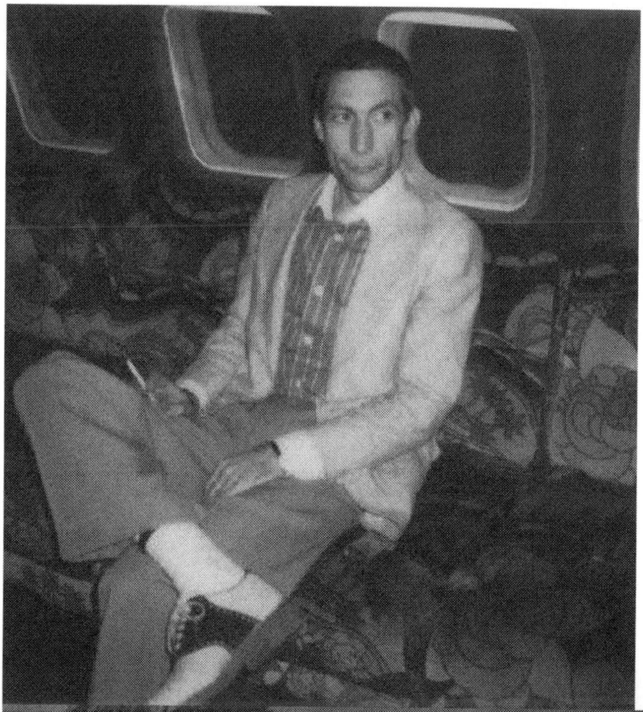

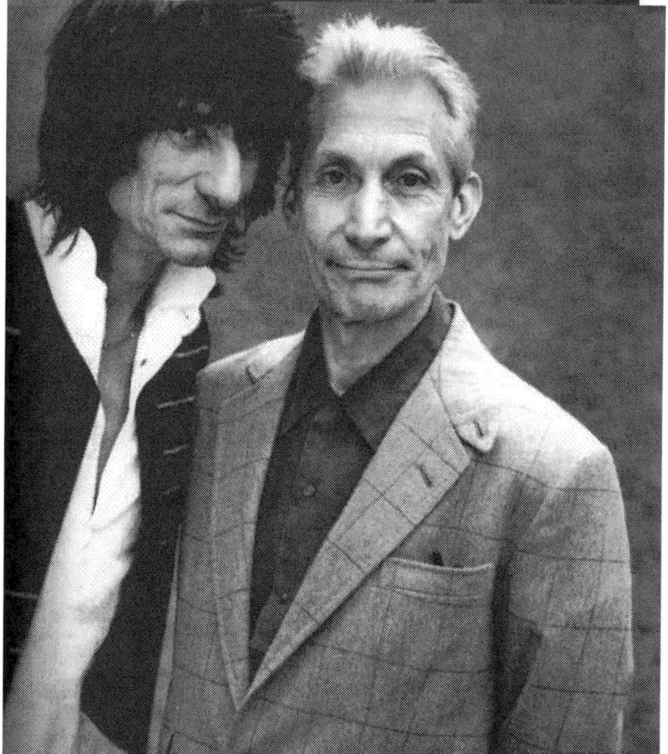

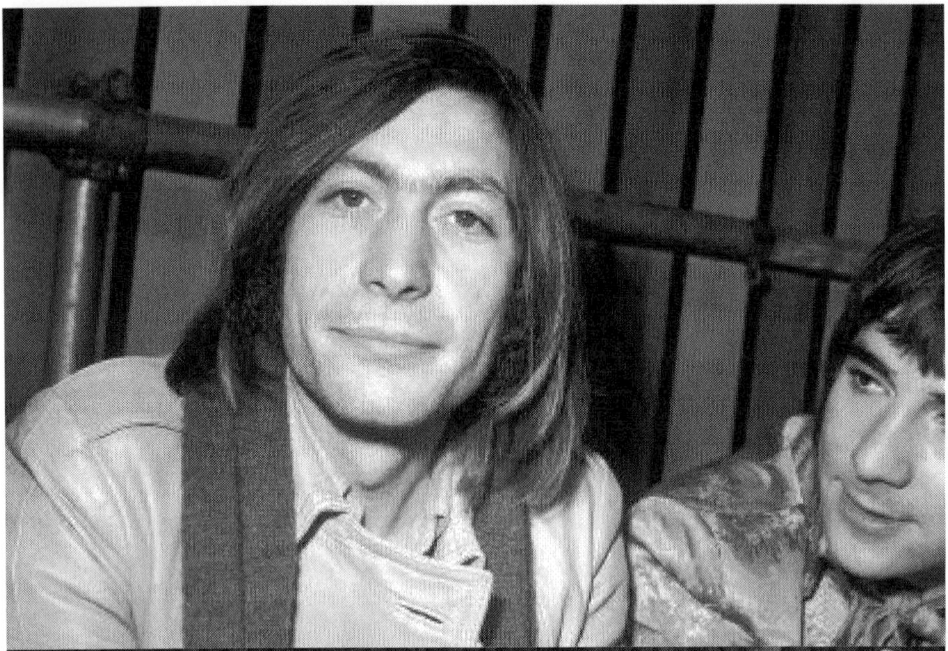

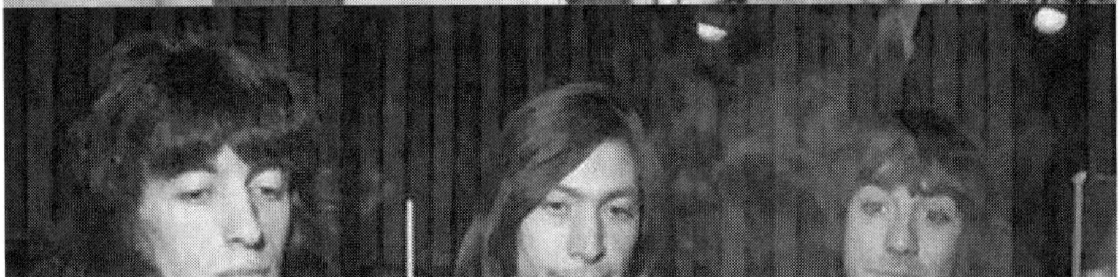

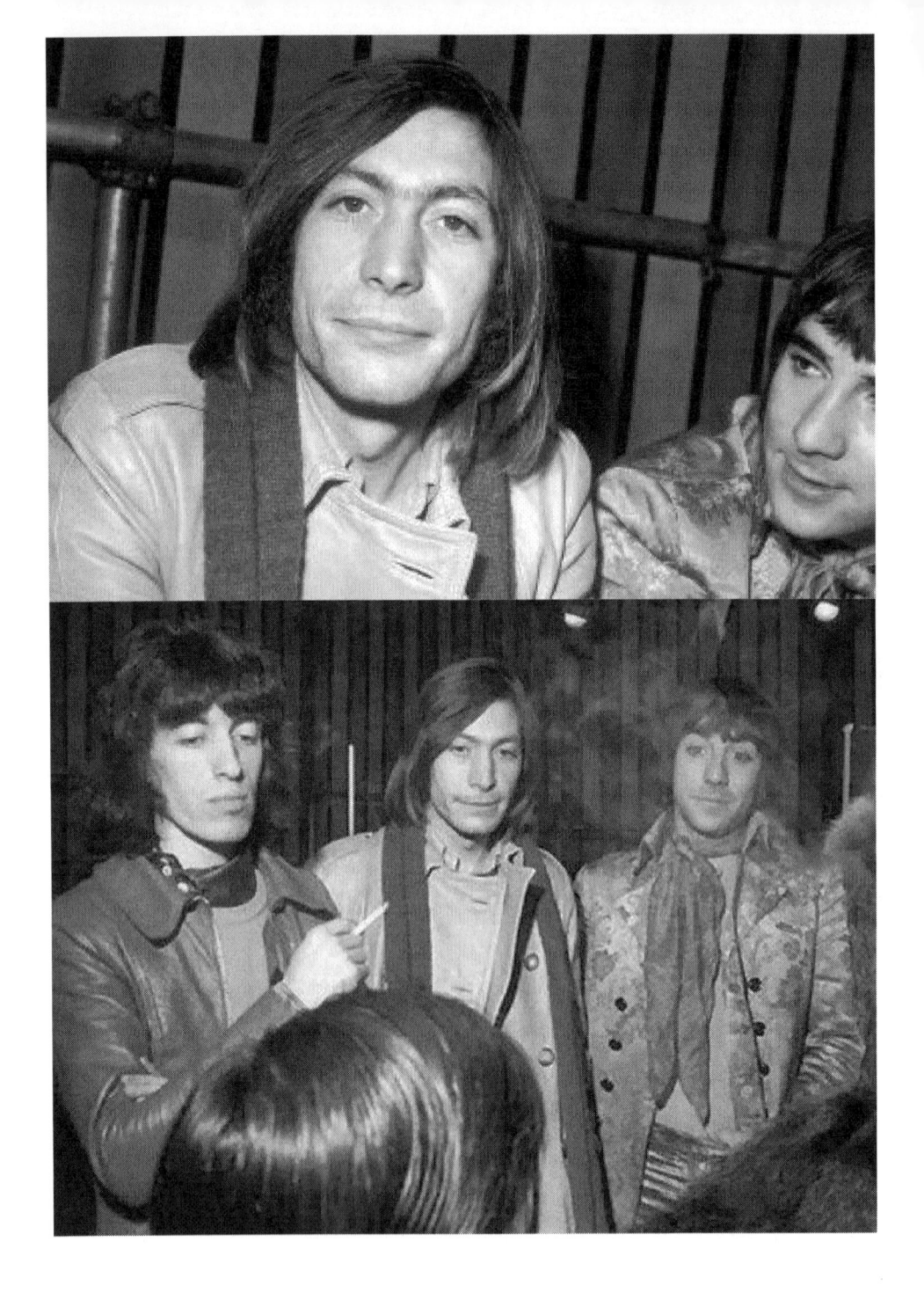

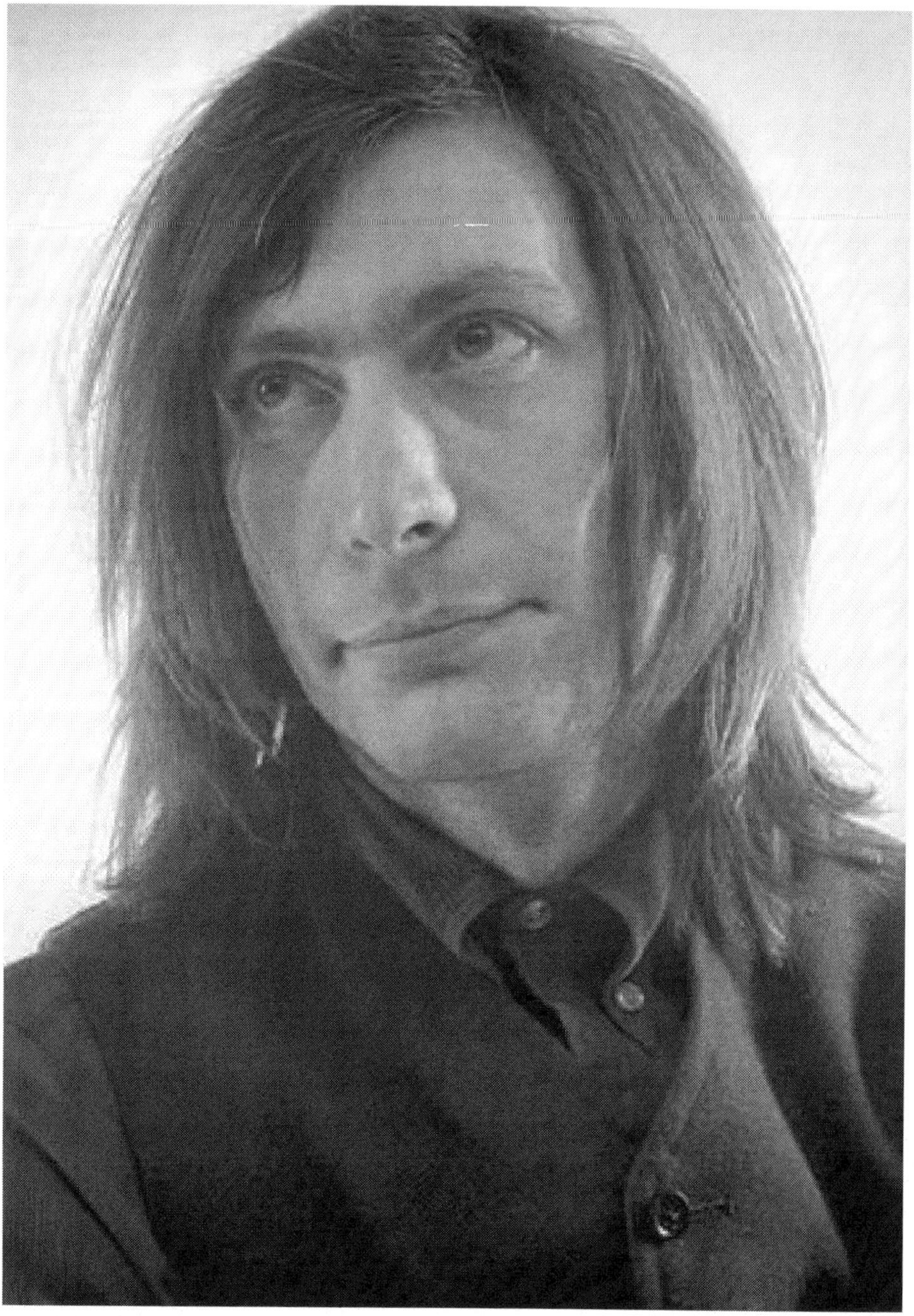

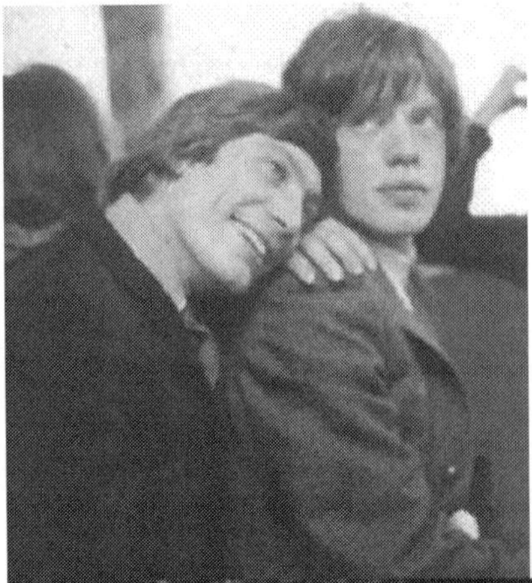

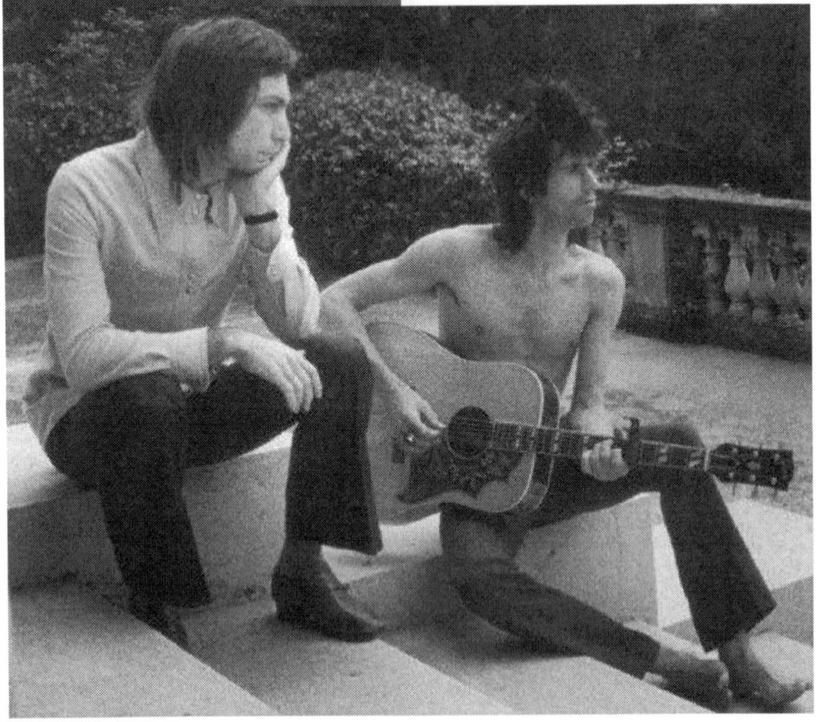

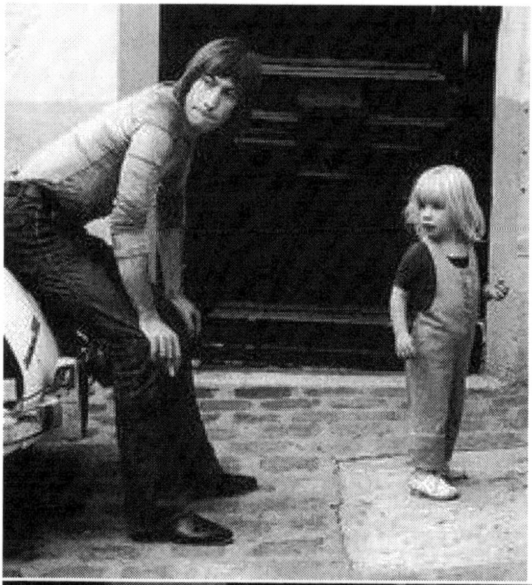

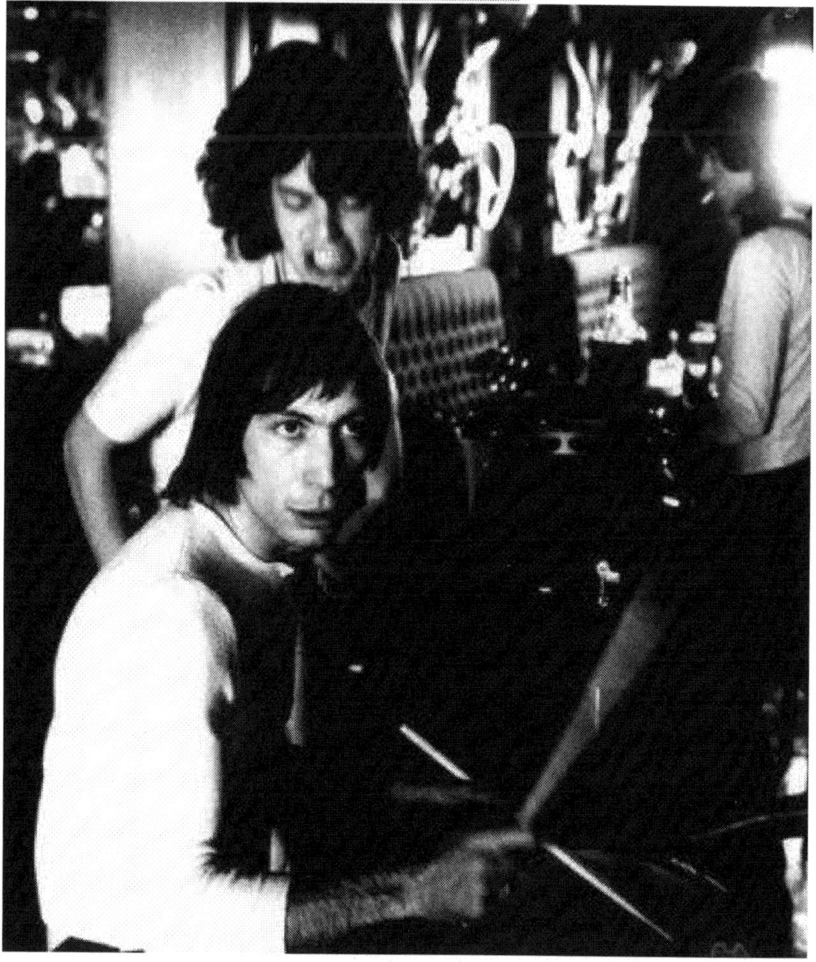

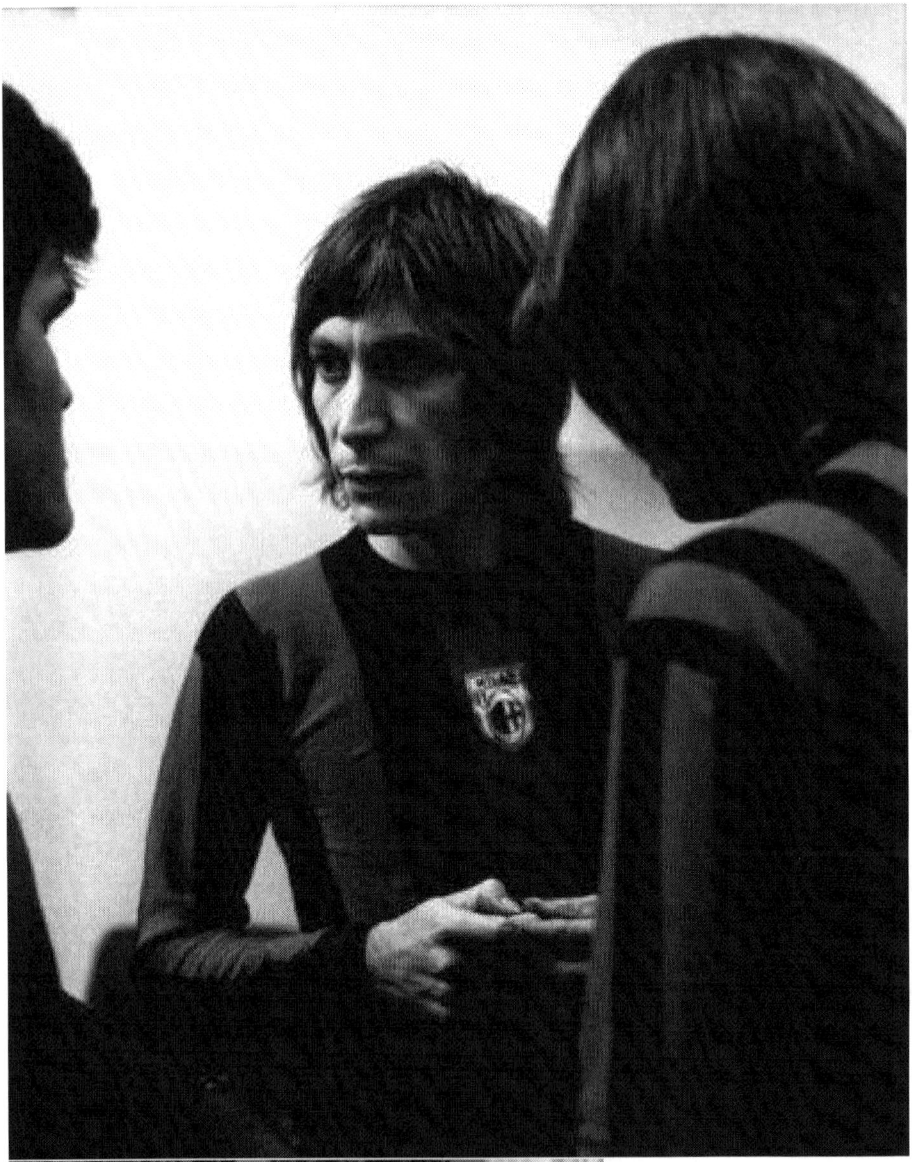

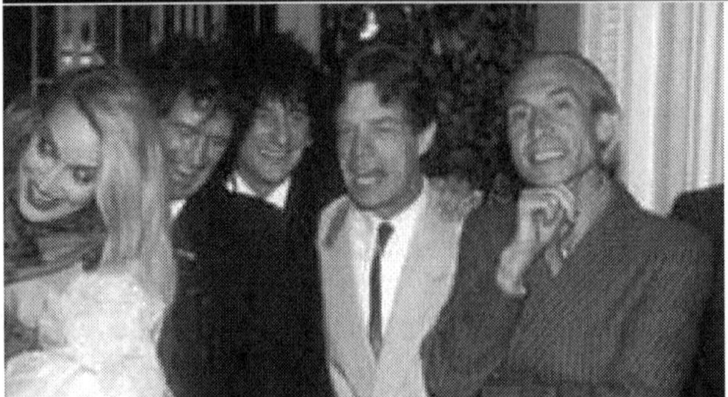

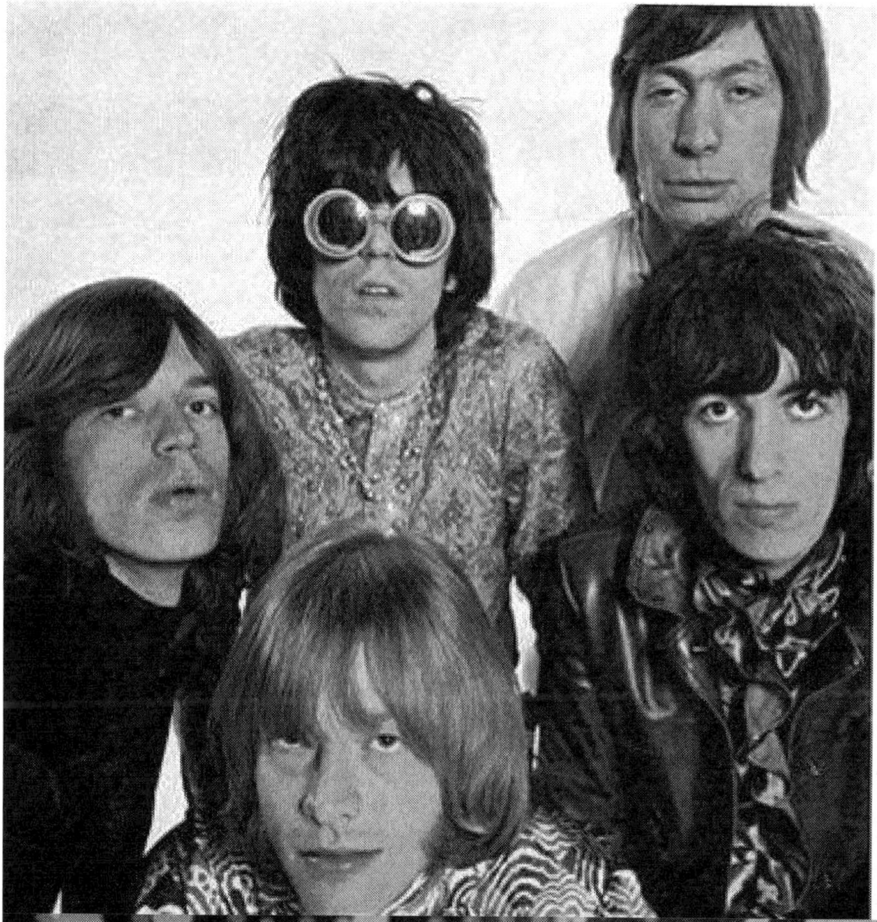

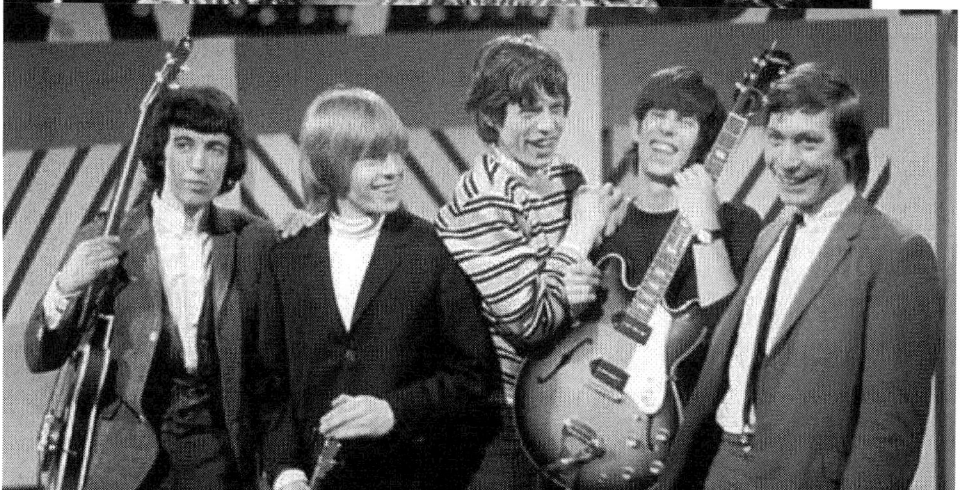

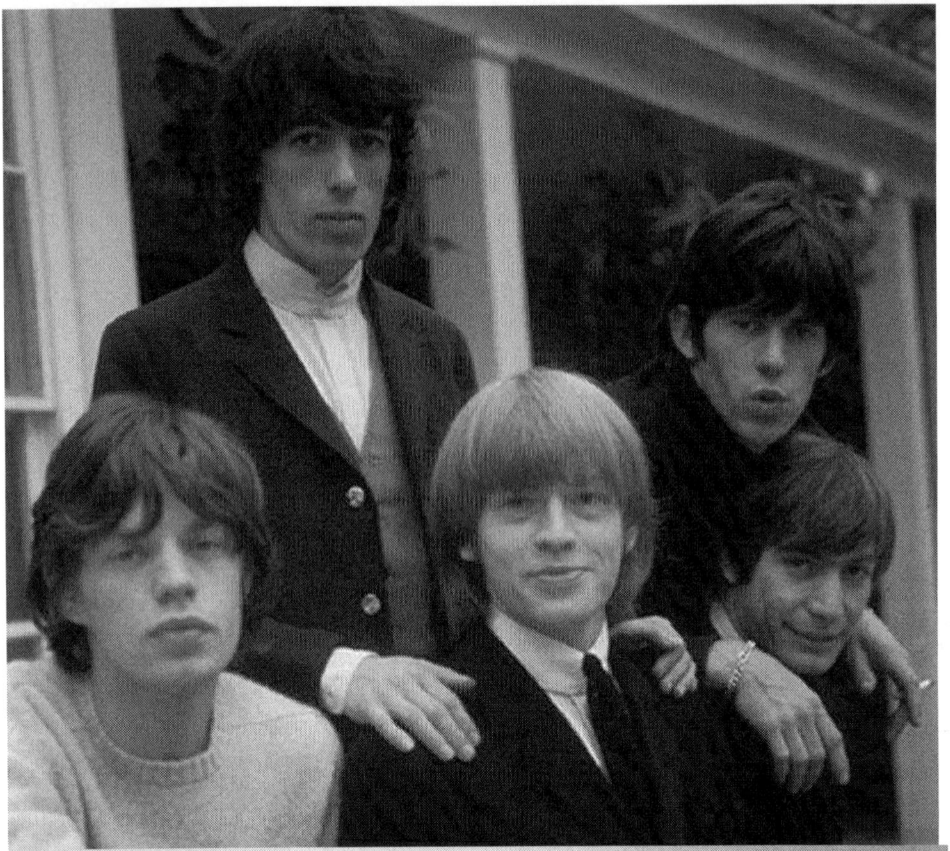

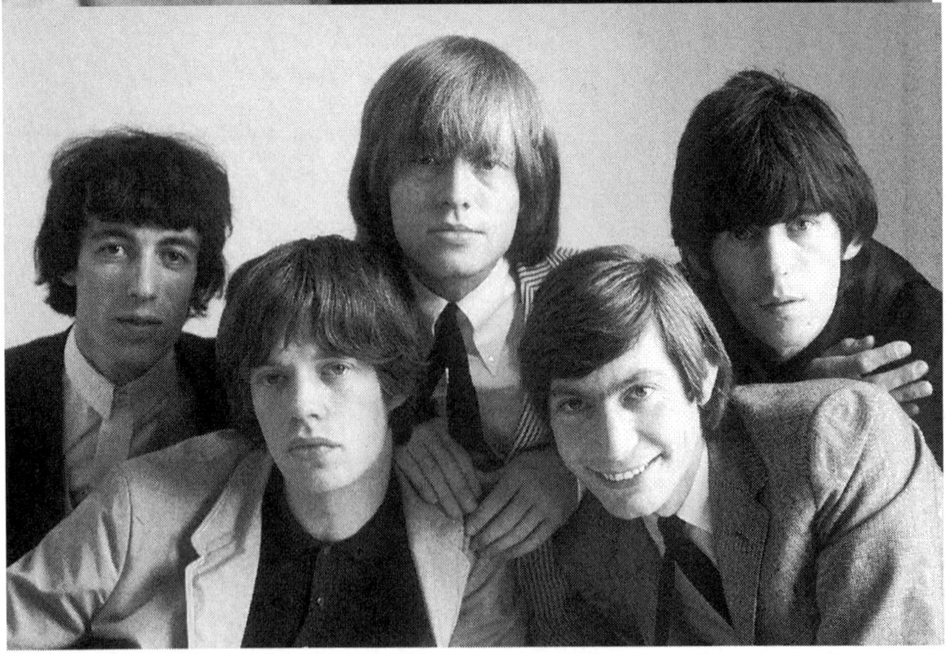

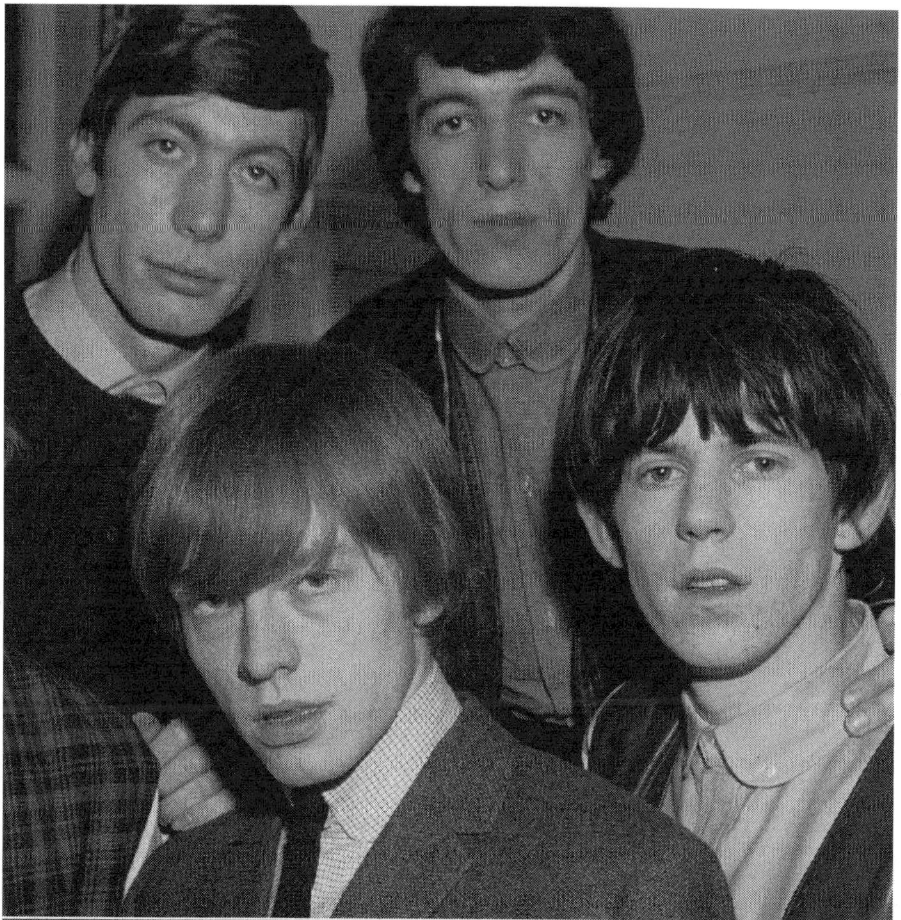

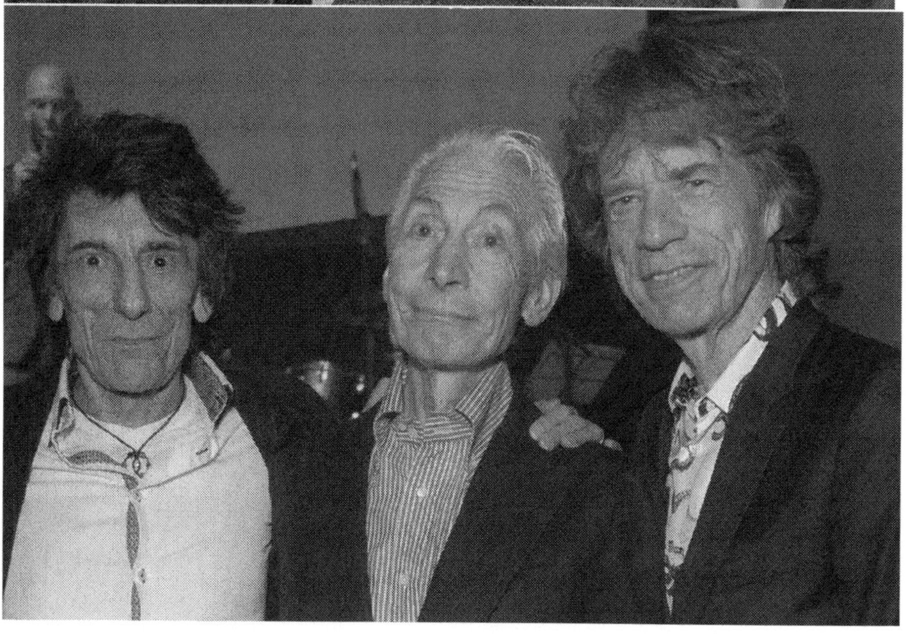

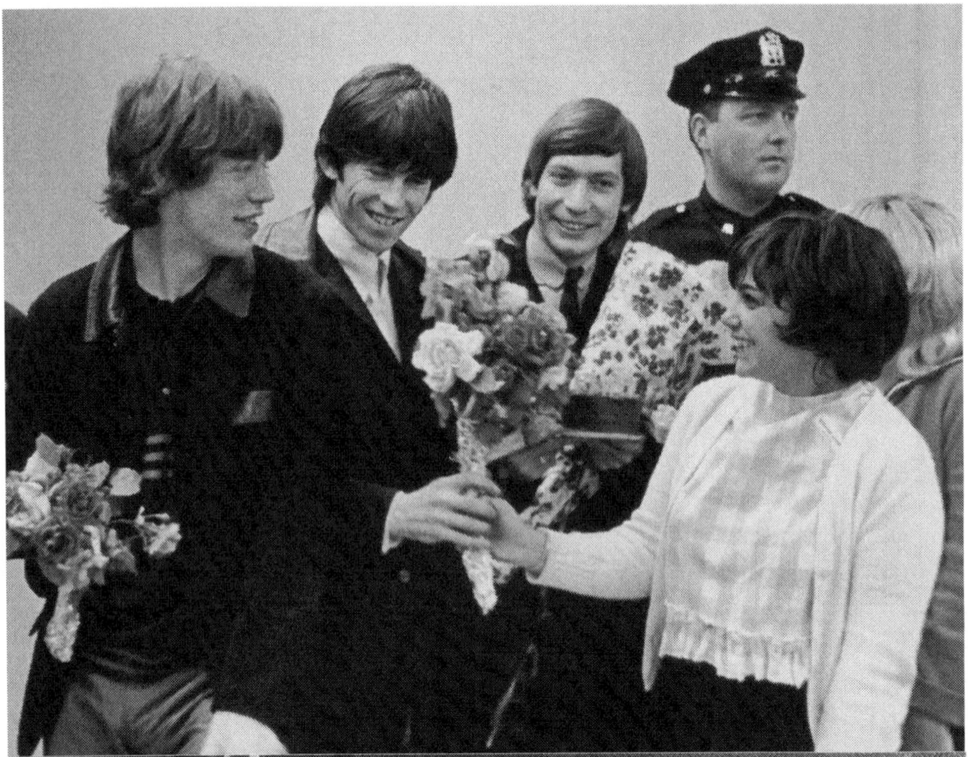

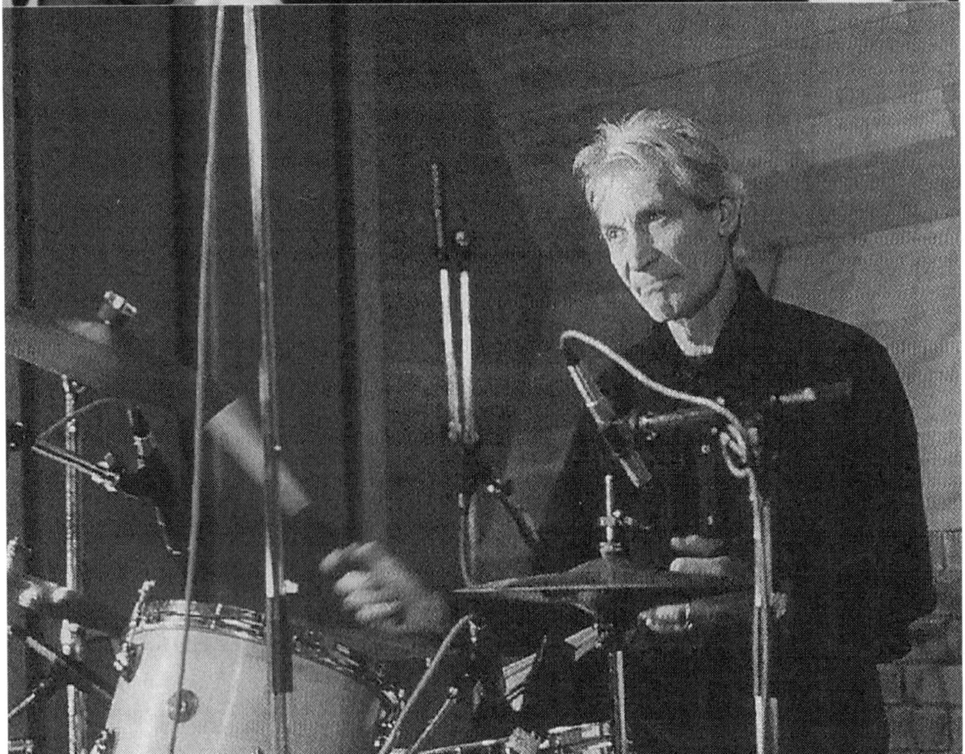

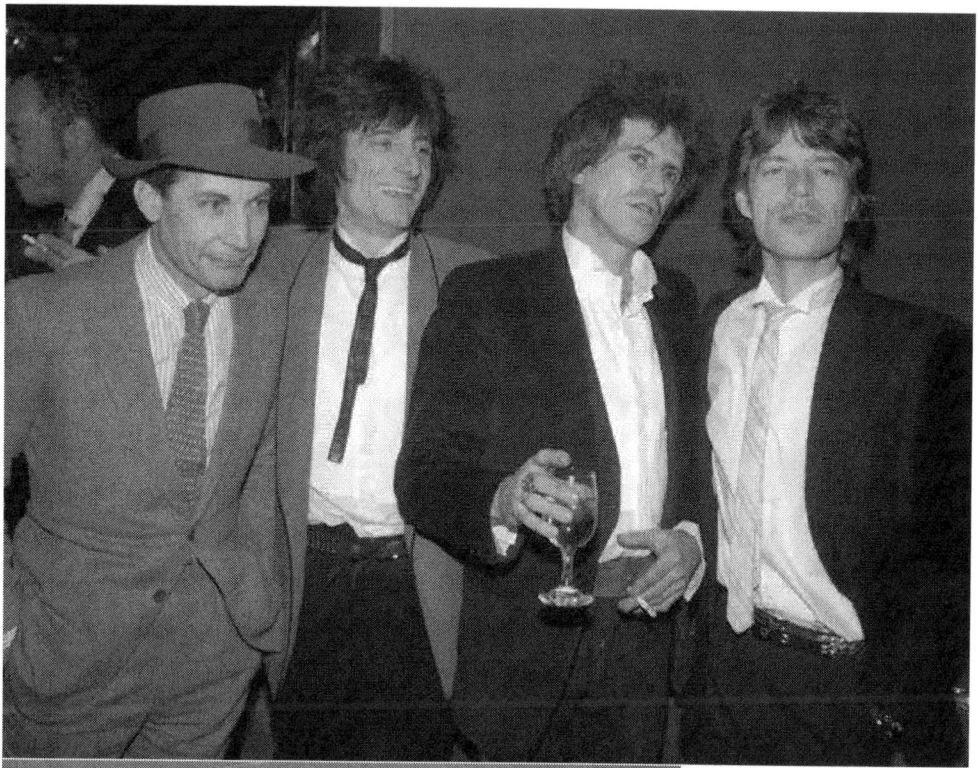

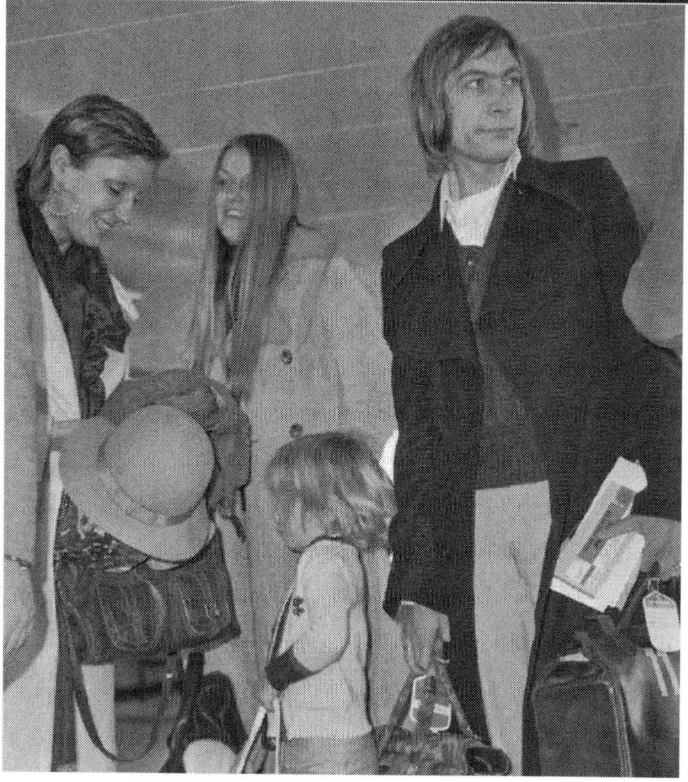

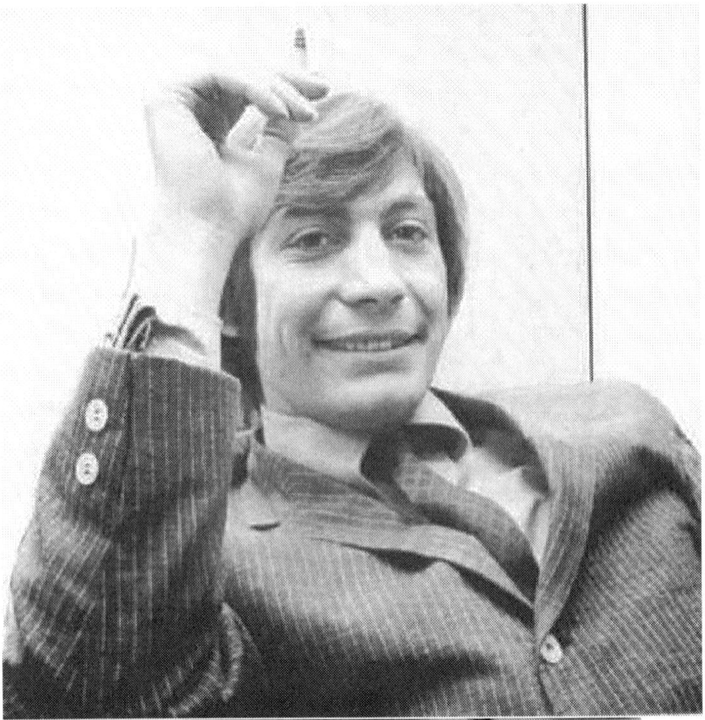

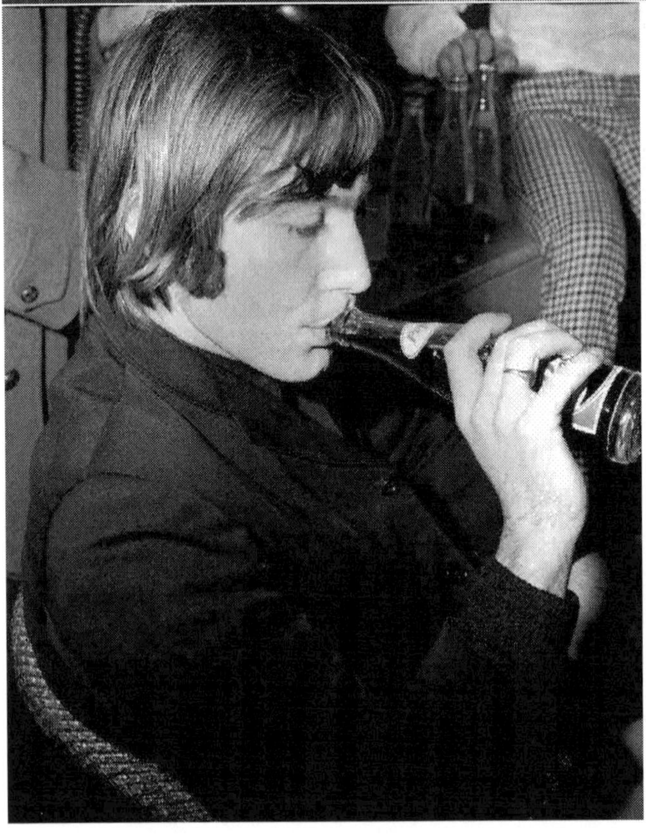

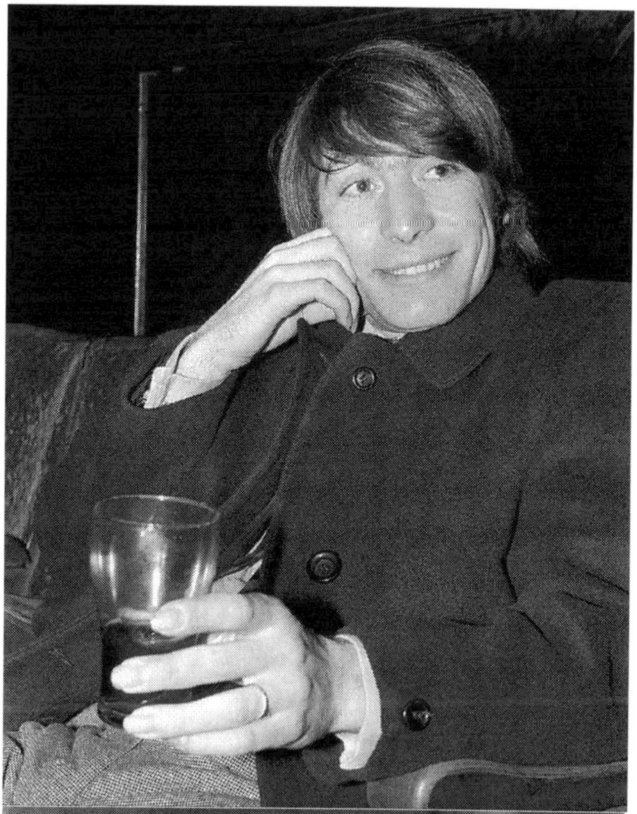

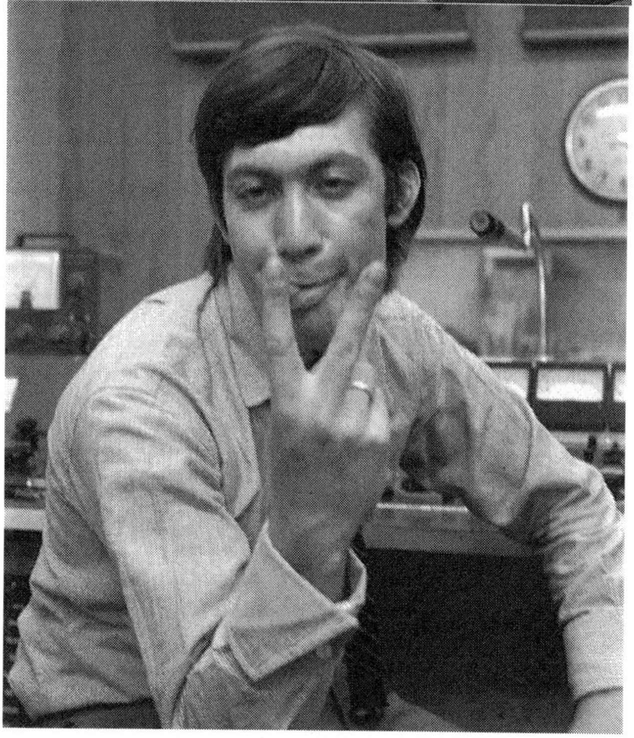

144

CHARLIE WATTS

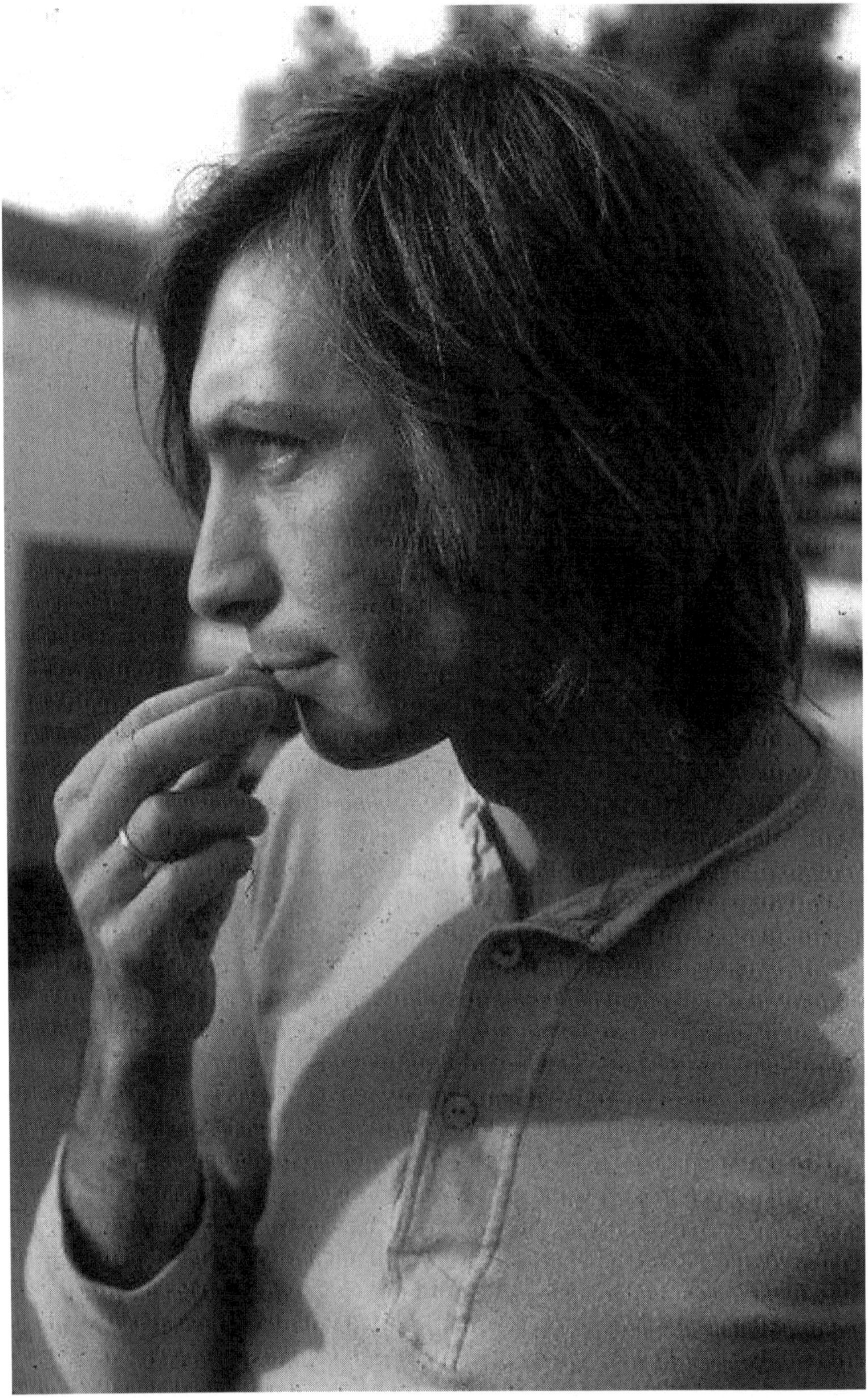

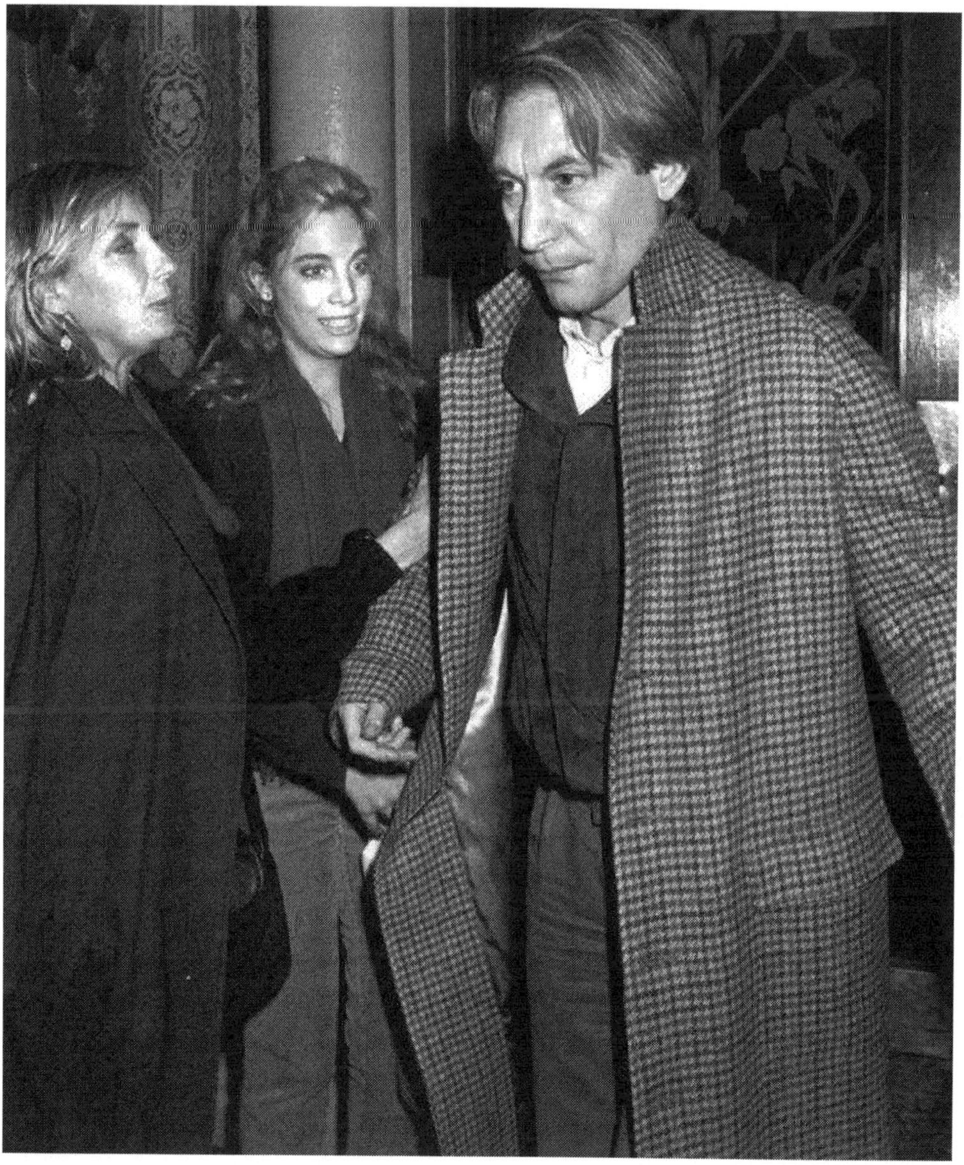

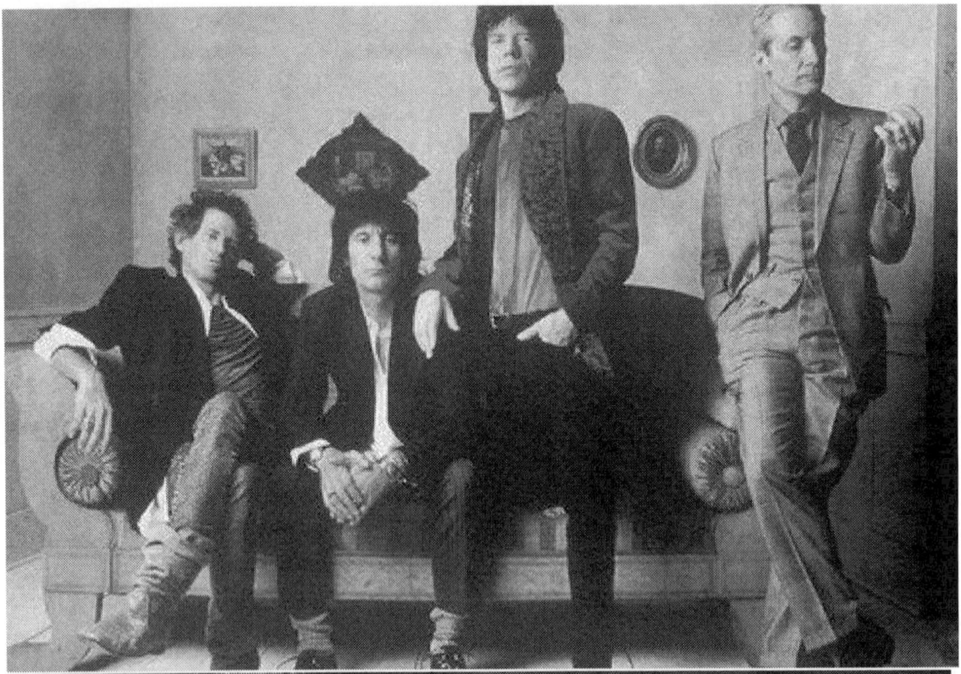

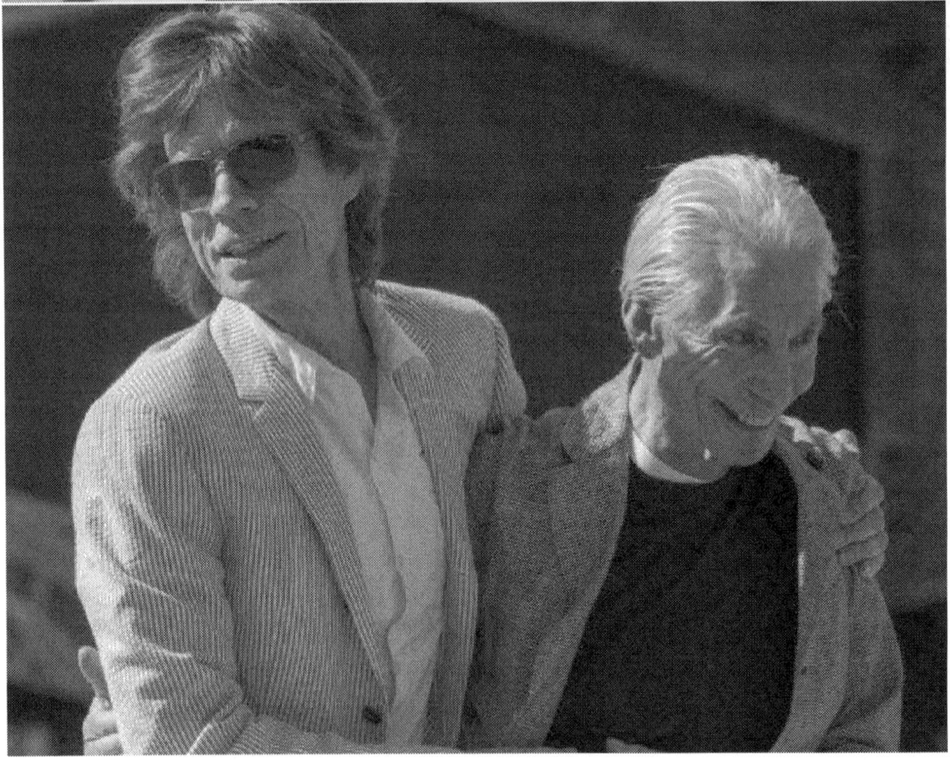

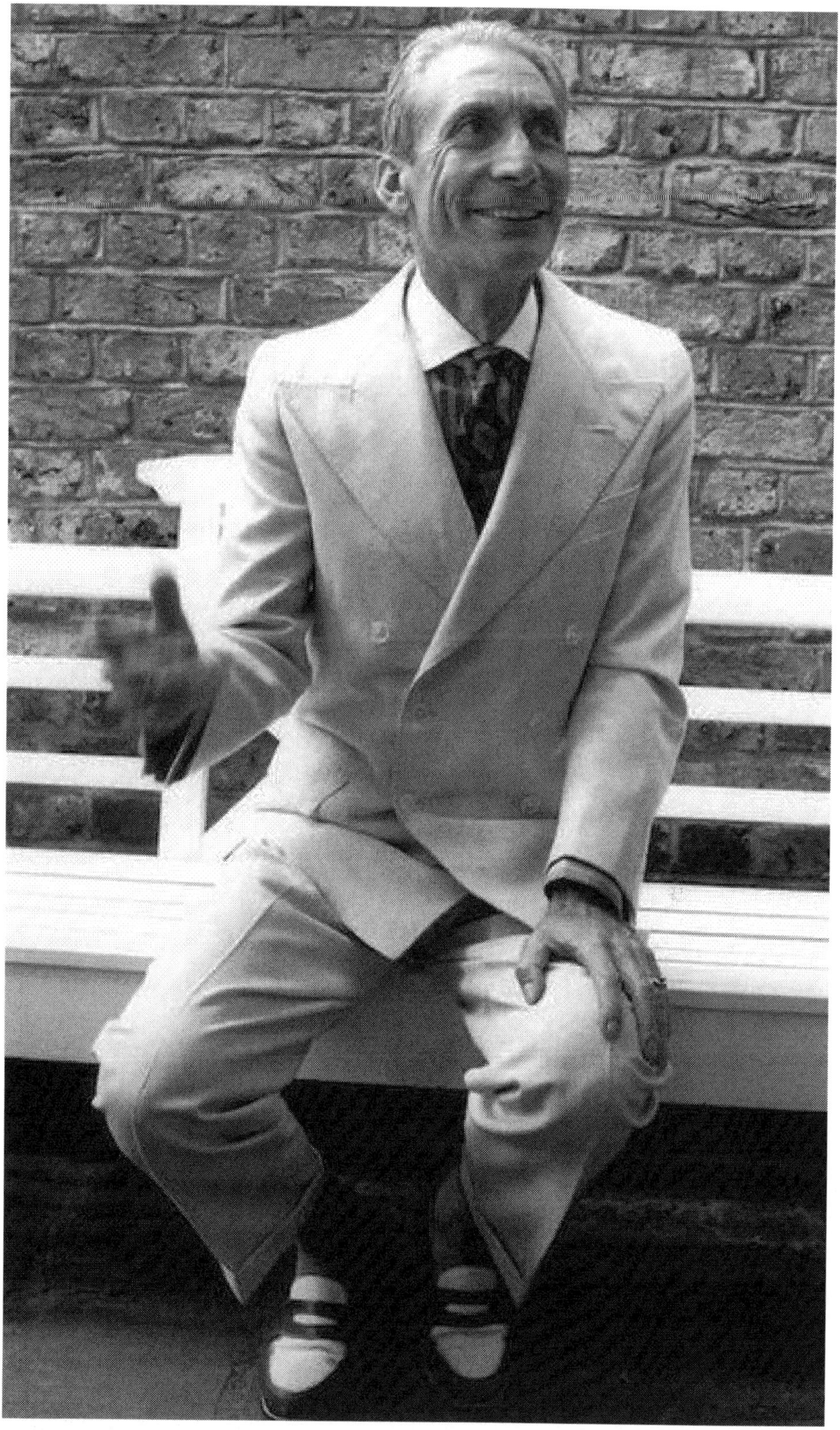

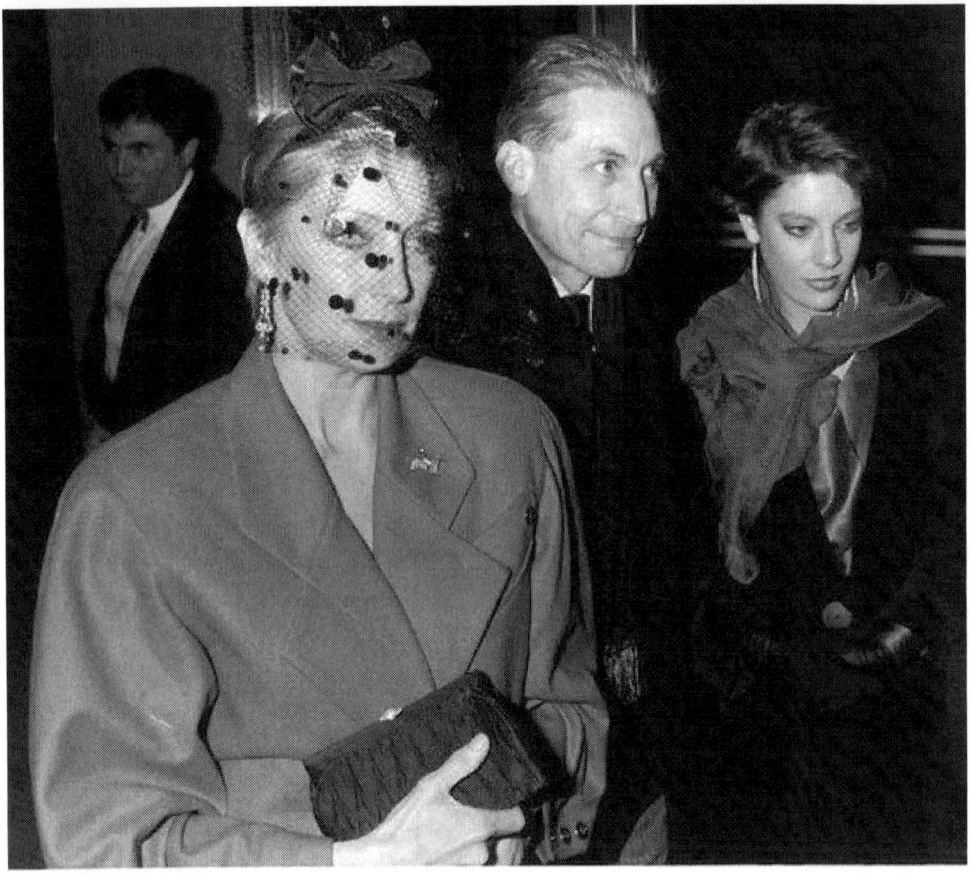

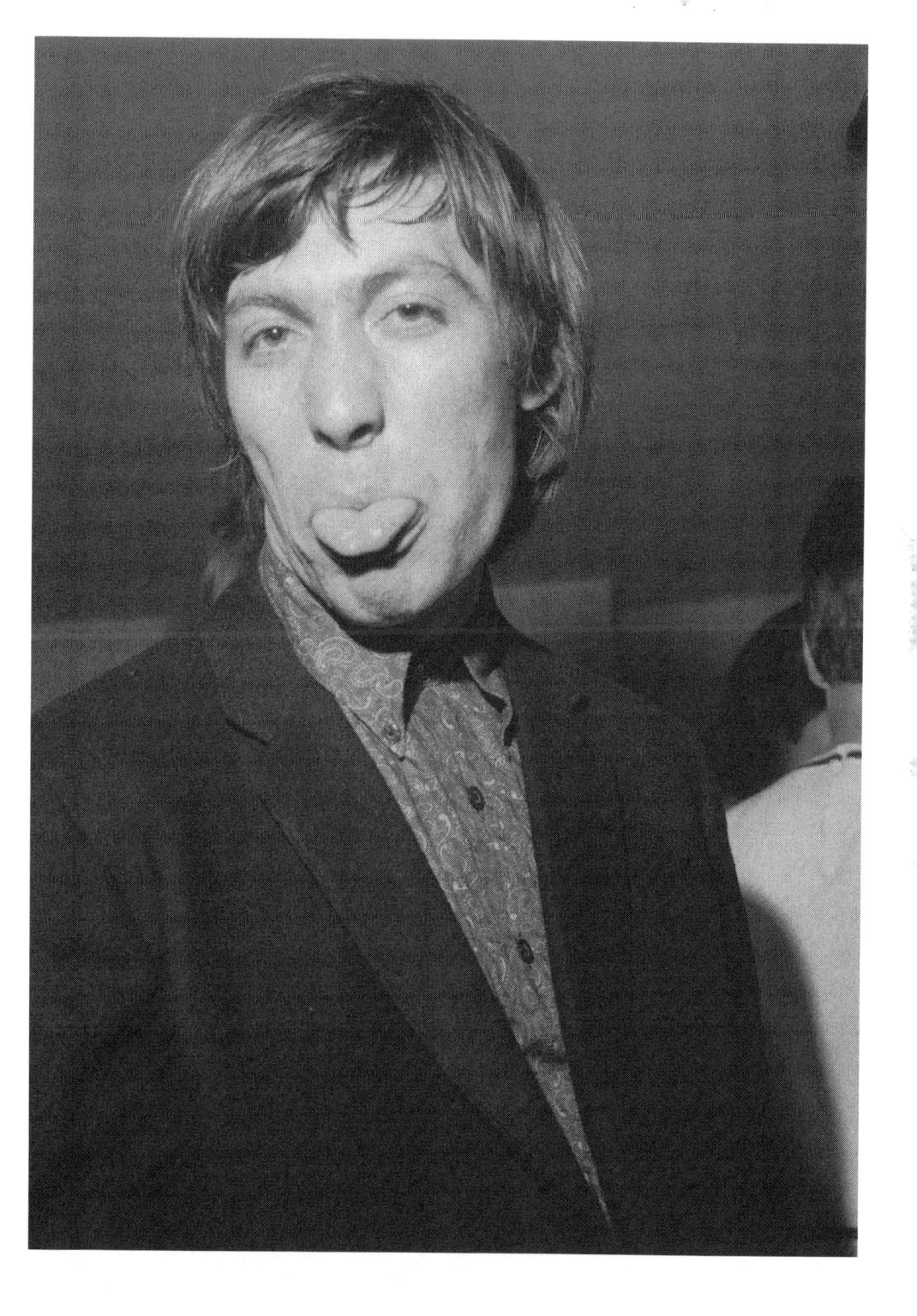

Printed in Great Britain
by Amazon